American Political Parties Under Pressure

Chapman Rackaway • Laurie L. Rice
Editors

American Political Parties Under Pressure

Strategic Adaptations for a Changing Electorate

palgrave
macmillan

Editors
Chapman Rackaway
Political Science
University of West Georgia
Carrollton, Georgia, USA

Laurie L. Rice
Political Science
Southern Illinois University
Edwardsville, Illinois, USA

ISBN 978-3-319-86950-6   ISBN 978-3-319-60879-2   (eBook)
DOI 10.1007/978-3-319-60879-2

Cover illustration: © Icon Fair / Noun Project

Printed on acid-free paper

This Palgrave Macmillan imprint is published by Springer Nature
The registered company is Springer International Publishing AG
The registered company address is: Gewerbestrasse 11, 6330 Cham, Switzerland

PREFACE AND ACKNOWLEDGMENTS

As this manuscript goes to press, Donald Trump just completed what most political scientists and pundits never saw coming—his first 100 days in office as the 45th president of the United States. This period has been fraught with partisan conflict—not just between parties but within them. As we write, news headlines warned that the Republican Party in the House was precariously close to losing the votes it needs for its second attempt at repealing and replacing the Affordable Care Act. It passed by a margin of just one vote. The compromises to draw in votes of the conservative Freedom Caucus members caused a number of moderate Republicans to jump ship and Democrats to sing "hey, hey, hey, goodbye." Meanwhile, a budget deal was just reached that caused both the White House and the Democrats to claim victory for what each side perceived as wins.

A year earlier, in April 2016, it was becoming increasingly clear that despite the Republican Party establishment's best efforts to stop him, Donald Trump was amassing a series of victories that made him the front-runner for the Republican presidential nomination. Meanwhile, what was supposed to be Hillary Clinton's easy path to the nomination was being challenged at every step of the way by self-proclaimed democratic socialist Bernie Sanders.

It was in this context we found ourselves on panels together at the Midwest Political Science Association (MPSA) Annual Meeting. While none of the work being presented at these panels dealt directly with what was happening in the unusually divisive interparty struggles manifesting themselves during the 2016 presidential primaries, it was not hard to see their relevance. Political scientists may not have seen most of these events

vi PREFACE AND ACKNOWLEDGMENTS

coming, but political science offers plenty of insights to better understand why these battles emerge and what we can expect from the political parties in the future. We invited Brian Arbour to provide insights into the role of unhyphenated Americans in party politics and how they contributed to Trump's victory. David Dulio and John Klemanski joined the project to help provide insights into the role of populism in fueling these interparty challenges and how they helped lead to the crumbling of the once solid "blue wall." Donald Gooch agreed to provide a new measure of polarization in the context of a culture war issue that challenged preexisting party coalitions—gay rights—and Joseph Romance offered his insights into the ideological battles taking place within both parties. We thank all of them for their insightful contributions that joined our own work on the consequences of presidential primary rules and the impact of campaign visits in previous elections to help explain the unusual events of 2016 and offer insights into political parties as they seek to move beyond 2016.

We thank Chris Robinson for his initial encouragement of this project and for helping steer it from idea to accepted proposal. We also thank John Stegner at Palgrave Macmillan for his quick replies, patience, and professionalism that helped make this book a reality.

Acknowledgments for Chapman Rackaway First and foremost, I am grateful for the love and support of my family. My wife Andrea, who is as steadfast as she is brilliant, supports me in countless ways, and I am exceedingly fortunate to have her in my life. The rest of my family, from my littlest Will, my middle child Cate, and my eldest Madison, are why I do what I do and why I strive to be a better person, father, husband, colleague, and scholar every day. To the rest of my family, both those I have known all my life and my biological family with whom I have only recently connected, I am grateful for the openness, love, and support you have shown me. I am better for being a Scott and a Rackaway.

My co-author, Laurie Rice, has been a phenomenal partner in this project as well, and I owe her a deep debt of gratitude for her vision, leadership, and cooperation. It has been a joy working on this project with Laurie, and I hope for many more in the future.

Acknowledgments for Laurie L. Rice I am blessed to have a supportive family who have always encouraged my passion for politics. I would not be where I am today without the love of my parents, Larry and Bobbie, who enthusiastically support everything I do. My interest in politics was also nurtured at extended family gatherings where my grandparents, Robert and Dorothy, never considered me too young for discussions about politics around the dinner table. They did not live to see the 2016 election but no doubt would have had plenty to say. I am sure they, too, would have been interested in this project and delighted that the conversations continued this year as my cousin Jason made a wonderful addition to our family by marrying Anna. I thank all of my family, as well as my friends and colleagues, for their patience, understanding, and support during this inordinately busy year.

I also thank my co-author, Chapman Rackaway. He has been wonderful to collaborate with since we first met at MPSA, and we have discovered more about how our research interests complement each other along the way. This book benefits significantly from the valuable insights he brought to this project and for that I am grateful.

CONTENTS

LIST OF FIGURES

LIST OF TABLES

Introduction: Turning Lemons into Lemonade? Party Strategy as Compensation for External Stresses

Chapman Rackaway and Laurie L. Rice

Political scientist V.O. Key (1955a, b, 1959) introduced the concept of American political parties as "tripod" entities, with legs composed of members of the electorate, the party organization, and elected officials who ran under their party's aegis. While the theory itself has withstood a number of challenges and adaptations (see Schlesinger 1984, 1994; Pomper 1998; Shea 1995), the basic structure of parties still resembles the three-legged stool Key described.

In Key's concept, the party organization was a byproduct of the elected officials, there to help overcome constitutional barriers to party founding and expansion. However, parties are also fluid entities, shifting and

C. Rackaway (✉)
Department of Political Science, University of West Georgia,
Carrollton, GA, USA

L.L. Rice
Department of Political Science, Southern Illinois University Edwardsville,
Edwardsville, IL, USA

© The Author(s) 2018
C. Rackaway, L.L. Rice (eds.), *American Political Parties Under Pressure*, DOI 10.1007/978-3-319-60879-2_1

1

morphing in response to changes within the political environment. From the 1970s to the 1990s, party organizations emerged as a powerful electoral coordinating mechanism as a byproduct of two significant forces: professional fundraising operations and large "soft-money" donations (Herrnson 1986, 1988; Kolodny 1998).

The soft-money era may have strengthened parties out of a century-long period of decay (Wattenberg 2009) but the effect was temporary. The 2002 Bipartisan Campaign Reform Act (BCRA) stopped the flow of soft money through the parties and redirected its flow into outside organizations (Holman and Claybrook 2004; Corrado 2006; Dwyre et al. 2006). The flow of money to 527 organizations and later SuperPACs have significantly undermined the ability of parties to serve as that electioneering coordinator highlighted under the soft-money era (Kolodny 1998; Malbin 2004; Skinner et al. 2012).

BRCA's weakening of parties under a new campaign finance regime is significant. The 1970s–1990s revival of parties followed a century of decline in the aftermath of the Progressive Reforms (Ranney 1975; Shefter 1994). Parties were seen as almost unnecessary artifacts of a long-extinct politics before they re-emerged. During that period of revival, though, the electorate did not embrace parties with concomitant energy: self-identified nonpartisans continued to increase in numbers over that time period (Bartels 2000). The party in government strengthened briefly (Aldrich and Coleman Battista 2002; Aldrich and Rohde 2000; Bianco and Sened 2005) but the real growth was located within the national party headquarters. Even the state parties did not experience similar expansion and revival seen in the Hill committees (Aldrich and Grynaviski 2015; Flavin and Shufeldt 2015).

If power abhors a vacuum, then the influence party organizations held during their brief period of revival had to go somewhere. Mostly, that power was ceded to outside groups. Organized interests, most notably SuperPACs, emerged as a powerful force. Initially, 527 organizations emerged as a response to BCRA's soft-money ban, but they were supplanted by SuperPACs after the *Citizens United* and *SpeechNOW!* decisions of 2010 and 2011 (Dwyre and Braz 2014; Hasen 2014; Kang 2013). SuperPACs could not only deal in unlimited funds but they were shielded from the strict disclosure rules of the Federal Elections Commission (FEC) giving them an advantage that surpassed even that of soft-money-era parties.

The brief reinvigoration of party organization was thus a bubble, an aberration of renewal during a steady state of decline. In the aftermath of the end of that growth period, what is the future of the American political party? Is continuing decline inevitable, or can the parties find new opportunities for expansion and influence? With their primary method of gaining a coordinating influence over other electioneering actors removed, how will parties strategically respond?

As party organizations struggled with their changing role, the nature of the electorate was also undergoing a transformation. The electorate was moving in two seemingly conflicting directions: away from parties and more polarized (Smidt 2015; Abramowitz and Fiorina 2013; Fiorina et al. 2005). The public was becoming simultaneously more ideologically extreme and less partisan. Typically, political parties are arranged on an ideological continuum, so the disaggregation of ideology from partisanship meant that not only were political scientists challenged to identify the new partisanship, also partisan campaigners faced a new challenge in identifying and mobilizing potential supporters.

Candidates for office were also changing simultaneously. As campaigns became more expensive, longer and more arduous, the type of person who ran for office and the number of them changed (Hopmann 2014). Fewer candidates run for office now because of the unpalatable process through which one must venture to win office (Evans et al. 2014). Those candidates who run reflect the interests of the outside groups and ideological extremity of the voters.

The brief run of candidates identified as the "Tea Party" or "Freedom Caucus" are an excellent example of the shifting power base away from party organizations. The Tea Party was never a party *per* se, but a high-profile and briefly successful faction within the Republican Party. That success did more to rend the Republican Party asunder than help its party organization revive itself in the wake of BCRA's shock (Collinson 2016).

Kansas' Tim Huelskamp, one of the most visible of the Tea Party generation of firebrand candidate, served in Congress from 2011 to 2017. Huelskamp first ran for Congress in 2010, prior to *Citizens United* and *SpeechNOW!* but during the Tea Party's rise. During his time in office, Huelskamp voted against his party frequently, publicly feuded with his party's leadership, and as a result was kicked off of the district-critical Agriculture Committee. Speaker John Boehner actively marshaled forces behind consecutive primary challenges to Huelskamp, resulting in his defeat in a 2016 primary versus a first-time candidate, Roger Marshall.

Huelskamp is an excellent example of the challenges facing the political party today. The one element of strength the party had to keep itself vital, let alone relevant, in politics was electioneering. Candidates like Huelskamp emerge when that one differential advantage is taken away from the parties, though. When faced with such challenges, both internal and external, how can and do parties adjust? (Choksi and Mele 2016).

The House Freedom Caucus, made up of primarily of more conservative Republicans who had served three terms or less (Desilver 2016), worked against then Speaker of the House John Boehner to shift power away from party leadership and complicated the ability of Republicans to choose a new Speaker in 2015. Despite the trouble they made for party leadership, 42% of Republicans say they have never heard of them, and among those Republicans who have heard of them, 67% of those who identify as conservative have a favorable opinion while other Republicans are nearly evenly split between favorable and unfavorable views of the Freedom Caucus (Gramlich 2017).

The challenges faced by parties are not abating in the least. The 2016 presidential election serves as an example of how parties must adapt strategy to meet the environment in which they operate. Both Republican and Democratic parties faced candidates that threatened the party organization and its strategic goals.

On the Democratic side, Vermont US Senator Bernard Sanders represented a significant disruption to the party's ability to align its candidates with its strategic direction. Democratic National Committee (DNC) leaders, notably Chair Debbie Wasserman Schultz, had decided early on that the party's best chance lay with former Senator and Secretary of State Hillary Clinton (Isaac-Dovere 2016). The DNC engineered the party's campaign apparatus around Clinton's candidacy. With President Barack Obama term limited out of office, Democrats sought to hold the White House after a two-term presidency for the first time since the 22nd Amendment limited presidential terms. The 2016 contest could have also marked the first time either party had held the White House after a term-limited president left office since George H.W. Bush's election in 1988.

Clinton adopted a very traditional campaign approach and message. Trodding a carefully constructed middle ground, Clinton had designs on general election strategy and largely regarded the primary contest as a brief but necessary annoyance on the way to the larger goal of winning the Electoral College. However, Sanders' candidacy kept the nomination contest from becoming an anointing exercise and actually forced Clinton to aggressively campaign (Nicholas and Tau 2016).

Despite the efforts of Clinton's campaign, Sanders' presence and message pushed the Democrats to take their agenda ever-further to the left throughout the course of the primary. Primary elections represent a persistent threat to the ability of party organizations to coordinate and strategically plan their campaign messages. Sanders ran irrespective of the goals or machinations of the DNC. The candidate confounded party strategy.

Party organizations struggle in primary elections, because the very concept is antithetical to what parties do and they pit the three legs of the party tripod against each other rather than coordinating between them. Parties are information shortcuts for voters and electoral support mechanisms for candidates (Popkin 1994; Aldrich 1995). The purpose of a party is to help make voter decisions easier by narrowing the vote choice and providing information cues to the voting public (Popkin 1995). Parties in government help overcome checks, balances, and other roadblocks to coordination set up in American constitutional government. Parties serve as linkage institutions and the party organizations are the core of that linkage.

Primaries damage that linkage. As the Huelskamp example shows, the party in government can engage in internecine campaign warfare during primaries. And as the Sanders example shows, no matter the intentions of the party organization, a well-motivated and mobilized electorate can overcome them.

Far more than Huelskamp or Sanders, no example shows the problem parties face in sharper relief than Donald Trump, 45th President of the United States. Indeed, Trump is undoubtedly the sharpest example of an actor that the party has not planned on emerging to take the party over, ready or not. Party strategy, no matter how carefully constructed or well deployed, could not overcome the effect of Donald Trump's presence in the Grand Ole Party (GOP) field.

Trump had never run for office before declaring his candidacy in 2015, and in fact had rarely shown any ideological cues that would suggest he was conservative or identified himself as a Republican (Krauthammar 2016). Trump actually supported issues such as abortion-on-demand, same-sex-marriage rights, gun control legislation, and expanded social welfare services in public statements prior to his candidacy. Trump's donation history to political candidates strongly suggests his preferences were much closer to those of the Democrats (Newkirk 2011). Until he declared his candidacy for the presidency, one could conceivably believe that Donald Trump would run as a Democrat and not a Republican. The Republican

National Committee's (RNC's) efforts to support other Republican candidates during the 2016 primary season also suggested that Trump was not preferred or even welcomed by the Republican Party organization.

No matter the preferences of the RNC's official staff, Chairman Reince Priebus, elected officials, or any other Republican with a stake in the party's electoral fortunes, Donald Trump won the party's nomination and eventually the presidency. Trump won the nomination because more than a century ago, the party organization had its ability to nominate candidates removed and handed over to the party in the electorate (Hofstadter 1955).

Trump never met with Priebus or other Republican elected officials before declaring his candidacy. Not once did Trump have to declare his allegiance to the party, show fealty as a precinct committeeman, run for lower office, or even contribute to a candidates' fund at the RNC or one of its affiliated Hill committees. Trump was able to bypass the party organization mechanism entirely and go straight to the voters. The party organization was obviated by the party in the electorate. When confronted with such challenges, can party strategy compensate for difficult candidates or overcome unwanted constraints?

Not only did Trump represent an atypical Republican, the New York real estate mogul's success was pronounced in states that held "open" primaries: ones where pre-registration with a fixed partisan identification was unnecessary. Trump may have won the Republican nomination with the active compliance of Democrats and unaffiliated voters. Effectively, open primaries allow for "hostile takeovers" of political parties, something with which Trump is intimately familiar from his business dealings.

Throughout the 2016 Republican primary contest, elected officials within the party and stalwarts of the party organization actively fought to undermine Trump's candidacy. Rick Wilson, a veteran Republican activist and consultant, organized opposition around a Twitter hashtag: #nevertrump. It bears repeating that Democrats were not the organizers of the anti-Trump activity, it was among members of his own party. Primaries present such a great challenge to the political parties that they foment open conflict within the party itself.

Party organizations have always had to deal with internal strife, but the parties were once able to keep them hidden from public sight. Until the 1960s, national presidential nomination conventions were raucous affairs with no access for the general public. Television brought viewers, scrutiny, and very quickly reforms that took the conflict away from party events and moved them into the electoral arena. The Democrats led the way with the McGovern-Fraser Reforms, effectively turning every primary into a binding one and removing the deliberative nature of party nominations from the organization.

The electorate now held sway in nominating Democratic presidential candidates, with Republicans quickly following suit. Once primary elections bound national convention delegates to particular candidates, the party organization lost all ability to direct nominations and candidates no longer needed to worry about the apparatus.

Parties are resilient entities, however. The post-McGovern-Fraser party was moribund, but immediately thereafter the party organizations developed new methods of fundraising, built permanent national headquarters, and steered themselves back to an important role. Democrats reasserted their organizational nomination power with the advent of the superdelegate system in 1984. Soft-money campaigning fed the parties' resurgent organizational elements, and the parties appeared to have rebounded well until 2002 and BCRA.

Therefore, we cannot say that parties are simply victims of the political environment in which they operate. The parties can push back against their circumstances, and when confronted with significant externally-imposed shocks the way parties respond provide us a good picture of how resilient parties can be in a decidedly anti-partisan age.

When the external shocks accumulate, they can make it much harder for the parties to effectively push back against the shocks. A century of weakening reforms has accumulated to fundamentally challenge the parties. Primaries disaggregated the organization from the electorate. Polarization has fragmented the electorate that the parties still can access and mobilize. The party in government has taken on the same internecine strife seen in the other two elements of the party structure.

Under the weight of those collective stresses, what does it mean to be an American political party in 2016? Is a party organization still a third co-equal element of today's political parties? What can parties do to regain the advantages they have lost over time? What strategies are available to political parties to overcome the financial disadvantages they have experienced since BCRA? How do changes in primary election and delegate allocation rules alter the competitiveness of candidates? How have changes in the electorate changed the political dynamics within which parties must operate? How extensive is political polarization, and what implications does polarization have for parties and politics more generally?

1.1   PLAN OF THE BOOK

In this volume, we intend to bring new light and clarity to some of the very vital questions introduced above. As linkage institutions, parties are one of the linchpin organizations in democracy. The health of the parties is the health of democracy. The chapters in this book will contribute a measure of that democratic health.

The book begins with a focus on the party in the electorate and how candidates have sought to exploit changes in it to their advantage. Even strong party organizations will struggle to acclimate to a hostile voting public. And by all measures, the public is deeply and profoundly hostile toward politics, parties, and candidates today.

Chapter 2, by Brian Arbour, immediately trains our focus on the phenomenon that is Donald Trump. Trump's support has been particularly strong among voters who self-identify as "unhyphenated" Americans: Anglo-Saxon-descended whites whose families have been in the same region of the United States for multiple generations. The unhyphenated American is a significant phenomenon because of their monolithic nature and geographic concentration. Arbour explores how the unhyphenateds emerged, why their support for Trump's candidacy contributed to his success, and how their partisanship has shifted over time.

In Chap. 3, David Dulio and John Klemanski discuss the emergence of candidates in both political parties challenging establishment candidates for the nomination with populist rhetoric. The voters sought by Sanders and Trump were, in many ways, similar. Dulio and Klemanski use Michigan as a case study of populist messaging, given the state's experience with trade issues, manufacturing jobs, and its history of Reagan Democrats. Their work helps us understand how a part of the so-called blue wall fell to Trump.

In Chap. 4, Donald Gooch investigates how to measure polarization, focusing on the issue of gay rights. Partisan polarization at the level of the mass electorate is a much discussed and controversial topic, but valid and reliable empirical measures of polarization have been wanting, limiting the reach and importance of empirical investigations of polarization. Gooch employs a unique and theoretically defensible measure of partisan polarization based on the distributional characteristics of mass opinion that permits the assessment of partisan polarization across any issue dimension. Gooch examines opinions on gay rights over the last 40 years against the backdrop of the culture war and discusses what this means for partisan polarization, the culture wars, and modern party politics.

The book then turns to other, broader challenges to the parties and how they contributed to the outcome of the 2016 presidential election. In Chap. 5, Joseph Romance's contribution details the challenges to holding together each party's ideological coalitions in 2016. One of the enduring questions in political science is the role of ideology in defining political parties. In recent years, scholarly research has delved into the issue of asymmetric polarization. This is the idea the Republican Party is more uniformly conservative than the Democratic Party is united by liberalism. This is appearing to be true at the mass level and, to a greater degree, among elected officials. Party asymmetry further explains a great deal about current politics—from elections to governing. Yet, Romance identifies three distinct veins of conservatism that have held an uneasy alliance in the Republican Party. Romance asks what the rise of Donald Trump, who fails to neatly fit any of these veins, tells us about the current role of ideology in the Republican Party. He also unpacks what the contest between Hillary Clinton and Bernie Sanders reveals about ideological differences in the Democratic Party and identifies narratives of disempowerment used by candidates from both parties in 2016.

Fully understanding what 2016 reveals about the political parties also requires a deeper look at the primary contests. In Chaps. 6 and 7, Laurie Rice and Chapman Rackaway investigate the 2016 presidential primaries for two important findings. Rice finds a relationship between areas presidential primary candidates have largely ignored over the last few presidential elections and Donald Trump's share of the vote. However, Bernie Sanders' share of the vote was largely driven by other factors. Specifically, Rice finds that a combination of past candidate activity, current candidate activity, party rules, and economic conditions advantage some candidates and disadvantage others, and not always in the direction party leaders think. Rackaway then looks deeper into the electoral rules set by parties for when their contests are held and how delegates are allocated, who can participate in them, and the type of contest used in Chap. 7. He uncovers how rules enacted by the Republican Party organization in 2016 may have inadvertently paved the way for Trump's victory while rules governing Democratic nominating contests made Sanders' strategy for winning the nomination less likely to succeed. Both chapters have strategic implications for party leaders as they seek to move forward from a particularly tumultuous election season.

Finally, in the concluding chapter (Chap. 8), we revisit the challenges faced by political parties and what they reveal about existing models of party politics. We also discuss what the findings of these chapters, taken together, may mean for political parties as they move beyond 2016.

REFERENCES

Abramowitz, Alan I., and Morris P. Fiorina. 2013. Polarized or Sorted? Just What's Wrong with our Politics, Anyway? *The American Interest.* Accessed September 30, 2013.

Aldrich, John H. 1995. *Why Parties? The Origin and Transformation of Party Politics in America.* Chicago: University of Chicago Press.

Aldrich, John H., and James S. Coleman Battista. 2002. Conditional Party Government in the States. *American Journal of Political Science* 46 (1): 164–172.

Aldrich, John H., and Jeffrey D. Grynaviski. 2015. Party Organizations' Electioneering Arms Race. *Emerging Trends in the Social and Behavioral Sciences: An Interdisciplinary, Searchable, and Linkable Resource.* John Wiley & Sons.

Aldrich, John H., and David W. Rohde. 2000. The Consequences of Party Organization in the House: The Role of the Majority and Minority Parties in Conditional Party Government. In *Polarized Politics: Congress and the President in a Partisan Era,* ed. Jon R. Bond and Richard Fleisher, 31–72. Washington, DC: CQ Press.

Bartels, Larry M. 2000. Partisanship and Voting Behavior, 1952–1996. *American Journal of Political Science* 44 (1): 35–50.

Bianco, William T., and Itai Sened. 2005. Uncovering Evidence of Conditional Party Government: Reassessing Majority Party Influence in Congress and State Legislatures. *American Political Science Review* 99 (3): 361–371.

Choksi, Niraj, and Christopher Mele. 2016. Tim Huelskamp, Anti-establishment Republican, Loses Primary for Congress. *The New York Times.* http://www.nytimes.com/2016/08/03/us/politics/tim-huelskamp-roger-marshall-kansas-primary.html?_r=0. Accessed August 15, 2016.

Collinson, Stephen. 2016. GOP at War with Itself. CNN.com. http://www.cnn.com/2016/03/04/politics/donald-trump-mitt-romney-republican-party/. Accessed August 15, 2016.

Corrado, Anthony. 2006. Party Finance in the Wake of BCRA: An Overview. In *The Election After Reform: Money, Politics, and the Bipartisan Campaign Reform Act,* ed. Michael J. Malbin. Lanham, MD: Rowman and Littlefield.

Desilver, Drew. 2016. What Is the House Freedom Caucus and Who's in It? Pew Research Center Facttank: News in the Numbers. http://www.pewresearch.org/fact-tank/2015/10/20/house-freedom-caucus-what-is-it-and-whos-in-it/. Accessed April 29, 2016.

Dovere, Edward-Isaac. 2016. Dems Turn on Wasserman Schultz. Politico.com http://www.politico.com/story/2014/09/democrats-debbie-wasserman-schultz-111077. Accessed August 20, 2016.

Dwyre, Diana, and Evelyn Braz. 2014. Super PAC Spending Strategies in the 2012 Federal Elections. Paper Presented at the 2014 American Political Science Association 2014 Annual Meeting.

Dwyre, Diana, Eric S. Heberlig, Robin Kolodny, and Bruce Larson. 2006. Committees and Candidates: National Party Finance After BCRA. In *The State of the Parties: The Changing Role of Contemporary American Parties*, ed. John C. Green and Daniel J. Coffey, 95–112. Lanham, MD: Rowman & Littlefield.

Evans, Heather K., Michael J. Ensley, and Edwards G. Carmines. 2014. The Enduring Effects of Competitive Elections. *Journal of Elections, Public Opinion & Parties* 24 (4): 455–472.

Fiorina, Morris P., Samuel J. Abrams, and Jeremy C. Pope. 2005. *Culture War? The Myth of a Polarized America*. New York, NY: Pearson Longman.

Flavin, Patrick, and Gregory Shufeldt. 2015. State Party Competition and Citizens' Political Engagement. *Journal of Elections, Public Opinion and Parties* 25 (4): 444–462.

Gramlich, J. 2017, April 18. *Most Americans Haven't Heard of the Freedom Caucus.* Pew Research Center. http://www.pewresearch.org/fact-tank/2017/04/18/many-americans-havent-heard-of-the-house-freedom-caucus/. Accessed June 22, 2017.

Hasen, Richard L. 2014. Super PAC Contributions, Corruption, and the Proxy War over Coordination. *Duke Journal of Constitutional Law & Public Policy* 9 (1): 1–21.

Herrnson, Paul S. 1986. Do Parties Make a Difference? The Role of Party Organizations in Congressional Elections. *The Journal of Politics* 48 (3): 589–615.

———. 1988. *Party Campaigning in the 1980s: Have the National Parties Made a Comeback as Key Players in Congressional Elections?* Cambridge, MA: Harvard University Press.

Hofstadter, Richard. 1955. *The Age of Reform: From Bryan to FDR*. Vol. 95. New York, NY: Vintage Books.

Holman, Craig, and Joan Claybrook. 2004. Outside Groups in the New Campaign Finance Environment: The Meaning of BCRA and the McConnell Decision. *Yale Law & Policy Review* 22: 235–259.

Hopmann, David Nicolas. 2014. Politicians, Parties and Political Candidates in the News Media. In *Political Communication*, ed. Carsten Reinemann, 389–408. Berlin: Walter de Gruyter.

Jacoby, William G. 2014. Is There a Culture War? Conflicting Value Structures in American Public Opinion. *American Political Science Review* 108 (4): 754–771.

Kang, Michael S. 2013. The Year of the Super PAC. *George Washington Law Review* 81 (6): 1902–1927.

Katz, Richard S., and Robin Kolodny. 1994. Party Organization as an Empty Vessel: Parties in American Politics. In *How Parties Organize: Change and Adaptation in Party Organizations in Western Democracies*, ed. Richard S. Katz and Peter Mair, 23–29. London: Sage Publications.

Key, V.O., Jr. 1955a. *Politics, Parties, and Pressure Groups*. 4th ed. New York, NY: Thomas Y Crowell Company.

———. 1955b. A Theory of Critical Elections. *The Journal of Politics* 17 (1): 3–18.

———. 1959. Secular Realignment and the Party System. *The Journal of Politics* 21 (2): 198–210.

Kolodny, Robin. 1998. *Pursuing Majorities: Congressional Campaign Committees in American Politics*. Norman, OK: University of Oklahoma Press.

Krauthammar, Charles. 2016. Donald Trump Is not a Conservative and the GOP Doesn't Care. NationalReview.com. http://www.nationalreview.com/article/435045/donald-trump-not-conservative-gop-doesnt-care. Accessed August 24, 2016.

Malbin, Michael J. 2004. Political Parties Under the Post-McConnell Bipartisan Campaign Reform Act. *Election Law Journal* 3 (2): 177–191.

Newkirk, Jeremy. 2011. Donald Trump's Donations to Democrats. OpenSecrets. org. http://www.opensecrets.org/news/2011/02/donald-trumps-donations-to-democrats/. Accessed September 1, 2016.

Nicholas, Peter, and Byron Tau. 2016. Democratic Presidential Race Ends with Clinton Victory in DC. *The Wall Street Journal*. http://www.wsj.com/articles/d-c-democrats-vote-ahead-of-sanders-clinton-meeting-1465921326. Accessed August 25, 2016.

Pomper, Gerald M. 1998. The Alleged Decline of American Parties. In *Politicians and Party Politics*, ed. John Geer, 14–39. Baltimore, MD: The John Hopkins University Press.

Popkin, Samuel L. 1994. *The Reasoning Voter: Communication and Persuasion in Presidential Campaigns*. Chicago: University of Chicago Press.

———. 1995. Information Shortcuts and the Reasoning Voter. In *Information, Participation and Choice: An Economic Theory of Democracy in Perspective*, ed. Bernard N. Grofman, 17–35. Ann Arbor, MI: University of Michigan Press.

Ranney, Austin. 1975. *Curing the Mischiefs of Faction: Party Reform in America*. Berkeley, CA: University of California Press.

Schlesinger, Joseph A. 1984. On the Theory of Party Organization. *The Journal of Politics* 46 (2): 369–400.

———. 1994. *Political Parties and the Winning of Office*. Ann Arbor, MI: University of Michigan Press.

Shea, Daniel M. 1995. *Transforming Democracy: Legislative Campaign Committees and Political Parties*. Albany, NY: SUNY Press.

Shefter, Martin. 1994. *Political Parties and the State: The American Historical Experience*. Princeton, NJ: Princeton University Press.

Skinner, Richard M., Seth E. Masket, and David A. Dulio. 2012. 527 Committees and the Political Party Network. *American Politics Research* 40 (1): 60–84.

Smidt, Corwin D. 2015. Polarization and the Decline of the American Floating Voter. *American Journal of Political Science* 61 (2): 365–381.

Wattenberg, Martin P. 2009. *The Decline of American Political Parties, 1952–1996.* Cambridge, MA: Harvard University Press.

Chapman Rackaway serves the University of West Georgia as a professor and chair in the Department of Political Science. Previously, Rackaway was a faculty member, department chair, and Dean at Fort Hays State University (FHSU). After serving as a political activist and consultant for ten years, Rackaway received his Ph.D. in Political Science from the University of Missouri in 2002. In 2007, 2010, and 2013, Rackaway was a nominee for the Pilot Award, FHSU's highest award for teaching faculty. In August 2015, Rackaway was named the FHSU President's Distinguished Scholar.

Chapman Rackaway is an avid believer in the role technology plays in both teaching and politics. Rackaway has published work on the use of technological and social media tools in state representative campaigns and multimedia supplements' effects on student learning outcomes in the American Government classroom. Rackaway uses instant polls, web video, lecture capture, social media, interactive graphics, and freeware tools to engage students in course materials.

A recognized expert in Kansas politics, Rackaway is regularly quoted in state, national, and international media. Rackaway's primary scholarly foci are on political parties as electioneering organizations and internal campaign strategy. Rackaway is the author of five books, including *Civic Failure and Its Threat to Democracy: Operator Error.* Dr. Rackaway is on social media on Twitter @DocPolitics or connect with him via Facebook or LinkedIn using the ID chapman.rackaway.

Laurie L. Rice is Associate Professor of Political Science at Southern Illinois University Edwardsville where she teaches classes in American politics including the presidency, presidential campaigns, and political parties and interest groups. She received her Ph.D. in Political Science from the University of California, San Diego. Her research appears in journals such as *Congress & the Presidency, Presidential Studies Quarterly, Social Science Computer Review,* and *Social Science Quarterly.* Rice is the co-author of the book *Web 2.0 and the Political Mobilization of College Students* and a contributor to *Technology and Civic Engagement in the College Classroom.* Rice has also written pieces for *The Hill* and *The Huffington Post* and provides expertise on elections, social media, and the presidency to regional, national, and international media.

CHAPTER 2

This Is Trump Country: Donald Trump's Base and Partisan Change in Unhyphenated America

Brian Arbour

"This is Trump Country" read the headline in the *New York Times* on March 4, 2016, just three days after Donald Trump emerged victorious from the Super Tuesday primaries. The *Times* article took "a closer look at a few of the places where Mr. Trump won big" (Kaplan 2016), and highlighted Trump's big vote totals in places such as Buchanan County in the Appalachian mountains in southwestern Virginia, Atkinson County in southern Georgia, and Macon County, TN, which sits on the Kentucky border.

More journalists did field reports from "Trump Country" in an effort to understand the people who would turn to a candidate who lacked political experience, detailed knowledge of policy issues, and the temperament traditionally associated with the job of Commander-in-Chief. The first few hits of a Google search for "Trump Country" produce links to articles written in the general election from journalists such as Larissa

B. Arbour (✉)
Department of Political Science, John Jay College, City University of New York, New York, NY, USA

© The Author(s) 2018
C. Rackaway, L.L. Rice (eds.), *American Political Parties Under Pressure*, DOI 10.1007/978-3-319-60879-2_2

15

MacFarquhar of the *New Yorker*, who explored Trump support in Logan County, WV, and Roger Cohen of the *New York Times* magazine, who went to examine Paris, KY (Bourbon County), and Hazard, KY (Perry County). In the wake of Trump's election victory, the Associated Press examined Elliott County, KY, which had voted Democratic in every election from its founding in 1869–2012, before giving 70% of its vote to Trump in 2016.[1]

The "This is Trump Country" article in the *Times* states that the counties it studied had "little in common but economic hardship [and] a sense of longing for the better times they once had." But this description misses one key attribute shared by all of the counties mentioned above—each has an above average population of what sociologists call "unhyphenated Americans." What is an unhyphenated American? These are white Americans who identify their ethnic origins not with the European countries from which their forefathers and mothers emigrated, but as distinctly and wholly "American." These American ethnic identifiers are not randomly distributed across the country, but instead are concentrated in a belt that runs along the Appalachian Mountains from West Virginia to points south, before turning west in the upper South and running through rural Tennessee, and throughout what can be called the highland South.

The media accounts on "Trump Country" in the 2016 election identified above focus heavily, if unconsciously, on areas with concentrations of these unhyphenated Americans. In Buchanan County, VA, 45.3% of residents identify their ethnicity as American. Elliott County, KY is 41.6% unhyphenated American, while 30.7% of residents of Macon County, TN, 23.7% of Perry County, KY, and 22.0% of Bourbon County, KY are unhyphenated Americans. Atkinson County, GA and Logan County, WV, have smaller shares of American ethnic identifiers—10.4% and 8.0%, respectively—but these are still above the national average of 7.5% per county. There is good reason for journalists trying to identify the base of support for Donald Trump in the primary election to go to what I call "unhyphenated America." An analysis by the Upshot, the data journalism portal hosted by the *New York Times*, found that percentages of unhyphenated Americans in a county was the second strongest correlate of Trump's vote share in the primary (Irwin and Katz 2016). A multivariate analysis posted in a political science blog showed that as the percentage of American ethnic identifiers in a county increased, so did Trump's vote share, even accounting for a number of correlated and confounding factors (Arbour and Teigen 2016).

Yet, there is reason to think that this region does not represent a general election base for Donald Trump specifically. Instead, it is a base for the modern Republican Party. Studies of the 2008 and 2010 elections show that the presence of concentrations of unhyphenated Americans in a county was strongly and negatively correlated with vote share for Barack Obama (Arbour and Teigen 2011) and for Democratic house candidates (Arbour 2011). Subsequent research has found that unhyphenated America started trending toward the Republicans in presidential elections in the late 1990s and continued into the first decade of the twenty-first century. The presence of Barack Obama on the ballot in 2008 and 2012 accelerated and intensified the Republican trend in the region. John McCain made significant gains in the region over George W. Bush's performance in 2004, despite a national trend that moved strongly toward the Democrats. In 2012, Mitt Romney improved on McCain's performance in the region (Arbour 2014, n.d.).

While regions with concentrations of unhyphenated Americans provided Trump a base in the primary election, it is unclear whether or not Trump significantly improved on the performance of previous Republican nominees in the region, or if his performance was in line with his predecessors at the top of the Republican ticket. A strong performance by Trump may indicate that the region is attracted to Trump's particular personality and his policy positions—maybe his strong anti-immigrant and anti-trade stands appeal to a region filled with blue-collar whites and lacking large populations of recent immigrants. But if Trump performs in line with previous Republican nominees, it may indicate that the region is broadly favorable to the contemporary Republican Party. It may further indicate the Republican trend in the region is a negative reaction to the contemporary Democratic Party, which has diversified its ethnic and racial makeup and focused more on social issues (e.g. gay rights, reproductive health, and climate change) which have little traction in unhyphenated America.

This chapter examines Donald Trump's performance in regions with concentrations of unhyphenated Americans in the 2016 election and compares it to the performance of previous Republican nominees in unhyphenated America. I find that despite Trump's strong performance in counties with concentrations of unhyphenated Americans in the primary election, his performance in the region does not represent a stark improvement over previous Republican presidential nominees. Trump does indeed improve over Mitt Romney's performance in the region, and it represents one of the strongest regions for Trump in the election. But

Trump's improvement in the region is in line with the improvement of previous Republican nominees such as Bob Dole, George W. Bush, and John McCain. The region may be "Trump Country," but it might be better to describe it as "Republican Country," and possibly as "Not a Democrat Country."

2.1   THE ETHNICITY OF AMERICANS

This chapter focuses on regions with concentrations of "unhyphenated Americans." In the 1980s, sociologists began identifying an "emerging new ethnic population" that possessed "a recognition of being white, but lack any clear-cut identification with and/or knowledge of a specific European origin" (Lieberson 1985, 159). Stanley Lieberson gave this group the name "unhyphenated Americans." Sociologists made this identification in large part because of a new Census question in 1980, which asked respondents "to what country does this person draw their heritage?" Unexpectedly, a large number of respondents wrote "American" or "the United States" as the answer to this question, rather than writing the name of a European (or other) nation from which their ancestors immigrated to the United States. In 1980, over 13 million respondents reported their ancestry was "American or the United States." That number increased to 20.2 million in the 2000 Census and 20.9 million in the 2009–2011 American Community Survey. Unhyphenated Americans are the fifth largest ancestry group in the country (Brittingham and Patricia de la Cruz 2004).[2] Sociologists defined those with American ancestry as unhyphenated Americans.

Ethnic identification results primarily from social construction (Omi 2001; Farley 1991), and is "mediated by a number of factors, including ethnic admixture (blending), the awareness and preservation of knowledge about ancestral origins, prevailing ideologies about race and racial divisions, and the number of generations removed from the arrival of immigrant ancestors" (Perez and Hirschman 2009: 3–4). Key to the identification of whites as ethnically "American" is the fading connection of contemporary Americans with their immigrant ancestors. Ethnic distinctions among American whites, especially those from old immigrant stocks of northern and western Europe, are eroding due to intermarriage and the passage of time (Alba 1990; Alba and Nee 1997). Individuals often blend together their diverse ethnic heritage, replaced their "detailed ethnic origins with simplified panethnic ... categories" (Perez and Hirschman 2009: 4).

Ethnic ties among American whites are weak enough that scholars have described them as merely "symbolic" (Gans 1979) or even "optional" (Waters 1990).

The choice to identify one's ethnicity as American reflects this fading connection to one's immigrant ancestors. Over time, individuals have come to identify themselves not with their European forefathers and mothers, but instead with their American grandparents and great-grandparents. The social construction of ethnic identity gives individuals great latitude to choose to which ethnicity they identify (Omi 2001; Omi and Winant 1994; Perez and Hirschman 2009). For example, the "American" ancestry "tends to absorb a very large number of the children in families ... of mixed parents in which one parent is American and the other is of some specific ancestry" (Lieberson and Waters 1993, 443–444), a conclusion which holds up controlling for education levels. As a result, Lieberson and Waters conclude that identifying as American is not the result of ignorance or some artifact of the design of the Census questionnaire, but instead represents a deliberate choice by the respondent. As a result, writing "American" demonstrates "true substantive changes in the determination of ancestry and ethnicity for later-generation Americans" (Lieberson and Waters 1993, 423).

2.2   The Demography, Geography, and Politics of the Unhyphenated

Sociologists study unhyphenated Americans because it allows them to see the development and creation of ethnic identity as it happens. Political scientists are interested in the political effects created by ethnic identity. Arbour and Teigen (2011) find that the presence of unhyphenated Americans in a county is negatively and significantly correlated with reduced vote share for Barack Obama in the 2008 general election, his 2008 primary contest against Hillary Clinton and in comparison to recent Democratic presidential candidates. Arbour (2011) extended these findings to the 2010 US House election, finding that the more unhyphenated Americans live in a congressional district, the worse the Democratic candidate fared.

Why do contemporary Democrats do so poorly in regions with concentrations of unhyphenated Americans? To answer this, one needs to understand the demography and geography of unhyphenated Americans.

American ethnic identifiers are not randomly distributed, but have distinct demographic characteristics—white (by definition), rural (Neidert and Farley 1985), Southern (Lieberson 1985), heavily Protestant (Lieberson 1985; Lieberson and Waters 1989), and less educated than average (Neidert and Farley 1985). According to one study, "the individuals who were most prone to write 'American' were young native [born] whites living in the South who had dropped out of high school. About 19% of this group said their ancestry was 'American,' compared to the overall rate of only 6%" (Farley 1991, 417). In addition, there are psychographic reasons why respondents would identify as "American." To some, this question may be a measure of patriotism, and they wish to identify with their own country and no other. Being "American" signifies that these respondents are "true-blue citizens of the United States, being neither sojourners nor of questionable loyalty" (Lieberson 1985, 172).

Figure 2.1 shows where these unhyphenated Americans are located geographically. To create the map, I defined unhyphenated Americans as those who write "American" in response to the Census Bureau's long-form question "what is this person's ancestry or ethnic origin" (Brittingham and Patricia de la Cruz 2004).[3] The answer is open-ended, but the Census Bureau codes these answers into general categories.[4] In Fig. 2.1, these counties are shaded. Since there is a close connection between unhyphenated concentrated and Appalachia, I also included the counties that make up the Appalachian Regional Commission, a federal agency; these counties are outlined in black.

The map shows the strong concentration of unhyphenated Americans in West Virginia and southwestern Virginia, as well as in rural Kentucky and Tennessee. There are also concentrations of unhyphenated Americans in upland regions of North Carolina, Georgia, Alabama, and Mississippi, as well as in significant parts of Arkansas. The map also shows concentrations of unhyphenated Americans scattered across the American midlands in places such as Louisiana, Texas, Oklahoma, Missouri, Indiana, and Ohio. Far distant unhyphenated communities exist in southern Georgia and central Florida, and there are a handful of unhyphenated concentrated counties in rural Illinois, and one county each in Iowa and Nebraska.

The strongest concentrations of American identifiers follow the line of pre-Civil War western migration of highland Southerners, the farmers of the hardscrabble Southern hills who never had enough money to buy land in the fertile Deep South and who moved from the Appalachian highlands across the upper South and into the near Southwest (Key 1949). These

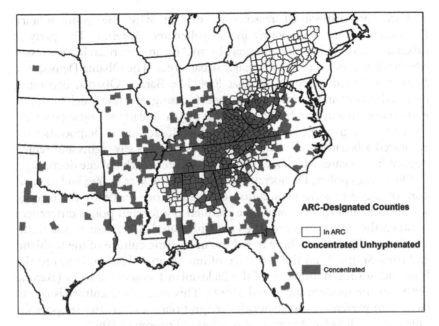

Fig. 2.1 Map of unhyphenated concentrated counties
Note: Unhyphenated concentrated counties are defined as those where 12.5% of residents or more identify their ethnic origin as "American." The ARC represents the counties that belong to the Appalachian Regional Commission

backwoodsmen and women often descended from later immigrants to the American colonies who often came from Scotland or the English border-lands (Fischer 1989). Thus, from a geographic standpoint, unhyphenated Americans are highly concentrated in the Appalachian Mountains and in the upper South.

Previous research has found a tight connection between the presence of unhyphenated Americans in a county and reduced vote share for Barack Obama. This result holds in both primary and general election electorates (Arbour and Teigen 2011). In recent years, Democratic congressional candidates have lost votes as the share of unhyphenated Americans in a district increases (Arbour 2011). My studies of previous elections show that there has been a long-term Democratic decline in areas with large concentrations of American ethnic identifiers, but that these trends accelerated after Barack Obama's election in 2008 (Arbour 2014, n.d.).

There are substantial reasons to explain why the contemporary Democratic Party does poorly in unhyphenated America. The party is urban and urbane, led for eight years by an African-American law professor who has lived his life entirely in major urban areas. The Obama Democratic Party has shifted in directions that look like Barack Obama, becoming more ethnically and racially diverse, and focusing on issues such as immigration reform and health care, which have a particularly strong appeal with the country's growing Hispanic population. In addition, Democrats have embraced a broad set of liberal social issues, such as gay rights and reproductive health care, which are popular with voters with college degrees.

On foreign policy, Democratic resistance to the War in Iraq and its criticism of the aggressive prosecution of the War on Terror by the George W. Bush Administration may have clarified the foreign policy differences between the parties and propelled unhyphenated Americans to the right. Scholars and journalists have noted the militaristic culture of the highland and rural South, from the first wave of immigrants (Fischer 1989) to the highland Southern founding of the Jacksonian Democratic party (Barone 2008) to the modern day (Lind 1999). This militaristic culture is correlated with preferences for hawkish foreign policy and greater support for military spending for American war efforts (Trubowitz 1992).

Another explanation for the shift of the upper South away from the Democrats is race. Race has not been as crucial to the politics of the upper South as it has been to that of the deep South, because of the smaller share of African-Americans in the population (Key 1949; Black and Black 2002). There are still substantial reasons to think that racial attitudes in regions with concentrations of unhyphenated Americans are still racially conservative. The presence of Barack Obama as the Democratic nominee would change this calculus, making race, in the words of Michael Tesler (2016) "chronically accessible." Obama's status as the first African-American president increases the relevance of race to voters and activates racial attitudes, especially those in unhyphenated American regions where racially conservative views are believed to exist, but have not been previously activated.

2.3   Unhyphenated Americans and Donald Trump

The 2016 election produced the unexpected phenomenon of Donald Trump. Trump proved to be particularly popular in unhyphenated America. In an analysis published during the Republican primary, Arbour and Teigen (2016) found that Trump exhibited great "strength across the Deep South, especially in bands of northern Mississippi and Alabama. And he does well in Appalachian regions such as southeast Ohio, eastern Kentucky and southwest Virginia." An analysis by the *New York Times*'s Upshot portal found that "places with high concentrations of these self-described Americans turn out to be the places Donald Trump's presidential campaign has performed the strongest" (Irwin and Katz 2016).

The *Times* article "compared hundreds of demographic and economic variables from census data, along with results from past elections" and determined that the percentage of unhyphenated Americans in a county was the second highest correlation with Trump's vote share in the primary election, trailing only the percentage of whites without a high school diploma. Arbour and Teigen (2016) used multivariate analysis to control for variables correlated to concentrations of unhyphenateds, such as median income and percent college graduates. They find that "[f]or every 10 percent increase in a county's share of unhyphenated voters, we found about 3 percent more support for Trump," controlling for other relevant variables.

These two studies conducted during the middle of the Republican primary show two consistent things. One, areas with concentrations of unhyphenated Americans constituted a significant base for Donald Trump's political ambitions. And second, Trump's success in the region is tied to its demographic characteristics. Not only does Trump do well in regions with concentrations of unhyphenated Americans, but he does well in regions where, according to Irwin and Katz (2016), "white identity mixes with long-simmering economic dysfunctions." Among the other "variables most closely linked to a county's support for Donald Trump" include the percentage of people living in a mobile home, the percentage working in "old economy" job such as agriculture, construction, manufacturing and trade, and support for George Wallace in the 1968 presidential election (Irwin and Katz 2016).[5] Arbour and Teigen (2016) find that median income and the percentage of college graduates in a county are negatively associated with Trump's primary vote, while percent black and percent foreign born are positively related to Trump's support. Arbour and Teigen (2016) argue that African-Americans and immigrants are not voting for Trump, but instead many "are pulling the lever for Trump's anti-immigrant and anti-minority platform and attitudes specifically because they feel threatened by those 'others.'"

Why did Trump appeal to voters in unhyphenated America? As noted above, unhyphenated America is notable for its relatively low scores on measures of socioeconomic status. The median income and the percentage of college graduates in the region are lower than the national average. The levels of residential mobility and economic growth in the region are low and thus, there is a sense of regional stagnation in the face of the loss of manufacturing jobs and an increase in suicide rates (Appalachian Regional Commission 2017) and opiate overdoses (Escoria 2016; Khazan 2014) that are concentrated in the region. In short, many in the region felt the world has passed them by, and are resentful of their current place in the world.

Ronald Brownstein (2016) noted the rhetorical importance for Donald Trump of words such as "again"—Make American Great *Again*, "If I'm elected president, we will win *again*"—and "back"—"we will bring *back* manufacturing jobs", or "bring *back* law and order to the cities." Brownstein argues:

> These phrases capture the mission of restoration underpinning Trump's campaign. They touch the pervasive sense of loss among many of his supporters—the belief that the changes molding modern America have marginalized them economically, demographically, and culturally. These words allow him to evoke a hazy earlier time when American life worked better for the overwhelmingly white, heavily blue-collar coalition now drawn to him. And they help explain the visceral connection he has established with those white working-class voters, a connection strong enough to survive a concatenation of controversies that might have exploded any other candidate.

In addition to a rhetoric of nostalgia, Donald Trump broke from traditional Republican positions on several issues that made him attractive to downscale white voters, especially those who live in regions with concentrations of unhyphenated American voters.

Trump promised, even before he declared his candidacy, that "I'm not going to cut Social Security like every other Republican and I'm not going to cut Medicare or Medicaid" (Brody 2015).[6] This stands in contrast to recent Republican efforts to privatize Social Security and cut Medicare spending under the euphemism "entitlement reform." Trump also vowed "to close tax loopholes that benefit the rich and by suggesting—and later retracting—that the wealthiest could pay higher taxes under his plan. He has also said he would be open to raising the minimum wage" (Rappeport and Parlapiano 2016).

But Trump's biggest deviations from Republican orthodoxy were on the issue of trade. Trump opposed free trade deals pushed by orthodox Republicans such as the Trans-Pacific Partnership. He argued that trade from countries such as Mexico, Japan, and China "is killing our country." Trump proposed "to redo our trade deals 100 percent. I have the greatest business people in the world lined up to do it. We will make great trade deals" (New York Times 2016). Republicans have traditionally supported free trade agreements, and orthodox Republican candidates for the presidential nomination were caught flat footed by Republican voters who "did not believe that the economic benefits of trade deals trickled down to their neighborhoods. They did not care if free trade provided them with cheaper socks and cellphones" (Confessore 2016).

Trump also staked out an extreme restrictionist position on immigration, most famously calling for a wall to be built on the US–Mexican border. After the San Bernardino shooting, Trump called for a "a total and complete shutdown of Muslims entering the United States until our country's representatives can figure out what is going on" (Trump 2015). The immigration issue has long divided the Republican Party between nationalists who wanted to restrict immigration and the party's business wing, which was happy to have an unending supply of cheap labor and who sought to reach out to more Hispanic voters in an increasingly diversifying country. Trump's bold rhetoric on the issue crystalized his support among those who supported more immigration restrictions, especially among blue-collar voters who saw growing numbers of immigrants as threats to their livelihood.

Trump may also appeal to this region of the country through his ability, in the words of New Republic columnist Jeet Heer (2016), to "turn subtext into text." This is particularly true on the issue of race, where Trump came to the political fore through fanning the flames of the birther movement. The fact that this conspiracy theory was incorrect was irrelevant and its clear racist and xenophobic elements were attractive to Trump's most fervent voters. In a region long suspicious of a black President (c.f. Arbour and Teigen 2011, Table 2) and in which there were relatively few Latino or Muslim immigrants to disabuse people of their stereotypes, Trump's descriptions of Mexican immigrants as "rapists" and his call to ban Muslims from the country were regarded as a plus. And clear evidence of Trump's personal bigotry—whether his history of redlining black tenants to the apartment complexes he owned (Mahler and Eder 2016), his attempts to claim that Judge Gonzalo Curiel should recuse himself from a Trump

University fraud case because of his ethnic heritage (Kendall 2016), and his use of a racial slur on cable television against Senator Elizabeth Warren (Yglesias 2016)[7]—meant little to these voters.

There is ample reason to believe that Donald Trump has a particular connection with downscale voters who identify themselves as American. His rhetoric harkens back to days when they felt better about their community, and his political positions speak more directly to these voters than those of orthodox Republicans. Unhyphenated America proved to be a base for Trump in the primary election.

On the other hand, unhyphenated America has trended toward the Republicans for several elections. These changes are the result of negative reactions to the contemporary Democratic Party and its embrace of gay rights, health care, environmentalism, and diversity. Democrats in 2016 maintained, and even doubled down, on these issue positions. This leads to the question of whether Donald Trump has particular appeal in unhyphenated America above and beyond an orthodox Republican nominee. Did Trump's blue-collar focused rhetoric and issue stands help him among the downscale voters in unhyphenated America, or did Trump run similar to any Republican nominee in the region?

2.4   THE 2016 GENERAL ELECTION IN UNHYPHENATED AMERICA

This chapter examines the performance of Donald Trump in the 2016 election in what I am calling "unhyphenated America." Figure 2.1 showed the counties that are unhyphenated concentrated—statistically greater concentration of American ethnic identifiers live in these counties than in the rest of the country. As discussed, these counties are focused in the Appalachian Mountains (from West Virginia to the South) and in the highland and rural portions of the South.

In 2016, Donald Trump ran up landslide margins in unhyphenated America. Of the 8,198,386 votes cast in unhyphenated concentrated counties, Trump won 5,595,213. That is 68.2% of the vote. Hillary Clinton won only 2,328,342. There are 530 unhyphenated concentrated counties across the country. Donald Trump won 529 of them. Hillary Clinton only won Richmond County, Virginia (Table 2.1).

Trump's performance in unhyphenated America is quite impressive. But, as noted above, research shows that unhyphenated America had

Table 2.1 2016 election results in unhyphenated concentrated counties

	Votes won	Percentage	Counties won
Donald Trump Republican	5,595,213	68.2	529
Hillary Clinton Democrat	2,328,342	28.4	1
Total	8,198,386		530

Note: Election data are from the Associated Press. Unhyphenated concentrated counties are defined as those where 12.5% of residents or more identify their ethnic origin as "American." Data calculations done by author

moved toward the Republicans in 2008 (if not earlier). Does Trump's landslide performance in the region indicate that he has a particular appeal in the region? Or does it indicate that the region is, at this time, a Republican region, and that Trump benefitted from the region's long-term Republican trend? To examine this question, it is necessary to look not just at the 2016 election, but also backward to previous elections and compare the results achieved by Donald Trump to previous Republican nominees.

To show these changes, I look at election results across time. I start with the 1988 election—West Virginia, the heart of unhyphenated America, was one of the only nine states to vote for Michael Dukakis. Table 2.2 shows the number of unhyphenated concentrated counties won by the presidential nominee of each party.[8] In 1988, Michael Dukakis, who lost nationally by about nine points, won only 118 unhyphenated concentrated counties. In 1992, Bill Clinton made gains over Dukakis nationally, and in unhyphenated America. While winning nationally by 5 points, he won a majority of unhyphenated concentrated counties in 1992, and came close to doing the same in 1996. But considering that Clinton ran better nationally in 1996 than he did in 1992, this represented a downgrade in performance. This Democratic downgrade continued in 2000, when George W. Bush won 450 counties in the region, and continued in 2004, when Bush won 489 counties. In 2008, John McCain lost nationally by seven points, but he made gains in unhyphenated concentrated counties and won 513 of these counties, and in 2012, Mitt Romney won 520 of these counties.

This represents an impressive level of gains for Republicans across time. They more than doubled the number of counties in the region they won

Table 2.2 Unhyphenated concentrated counties won by party, presidential elections 1988–2012

	Democratic wins	Republican wins
1988	118	413
1992	290	240
1996	252	279
2000	80	450
2004	42	489
2008	18	513
2012	10	520
2016	1	529

Note: Election data are from Dave Leip's Political Atlas (1988 to 2004) and from Associated Press vote totals (2008–2016). Unhyphenated concentrated counties are defined as those where 12.5% of residents or more identify their ethnic origin as "American." Data calculations done by author

between their low point of 1992 and the 2012 election. But despite nearly maxing out on the counties they could win, Donald Trump managed to win even more counties. As noted, he won 529 of the 530 unhyphenated concentrated counties in the nation.

I also examine aggregate results across unhyphenated concentrated counties, again going back to 1988. Figure 2.2 looks at Republican vote share in each of these elections nationally and in unhyphenated concentrated counties. Across the entire timeline, Republican presidential candidates ran ahead of their national numbers in unhyphenated concentrated counties. But across time, that gap grows. And in the twenty-first century, Republican performance nationally in presidential elections stabilizes. But over the same time period, it grows and expands in unhyphenated concentrated counties. For example, John McCain ran 5.1% behind George W. Bush's 2004 performance; in 2008, McCain ran only 0.4% behind Bush in unhyphenated concentrated counties. In 2016, Donald Trump ran behind Mitt Romney's 2012 national performance by 1.3%. But in unhyphenated concentrated counties, there was almost a mirror image. There, Trump ran ahead of Romney by 1.6%.

Figure 2.3 measures the difference between the two lines on Fig. 2.2. It is calculated by subtracting the Republican presidential nominee's national vote share from his percentage in unhyphenated concentrated counties and measures how much better the Republican nominee did in these counties than nationally. For example, in 1988, George H.W. Bush ran

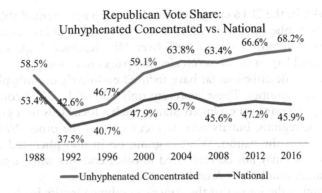

Fig. 2.2 Republican vote share across time
Note: Election data are from Dave Leip's Political Atlas (1988–2004) and from Associated Press vote totals (2008–2016). Unhyphenated concentrated counties are defined as those where 12.5% of residents or more identify their ethnic origin as "American." Data calculations done by author

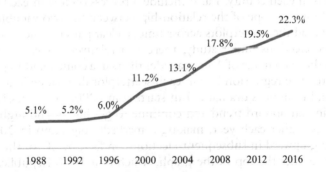

Fig. 2.3 Republican trend in unhyphenated concentrated counties
Note: Election data are from Dave Leip's Political Atlas (1988–2004) and from Associated Press vote totals (2008–2016). Trend is calculated by subtracting the Republican president nominee's national vote share from his percentage in unhyphenated concentrated counties. Unhyphenated concentrated counties are defined as those where 12.5% of residents or more identify their ethnic origin as "American." Data calculations done by author

5.1% better in unhyphenated concentrated counties than he did nationally. The figure shows the steadiness of region in the last three elections of the twentieth century, followed by continual Republican growth in the region in the twenty-first century. The biggest jumps are recorded in the 2000 election (up 5.2% over the 1996 election) and the 2008 election (up 4.7%

over 2004). In the 2016 election, Donald Trump ran a remarkable 22.3% better in unhyphenated concentrated counties than he did nationally. This represents an improvement of 2.8% over Mitt Romney. Impressive, but only the third largest of the seven election pairs under study.

The results described so far have focused exclusively on unhyphenated concentrated counties. These represent only 530 of the 3114 counties or county-equivalents in the United States. Such a focus tells us a great deal about these regions, but its narrow focus ignores the other 2600 or so counties across the nation. What is going on in unhyphenated concentrated counties may not be replicated in other counties with large, if not concentrated, numbers of American ethnic identifiers.

To examine the impact of the American ethnic identity in all counties, I employ bivariate scatterplots. Figure 2.4 shows a scatterplot for each election between 1988 and 2016.[9] For each scatterplot, the y-axis measures county-level vote share for the Republican presidential nominee in that year's election, and the x-axis shows the percentage of unhyphenated Americans in each county. I also include a regression line in each scatterplot to show the slope of the relationship between the two variables.

If you read the scatterplots across time, a clear pattern emerges. In the first three elections under study, there is a relatively small relationship between the percentage of American identifiers in a county and Republican vote share. The regression line in each scatterplot does slope in a positive direction, but none is dramatic. But starting in 2000, the regression lines start taking an upward trend and continue to get higher and higher. The line moves higher each year, making a markedly big jump in 2008 and continuing upward in subsequent elections. In fact, by 2016, the regression line reaches the top of the graph, which is at 100% Republican vote share, before it reaches the highest levels of American ethnic identifiers in a county.

Table 2.3 includes the coefficients and the R^2 for the regression lines for each of the scatterplots shown in Fig. 2.4. The regression coefficient declines from 0.207 in 1988 to 0.122 in 1996. It then starts to increase sharply in each of the next three elections, climbing to 0.787 in Barack Obama's first White House run in 2008. The number stabilized in 2012, but then shot up again in 2016 to a coefficient of 0.963. This means that in 2016, for every 1% increase in the percentage of unhyphenated Americans living in a county, Donald Trump's vote share went up by 0.96%. Compare that to 1988, when a 1% increase in the percentage of unhyphenated Americans in a county increased George H.W. Bush's vote

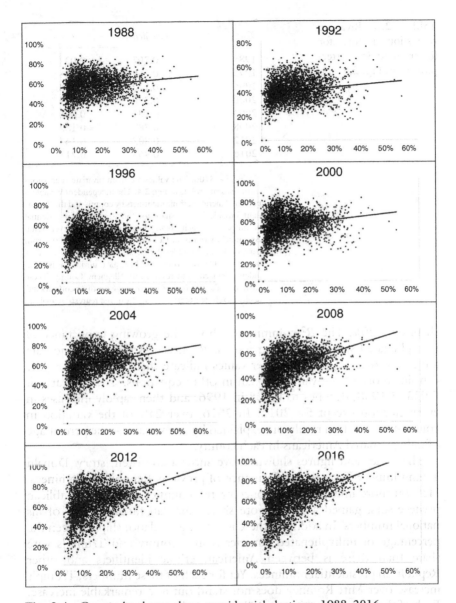

Fig. 2.4 County-level vote share, presidential elections, 1988–2016
Note: The x-axis is the percent American ethnic identifiers by county. The y-axis is the vote share won by the Republican nominee by county. Data calculations, including trend lines done by author

Table 2.3 Bivariate regression results for linear trend in scatterplots from Fig. 2.4

Year	Coefficient	R^2
1988	0.207	0.022
1992	0.179	0.024
1996	0.122	0.008
2000	0.290	0.032
2004	0.431	0.066
2008	0.787	0.182
2012	0.807	0.167
2016	0.963	0.211

Note: $N = 3106$. The values are from bivariate regressions form the scatterplots in Fig. 2.4. The independent variable is percent American ethnic identifiers by county, and the dependent variable is vote share for the Republican presidential nominee for each year. I employ county-level data. Broomfield County in Colorado was created in 2001 from parts of Adams, Boulder, Jefferson, and Weld counties. That same year, Clifton Forge, Virginia, gave up its status as an independent city and reverted to Allegheny County. These changes make comparisons across time for these counties difficult. I excluded these counties from the regression analysis

share by 0.20%. The R^2 column also shows the growing importance of unhyphenated status in election results. R^2 measures how close the data are to the regression line; higher values indicate that the regression line explains more of the variation than in other equations. The R^2 starts at 0.023 in 1988, declines to 0.008 in 1996, and then rapidly increases in every election except for 2012. In 2016, over 21% of the variation in county-level election results are explained by one variable—the percentage of unhyphenated Americans in each county.

The tables and figures shown above show a consistent story. Donald Trump improved on the performance of previous Republican nominees. He won more unhyphenated concentrated counties than his Republican predecessors, gained a higher vote share, and ran further ahead of his national numbers. In addition, there is a stronger relationship between the percentage of unhyphenated Americans in a county and Trump's vote share than there is between American ethnic identifiers and other Republican presidential nominees. Yet for each of these numbers, Trump's increase over Mitt Romney does not stand out as a remarkable increase. Each of the increases achieved by Trump is in line with the increase shown in previous elections in the twenty-first century. So while Trump has increased Republican vote share in regions with concentrations of unhyphenated Americans, he has not done so in a way that indicates that his personal characteristics or deviations from Republican orthodoxy gave him a particular appeal in this region in the general election.

Instead, the 2016 election looks like a long series of elections in which the Republican nominee, regardless of his personal characteristics or ideological positioning, increased his vote share in unhyphenated America. Since Trump sits at the end of a long list of Republican nominees who have improved his standing in unhyphenated America, and because of his primary strength in the region (Arbour and Teigen 2016; Irwin and Katz 2016) and his rhetorical boosterism of manufacturing and mining, many have perceived him as having a special base in the region. The data presented here indicate that is not the case. Looking at the trends across time, Trump's numbers seem to be similar to those that a different Republican nominee would have achieved in unhyphenated America.

The conclusions one can derive from these data are that voters in unhyphenated America are attracted to the contemporary Republican Party, or repelled from the Democrats. No individual candidate has created the Republican shift in the region. Instead, it stems from a long-term trend that goes beyond any single candidate, issue, or event.

2.5   UNHYPHENATED AMERICA AND THE CHALLENGE TO THE PARTIES

The clear conclusion of the results presented in this chapter is that unhyphenated America is a Republican region. Republican candidates keep reaching new electoral heights in the region, only to have those numbers topped by their successor as Republican nominee. Donald Trump certainly won counties with concentrations of unhyphenated American by landslide margins, but his improvement in the region is in line with the improvements made by nominees such as John McCain and Bob Dole.

Trump certainly won big margins in unhyphenated America during the primary (Arbour and Teigen 2016; Irwin and Katz 2016). Congressional scholar Richard Fenno (1977) found that members of Congress saw their districts as four concentric but distinct constituencies. Using this rubric, one can identify unhyphenated America as part of Donald Trump's "primary constituency." Fenno (1977, 887) says that while "routine supporters only vote for [a candidate] ... others will support them with a special degree of intensity." In the primary, regions with concentrations of unhyphenated Americans demonstrated that "special degree of intensity" toward Trump. If Trump receives a challenge in the 2020 primary from a more establishment or a more doctrinaire conservative candidate, he should be able to count on strong support from this region.

Fenno's rubric also describes a re-election constituency, which includes "the people [a politician] thinks vote for him." According to Fenno (1977, 886), politicians can assess these voters based on "party identification as revealed in registration or poll figures and party voting" and "the political tendencies of various demographic groupings." Based on this definition, one can describe unhyphenated America as part of the re-election constituency for a Republican presidential nominee. So while Donald Trump did very well in the region, the results presented here indicate that any Republican nominee would have done similarly well. Looking forward, one can expect Trump to do well in this region when he runs for re-election in November 2020.

The results presented here suggest the continued importance of ethnicity among whites in American politics. Patterns of immigration and settlement helped establish not only the type of people who settled a region but also the political norms and values of that region. Traditionally, studies of ethnic voting in American elections has assessed how the values, norms, and political loyalties of the "Old Country" transferred to the voting behavior of immigrants and their descendants in their new country (c.f. Gimpel and Tam Cho 2004; Miller 1971, 1974; Sonenshein and Valentino 2000; Wolfinger 1965). Those who identify as Americans are qualitatively different. Rather than identify with their European ancestors and the traditions they brought with them to America, unhyphenateds identify with their own country. Sociologists Anthony Perez and Charles Hirschman (2009) have noted the development of different pan-ethnic "New World" ethnicities; the "American" ethnicity was a major part of this trend.

The capability of groups to morph their ethnic identification over time and the results of the 2016 election raise a question that is not explored in this chapter—have whites across the country developed a pan-ethnic racial identity? And if so, does that pan-ethnic racial identity help to explain why a bigoted candidate Donald Trump made so many gains across homogenously white areas of the country, whether in unhyphenated America or in regions of the upper Midwest (Cohen 2016)? It will take more elections (and more outwardly racialized appeals from Republican candidates other than Donald Trump) to determine the level of racial solidarity that has developed between whites, especially those on the bottom half of the socioeconomic ladder. It will also take future Censuses to determine if the American ethnic identification is becoming more common outside of unhyphenated concentrated regions.

The importance of the American ethnic identification, and its possible growth, leads to a different set of political choices for the two major parties in the future. For Democrats, the 2016 election demonstrated the promise and peril of their reliance on a coalition of the young, minorities, and the urban and urbane. The Electoral College muted the advances Democrats made among these voters in states such as Arizona and Texas, while accentuating their problems with blue-collar whites in the more valuable Midwest. These patterns were repeated in Senate elections—Senate Democrats, like Hillary Clinton, won more votes than their opponents, yet do not hold more seats.

In the absence of a national movement to move to a one-person, one-vote electoral system, Democrats face a difficult dilemma in near term elections. They need to win back the votes of unhyphenated Americans in swing states such as Ohio, Pennsylvania, and North Carolina, but appealing to racially and socially conservative rural white voters can create problems with socially and racially liberal voters. Democrats have hopes that they can continue to make gains among young and minority voters that will lead to them flipping Sunbelt states (e.g. Georgia, Texas, and Arizona). Yet these states still seem to be several elections away from going blue. And it is worth noting that this challenge might become more difficult in the future—future Republican nominees may adapt Trump's nationalist positions on trade and immigration, but will likely lack the baggage created by Trump's lack of political experience, his childish temperament, and his willingness to brag about routinely sexually assaulting women (Burns et al. 2016).

For Republicans, the challenge is on a policy level. Trump won votes in the Republican primary primarily by standing out from traditional Republican politicians on issues such as trade—where his position is clearly different from the free trade thrust of movement conservatives—and immigration—where his nationalistic and bigoted rhetoric signaled a commitment that establishment politicians would not make. But the opening for Trump was created by the disconnect between the plutocratic priorities of the conservative establishment—tax cuts that predominantly benefit the wealthy and cuts to social welfare programs such as Medicare—and a Republican base that is increasingly downscale.

Trump's rise to the top of the Republican Party may represent the solution to this dilemma. Trump's position on issues of trade and immigration appeals to blue-collar whites centered in unhyphenated America. At the same time, Trump's positions are consistent with the Republican establishment on issues such as taxes; his campaign's tax plan was larger than his primary rivals and showered most of its benefits on his fellow millionaires (Matthews and Zarracina 2016). His policy agenda is business friendly, calling for a reduction in government regulations (Kaufman 2016), and, like most Republicans, his environmental policy is based on the hope that scientific consensus on global warming is wrong (Bump 2016). Unlike his fellow Republicans, Trump made occasional sympathetic gestures toward those who would lose their health care through repealing the Affordable Care Act, but as president, Trump supported a health care bill that would strip coverage from millions of working class Americans *and* significantly reduce taxes on high-income Americans (Alonso-Zaldivar 2016). No wonder why almost every establishment Republican politician came around to endorsing Trump.

Yet Trump's rise also creates tensions in the Republican coalition. Trump owes none of his rise to the Republican establishment and his relationship with the conservative movement is transactional, at best. Trump's rhetorical focus on "bringing jobs back" and his claims that "we're going to start making things again" and that "miners are going back to work" (Lindstrom 2016) raise hopes in unhyphenated America about the prospects for a Trump administration. Yet manufacturing and mining jobs are declining due to technological changes and structural changes in the economy. Donald Trump can no more bring these jobs back than he can ask the sun to rise in the West tomorrow. And while the Republican Congress, dominated by establishment Republicans, has proven its willingness to lower taxes for the wealthy and to repeal (if not replace) Obamacare, there is little indication it is willing to move toward Trump's priorities on issues such as infrastructure.

There are also substantial questions about the ability of any Republican to govern on an agenda of disdain for the government, massive specific tax cuts, and unspecified budget cuts. These concerns are only greater for a president who has never held political office and whose closest advisors have as much experience in government as he does. Trump seems to constantly generate scandal and his voters seem to trust him despite his foibles because of their belief that he, as a non-politician, can deliver on his promises.

It is worth noting at this point that historically those who have relied upon the promises of Donald Trump, whether his creditors, former employees, or even his ex-wives, have left the exchange disappointed. And Donald Trump was not exactly circumspect in his campaign promises. He promised to bring manufacturing and mining jobs back to the country, keep the country existing, and restore the nation's sense of pride. At one point, Trump said "you have 40 days to make every dream you ever dreamed for your country come true" (Benen 2016). Trump must meet this seemingly impossible set of promises. Trump may not be a conventional politician and the 2016 election indicates that a broad number of political "rules" seem to either no longer apply, or not to apply to Donald Trump. Yet we can be certain that one rule is still in force: politicians who cannot meet the promises they make to supporters cannot count on winning re-election.

NOTES

1. I will also note without further comment that the fourth hit on this search is for the Trump National Golf Club in Bedminster, NJ.
2. After Germans, Irish, African-Americans, and English. Following Americans are Mexicans, Italians, and Poles.
3. Underneath the answer grid, the form says "For example: Italian, Jamaican, African Am., Cambodian, Cape Verdean, Norwegian, Dominican, French Canadian, Haitian, Korean, Lebanese, Polish, Nigerian, Mexican, Taiwanese, Ukrainian, and so on."
4. Among all respondents, 80% write in an ethnicity on this question.
5. All data in the Upshot analysis are at the county level.
6. It is worth noting that Trump broke this promise by supporting the American Health Care Act. The version that passed the US House on May 4, 2017, would cut $880 million from Medicare over a decade. It remains to be seen what, if any, political price Trump pays for breaking this promise (Kliff 2017).
7. To be fair to Trump voters, the fault on this last one lies mostly with members of the national media, who gave little coverage to Trump's use of the ethnic slur "Pocahontas." When they did, they tended to regard this clear ethnic slur as a "nickname" (Nelson 2016; Lemire 2017).
8. In 2001, Clifton Forge, VA gave up its status as an "independent city" and reverted to the surrounding Allegheny County. As a result, the number of unhyphenated concentrated counties declined from 531 to 530.

9. Broomfield County in Colorado was created in 2001 from parts of Adams, Boulder, Jefferson, and Weld counties. That same year, Clifton Forge, Virginia gave up its status as an independent city and reverted to Allegheny County. These changes make comparisons across time for these counties difficult. I excluded these counties from the regression analysis.

REFERENCES

Alba, Richard D. 1990. *Ethnic Identity: The Transformation of White America.* New Haven, CT: Yale University Press.

Alba, Richard D., and Victor Nee. 1997. Rethinking Assimilation Theory for a New Era of Immigration. *International Migration Review* 31 (4): 826–874.

Alonso-Zaldivar, Ricardo. 2016. Study Finds 20M Would Lose Health Coverage Under Trump Plan. *US News & World Report.* https://www.usnews.com/news/politics/articles/2016-09-23/study-finds-20m-would-lose-health-coverage-under-trump-plan. Accessed March 11, 2017.

Appalachian Regional Commission. 2017. Suicide Mortality in Appalachia. https://www.arc.gov/assets/research_reports/Mortality_SUICIDE.pdf. Accessed March 1, 2017.

Arbour, Brian K. 2011. Unhyphenated Americans in the 2010 U.S. House Election. *The Forum* 9 (2): Article 4.

———. 2014. "The Rise of Appalachian Republicans: Party Realignment and Unhyphenated Americans," presented at the *American Political Science Association* Annual Meeting, Washington, DC, August 28–31, 2014.

———. n.d. Unhyphenated Americans, Barack Obama, and the Rise of Republicans. *Social Science Quarterly.* Forthcoming.

Arbour, Brian K., and Jeremy M. Teigen. 2011. Barack Obama's 'American' Problem: Unhyphenated Americans in the 2008 Elections. *Social Science Quarterly* 92 (3): 563–587.

———. 2016. These Two Maps Are Incredibly Revealing About Who's Voting for Trump, and Why. WashingtonPost.com (The Monkey Cage). https://www.washingtonpost.com/news/wp/2016/04/05/these-two-maps-are-incredibly-revealing-about-whos-voting-for-trump-and-why/?utm_term=.3e78daba5c59. Accessed February 3, 2016.

Barone, Michael. 2008. In Terms of Geography, Obama Appeals to Academics and Clinton Appeals to Jacksonians. USNews.com. http://www.usnews.com/opinion/blogs/barone/2008/04/02/reviewing-the-primary-results-academics-versus-jacksonians. Accessed December 20, 2010.

Benen, Steve. 2016. Trump Vows to Fulfill 'Every Dream You Ever Dreamed.' MSNBC.com. http://www.msnbc.com/rachel-maddow-show/trump-vows-fulfill-every-dream-you-ever-dreamed. Accessed March 11, 2017.

Black, Earl, and Merle Black. 2002. *The Rise of Southern Republicans*. Cambridge, MA: Harvard University Press.

Brittingham, Angela, and G. Patricia de la Cruz. 2004. *Ancestry: 2000*. Washington, DC: US Census Bureau. http://www.census.gov/prod/2004pubs/c2kbr-35.pdf

Brody, David. 2015, May 21. Why Donald Trump Won't Touch Your Entitlements. DailySignal.com. http://dailysignal.com/2015/05/21/why-donald-trump-wont-touch-your-entitlements/. Accessed March 1, 2017.

Brownstein, Ronald. 2016. Trump's Rhetoric of White Nostalgia. *The Atlantic.com*, June 2, 2016. https://www.theatlantic.com/politics/archive/2016/06/trumps-rhetoric-of-white-nostalgia/485192/. Accessed June 14, 2017.

Bump, Philip. 2016. A Brief History of Donald Trump's Denialist Position on Climate Change. WashingtonPost.com (The Fix). https://www.washingtonpost.com/news/the-fix/wp/2016/09/27/a-brief-history-of-donald-trumps-denialist-position-on-climate-change/?utm_term=.0782af481c6e. Accessed March 11, 2017.

Burns, Alexander, Maggie Haberman, and Jonathan Martin. 2016. Donald Trump Apology Caps Day of Outrage Over Lewd Tape. *New York Times*. https://www.nytimes.com/2016/10/08/us/politics/donald-trump-women.html. Accessed March 11, 2017.

Cohen, Roger. 2016, September 9. We Need 'Somebody Spectacular': Views from Trump County. NYTimes.com. https://www.nytimes.com/2016/09/11/opinion/sunday/we-need-somebody-spectacular-views-from-trump-country.html. Accessed March 1, 2017.

Confessore, Nicholas. 2016. How G.O.P. Elites Lost the Party's Base to Trump. *New York Times*, March 28, 2016, p. A1(L). Infotrac. http://go.galegroup.com/ps/i.do?p=STND&sw=w&u=cuny_johnjay&v=2.1&id=GALE%7CA44 7618737&it=r&asid=4c2c82347113a0283c7b31f24cfd2019. Accessed March 1, 2017.

Escoria, Juliet. 2016. The Hard Times, Struggles, and Hopes of Addicts in Appalachia. Vice.com. https://www.vice.com/en_us/article/the-hard-times-struggles-and-hopes-of-appalachian-addicts-ang. Accessed March 1, 2017.

Farley, Reynolds. 1991. The New Census Question about Ancestry: What Did It Tell Us? *Demography* 28 (3): 411–429.

Fenno, Richard F., Jr. 1977. US House Members in Their Constituencies: An Exploration. *American Political Science Review* 71 (3): 883–917.

Fischer, David Hackett. 1989. *Albion's Seed: Four British Folkways in America*. New York, NY: Oxford University Press.

Gans, Herbert J. 1979. Symbolic Ethnicity: The Future of Ethnic Groups and Cultures in America. *Ethnic and Racial Studies* 2 (1): 1–20.

Gimpel, James G., and Wendy K. Tam Cho. 2004. The Persistence of White Ethnicity in New England Politics. *Political Geography* 23 (8): 987–1008.

Heer, Jeet. 2016. https://twitter.com/HeerJeet/status/715279919299710976. Accessed March 12, 2016.

Irwin, Neil, and Josh Katz. 2016. The Geography of Trumpism. March 12, 2016. NYTimes.com (The Upshot). https://www.nytimes.com/2016/03/13/upshot/the-geography-of-trumpism.html?ref=politics&_r=2. Accessed February 3, 2016.

Kaplan, Thomas. 2016. This Is Trump Country. *New York Times*, March 4, 2016. https://www.nytimes.com/interactive/2016/03/04/us/politics/donald-trump-voters.html?_r=0. Accessed June 14, 2017.

Kaufman, Chris. 2016. Republican Trump Says 70 Percent of Federal Regulations 'Can Go.' Reuters.com, October 7, 2016. http://www.reuters.com/article/us-usa-election-trump-regulations-idUSKCN12629R. Accessed March 11, 2017.

Kellman, Laurie, and Adam Beam. 2016, November 13. Trump Country: What One County Tells Us About the Election. AP.com (Associated Press). http://bigstory.ap.org/article/06e8c4950c364f66994d194b0ec64f50/trump-country-democratic-elliott-county-ky-23-points. Accessed March 1, 2017.

Kendall, Brent. 2016. Trump Says Judge's Mexican Heritage Presents 'Absolute Conflict'. *Wall Street Journal*, June 3, 2016. https://www.wsj.com/articles/donald-trump-keeps-up-attacks-on-judge-gonzalo-curiel-1464911442. Accessed March 11, 2017.

Key, V.O. 1949. *Southern Politics in State and Nation*. New York, NY: A. A. Knopf.

Khazan, Olga. 2014. The New Heroin Epidemic. TheAtlantic.com, October 30, 2014. https://www.theatlantic.com/health/archive/2014/10/the-new-heroin-epidemic/382020/. Accessed March 1, 2017.

Kliff, Sarah. 2017. CBO Estimates 24 Million Lose Coverage Under GOP Plan. The Devastating Report, Explained. Vox.com, March 13, 2017. https://www.vox.com/2017/3/13/14912520/cbo-ahca-gop-plan. Accessed May 5, 2017.

Lemire, Jonathan. 2017. Trump Revives 'Pocahontas' Insult of Elizabeth Warren. AP.com, April 28, 2017. https://apnews.com/95a2c08c98714990a1e1cc644 02da516?utm_campaign=SocialFlow&utm_source=Twitter&utm_medium=AP_Politics. Accessed May 5, 2017.

Lieberson, Stanley. 1985. Unhyphenated Whites in the United States. *Ethnic and Racial Studies* 8 (1): 159–180.

———. 1989. The Rise of a New Ethnic Group: The 'Unhyphenated American'. *Social Science Research Council Items* 43: 7–10.

———. 1993. The Ethnic Responses of Whites: What Causes Their Instability, Simplification, and Inconsistency? *Social Forces* 72 (2): 421–450.

Lind, Michael. 1999. Civil War by Other Means. *Foreign Affairs* 78 (5): 123–142.

Lindstrom, Lauren. 2016. Trump Wants to Bring Jobs Back to Ohio. *Toledo Blade*, October 14, 2016. http://www.toledoblade.com/Politics/2016/10/14/

Donald-Trump-wants-to-bring-jobs-back-to-Ohio-Economy-is-Republican-s-focus-in-speech-in-Cincinnati.html. Accessed March 11, 2017.

MacFarquar, Larissa. 2016, October 10. In the Heat of Trump Country. *New Yorker*. http://www.newyorker.com/magazine/2016/10/10/in-the-heart-of-trump-country. Accessed March 1, 2016.

Mahler, Jonathan, and Steve Eder. 2016. 'No Vacancies' for Blacks: How Donald Trump Got His Start and Was First Accused of Bias. *New York Times*, August 27, 2016. https://www.nytimes.com/2016/08/28/us/politics/donald-trump-housing-race.html?_r=0. Accessed March 11, 2017.

Matthews, Dylan, and Javier Zarracina. 2016. The Huge Republican Tax Cut Plans, in 4 Charts. Vox.com, February 25, 2016. http://www.vox.com/2016/2/25/11109160/donald-trump-marco-rubio-tax-comparison. Accessed March 11, 2016.

Miller, Abraham H. 1971. Ethnicity and Political Behavior: A Review of Theories and an Attempt at Reformulation. *Western Political Quarterly* 24 (3): 483–500.

———. 1974. Ethnicity and Party Identification: Continuation of a Theoretical Dialogue. *Western Political Quarterly* 27 (3): 479–490.

Neidert, Lisa J., and Reynolds Farley. 1985. Assimilation in the United States: An Analysis of Ethnic and Generation Differences in Status and Achievement. *American Sociological Review* 50 (6): 840–850.

Nelson, Colleen McCain. 2016. Trump Is Challenged on 'Pocahontas' Nickname for Elizabeth Warren. *Wall Street Journal*, May 26, 2016. http://blogs.wsj.com/washwire/2016/05/26/trump-is-challenged-on-pocahontas--nickname-for-elizabeth-warren/. Accessed March 12, 2017.

New York Times. 2016. Transcript of the Republican Presidential Debate in Detroit. *New York Times*, March 4, 2016. http://go.galegroup.com/ps/i.do?p=STND&sw=w&u=cuny_johnjay&v=2.1&id=GALE%7CA444995708&it=r&asid=6a3ddc298491c1aa65a35b1695af04e9. Accessed March 1, 2017.

Omi, Michael A. 2001. The Changing Meaning of Race. In *America Becoming: Racial Trends and Their Consequences*, ed. N.J. Smelser, W.J. Wilson, and F. Mitchell. Washington, DC: National Academy Press.

Omi, Michael A., and Howard Winant. 1994. Racial Formation. In *Racial Formation in the United States*, ed. Michael Omi and Howard Winant, 53–76. New York, NY: Routledge.

Perez, Anthony Daniel, and Charles Hirschman. 2009. The Changing Racial and Ethnic Composition of the US Population: Emerging American Identities. *Population and Development Review* 35 (1): 1–51.

Rappeport, Alan, and Alicia Parlapiano. 2016. Where Trump Breaks with the Republican Party. *New York Times*, May 12, 2016, p. A17(L). Infotrac. http://go.galegroup.com/ps/i.do?p=STND&sw=w&u=cuny_johnjay&v=2.1&id=GALE%7CA452138329&it=r&asid=f832964326fedbb9c4aa83582370fb8a. Accessed March 1, 2017.

Sonenshein, Raphael J., and Nicholas A. Valentino. 2000. The Distinctiveness of Jewish Voting. *Urban Affairs Review* 35 (3): 358–389.

Tesler, Michael. 2016. *Post Racial or Most-Racial? Race and Politics in the Obama Era*. Chicago: University of Chicago Press.

Trubowitz, Peter. 1992. Sectionalism and American Foreign Policy: The Political Geography of Consensus and Conflict. *International Studies Quarterly* 36: 173–190.

Trump, Donald J. 2015. Donald J. Trump Statement on Preventing Muslim Immigration. https://www.donaldjtrump.com/press-releases/donald-j.-trump-statement-on-preventing-muslim-immigration. Accessed March 1, 2017.

Waters, Mary C. 1990. *Ethnic Options: Choosing Identities in America*. Berkeley, CA: University of California Press.

Wolfinger, Raymond E. 1965. The Development and Persistence of Ethnic Voting. *American Political Science Review* 59 (4): 896–908.

Yglesias, Matthew. 2016. Donald Trump Gave an Interview This Morning that Should Be Shocking—But We're Numb. Vox.com, September 12, 2016. http://www.vox.com/2016/9/12/12887522/donald-trump-interview-shocking-numb. Accessed March 11, 2017.

Brian Arbour is Associate Professor of Political Science at John Jay College, City University of New York. He conducts research on campaigns and elections, political parties, campaign strategy, campaign message strategy, and political geography. He is the author of *Candidate-Centered Campaigns: Political Messages, Winning Personalities, and Personal Appeals* (Palgrave) and is a member of the election night Decision Team for Fox News Channel.

CHAPTER 3

Parties and Populism in 2016

David A. Dulio and John S. Klemanski

*This was the year of bipartisan, ecumenical, populist rage and it was enough
that the figure of Donald Trump was able to marshal that populist outrage
and engineer a hostile takeover of the Republican Party. Bernie Sanders on
the left was able to marshal that populist rage and nearly beat Hillary Clinton
in the Democratic Party nomination fight. On the back of widespread outrage
and anger at Democrats, at Republicans, at Washington, at Wall Street, at
the Fortune 500, at the mass media, at every major establishment institution
in the county, people are ... pissed off.... For about half the country, their lives
have sucked for the last 25 years while all the rest of us have been doing fine.
They have no real hope that their lives are going to get better and their attitude
was: "You know what? That guy is risky, but doing the same thing over and
over again for another 20 years that we did for the last 20 years that didn't fix
anything either, that's risky too and I'm willing to take these risks and just roll
a ... stick of dynamite into Washington, D.C. and blow the [whole thing] up
and see where the rubble falls."*
—John Heilemann, managing editor of Bloomberg Politics, on election night 2016 during the *Showtime* series *The Circus: Inside the Greatest
Political Show on Earth.*

D.A. Dulio (✉) • J.S. Klemanski
Department of Political Science, Oakland University, Rochester, MI, USA

43

These words are an excellent description of the dynamics surrounding the 2016 presidential election. They are even more enlightening for our purpose here—to examine questions related to parties and populism during the campaign and their impact on the outcome.

To say the 2016 election was different from previous elections in many ways is an understatement. After all, who could have predicted that a candidate such as Donald Trump—a candidate with no previous government experience and who frequently insulted his primary and general election opponents—would win not only the primary but go on to win the White House? In that same campaign season, Bernie Sanders, a self-described "democratic socialist", nearly won the Democratic nomination against Hillary Clinton, whom some described as "the most qualified person to run for president since George Washington" (Jacoby 2016). How is it possible that Sanders and Trump were so surprisingly successful in the 2016 election cycle?

"Populism" or "populist" has tended to be a broad and often vague term applied to many candidates and political issues over time. There is some agreement by scholars over common elements of populism in US political history. Broadly speaking, populism adopts a moral vision of the superiority of the common people, while vilifying economic or political elites.[1] A major target of populist messages could include any established institution (e.g., mainstream political parties, the media, "big banks", or global corporations) perceived to be unresponsive to the needs of average people. Other targets include political leaders who are career politicians, those perceived to be corrupt (and who help those in power), and politicians who are thought by voters to lie and cheat in order to gain or maintain power.

Bernie Sanders and Donald Trump both offered populist messages to voters, although they rarely agreed on policy positions. Their approach was widely described as "populism" by the media, and some of Sanders's criticisms of wealth inequality evoked the People's Party of the 1890s. However, Donald Trump's nativist "America First" and his anti-illegal immigration positions also seemed to echo the American Party of the 1840s and 1850s, also known as the "Know Nothing" party (Cannon 2015). While neither Sanders nor Trump fit the populist label exactly, both adopted a version of populism that targeted establishment institutions, and both specifically challenged the mainstream elements of their respective political parties. As outsiders, Sanders and Trump often proposed opposing policy solutions during the campaign, but their criticism of establishment party politics, mainstream candidates, and current government policies was a major theme of both candidates.

In this chapter, we first examine a brief history of parties and populism in US politics to better understand why the recent populist messages emerged—and why they were so compelling to voters in 2016. We then explore the dynamics of the Democratic nomination process and chart how the popularity of Bernie Sanders's populism made him a serious contender for the nomination. We believe his unexpected success also served as a predictive measure of Hillary Clinton's vulnerability against Donald Trump's populist messages in the general election. We then move to Donald Trump's primary election campaign and what appeared to be an anti-party establishment approach. Part of this approach also included what some described as a populist message to voters. In the general election, Donald Trump's Electoral College victory came in large part due to voter support in the traditionally blue states of Pennsylvania, Wisconsin, and Michigan. These industrialized blue-collar states had long supported Democratic presidential candidates, but Trump's message effectively flipped these states to the Republican column. We analyze the appeal of Donald Trump to voters in Michigan, where a majority of the state's voters formerly had supported each Democratic presidential candidate since the 1988 election.

Finally, we discuss how the success of populism in the 2016 presidential election has caused both major political parties to examine their own messages. For many years, scholars have debated about whether certain past elections have served as realigning elections, or if there has been a long-term dealignment among voters, who now focus less on party attachment as a voting cue, and more on specific policy positions of candidates, individual candidate qualities, or personality politics. That ongoing debate will influence the future direction and policy positions adopted by the two major parties.

3.1   Populism and Parties in US History

In a representative democracy, political parties and candidates often lay claim to being able to best represent "the people". As long as enough voters believe that their interests are represented adequately, the people's voice will be expressed through party platforms and candidate positions on issues that form winning coalitions at election time. However, the adequacy of representation available through extant political parties and candidates is not always successfully maintained over long periods of time. When parties and mainstream candidates are seen by voters to fail the people's interest, then alternatives may be sought by voters and political activists.

One alternative is to support candidates or politicians who advocate for "common" people and who often oppose the current political structures, institutions, and leaders on behalf of "the people". Throughout US history, there have been many individuals who have taken on the existing political establishment on behalf of the people's interest. In the earliest years of the United States, anti-federalist groups fought against the centralized power of the Federalist Party, a fight that continued in the form of Jeffersonian opposition to aristocratic elites. In the 1830s, Jacksonian democracy expanded voting rights to include white men without property, a departure from previous laws restricting voting to male property owners or those wealthy enough to pay a poll tax.

Another alternative is for those unhappy with the current party system to create a new political party. Minor parties form and grow because the major political parties at the time are not addressing at least some issues considered important to a portion of the voting population. Notably, this led to the formation of the People's Party, also known as the Populist Party, which was founded in the early 1890s. The party grew out of a populist movement that had opposed the increased income and wealth inequality that came from the "industrial age's regime of market cartels, debt peonage and degraded wage labor" (Lehmann 2015). In this regard, populists of the time were more focused on economic elites and their belief that improper and corrupt business practices led to a serious economic depression known as the Panic of 1893. Populists believed that neither the Republican nor the Democratic parties appeared to have solutions to the economic problems occurring at the time. The People's Party nominated presidential and vice-presidential candidates in 1892, winning almost 10% of the popular vote and 22 Electoral College votes that year. The party then endorsed the Democratic Party nominee William Jennings Bryan in 1896. The People's Party, however, was able to elect a number of state governors, members of the US House and Senate, and state legislators in several states during the late 1800s.

Another politician with a strong populist message emerged around the time of the Great Depression. Huey Long served as Louisiana Governor and US Senator in the late 1920s and early 1930s, and fought against the wealthy elite and big banks. A Democrat, he advocated for a "Share Our Wealth" program, and as governor, expanded schools and charity hospitals for those who were poor. He proposed a wealth redistribution system that would have helped those who were homeless and living in poverty during the Great Depression that would have been funded by a "wealth tax", on corporations and businesses. Most of the early populist messages seemed to focus on economic inequalities and therefore have been associated with more egalitarian and leftist politics.

Of course, many candidates claim to speak for "the people" or try to use their outsider status to attract voters frustrated with the status quo. Richard Nixon talked about a "silent majority" of the US population that was not represented sufficiently in the late 1960s and early 1970s. Georgia governor Jimmy Carter ran for president in 1976 as a candidate who was a "Washington outsider" who was proud he did not have Washington DC experience. In the 1980s, Ronald Reagan proposed significant changes to established economic and foreign policy. Over the past 40 years, Ross Perot, Pat Buchanan, George Wallace, Sarah Palin, the Occupy Wall Street movement, and the Tea Party movement all can be considered to be outsiders or have had some elements of a populist message and philosophy.

3.2   POPULISM IN 2016

News accounts of the 2016 presidential nominations and general election frequently referred to both Donald Trump and Bernie Sanders as outsiders and populists.[2] Voters frustrated with the ineffectiveness of government were thought to be particularly attracted to candidate messages that sought to make substantial—rather than incremental—changes to the status quo. Many voters seemed to indicate that both parties were to blame for being unwilling or unable to respond to their needs or those of other Americans.

In general, we agree with scholars who have suggested that, in part, "… populism always involves a critique of the establishment and an adulation of the common people" (Mudde and Kaltwasser 2017, 4). Criticism of established institutions can be far reaching—for example, it can include political institutions and established political actors, global corporations, mainstream media, and mainstream political parties or candidates. Populist political candidates advocate for major changes in the current system, which they identify as corrupt, ineffective, unfair, or all of the above. For all of their policy differences, Donald Trump and Bernie Sanders both criticized the media as part of their appeals to voters. This is where the similarity ends, however, as Trump claimed that mainstream media misrepresented his positions or did not cover him properly, while Sanders argued that the corporate-based news outlets often portrayed his ideas for social reform as too extreme or on the fringe of American politics. Both Trump and Sanders also criticized the political parties under whose banner they were running. Interestingly, both candidates had an unorthodox relationship with their respective political parties. Since the 1980s, Trump had switched his party registration several times. As we discuss in more detail below, his positions on several issues—most notably as an opponent of free trade and his support of increased taxes to sustain the solvency of Social Security—were contrary to the views of the mainstream Republican Party. While Bernie Sanders caucused with the Democrats in Congress, he had always run as an Independent candidate—often facing both Republican and Democratic Party opposition in his elections.

Both candidates were able to tap into an anti-government and anti-party mood of the voters during the 2016 election cycle. In one late October 2016 poll (just a week or so prior to the election), 61% of survey respondents indicated that neither major political party reflected their opinions. This view was espoused by more Republicans (54%) than Democrats (46%), but a large percentage of Independents (77%) also responded that neither party reflected their beliefs. According to this same poll, almost three-quarters of survey respondents (74%) reported that the United States was on the wrong track compared to 57% who had the same opinion prior to the 2012 presidential election (Smith 2016). Early on in 2016, voters appeared to be ready for a candidate who would shake up the status quo, and Donald Trump turned out to be that candidate. In addition, Bernie Sanders offered Democratic Party primary voters a distinct choice in contrast to Hillary Clinton, the party's mainstream candidate.

3.3   SANDERS TAKES ON ESTABLISHMENT DEMOCRATIC PARTY POLITICS

About one month after Hillary Clinton announced her candidacy for president in 2016 via a YouTube posting (Clinton 2015), Bernie Sanders stood on the shore of Lake Champlain on May 26, 2015, in his home state of Vermont to officially announce he was running for the Democratic Party presidential nomination (Sanders 2015). Sanders has been a longtime politician and public servant—he served as Mayor of Burlington, Vermont, then later as the state's lone member of the US House of Representatives, and finally, US Senator, for a total of 34 years at the time of his 2015 announcement for president.

Despite this long service, Sanders considered himself an outsider, since he has claimed to be a democratic socialist throughout his career, and formally had Independent partisan status in the US Congress. His announcement speech evoked some of the views of the nineteenth-century populists, the New Deal of the 1930s, and the Occupy Wall Street movement of the twenty-first century. Sanders told the crowd that:

> Today, with your support and the support of millions of people throughout this country, we begin a political revolution to transform our country economically, politically, socially and environmentally. Today, we stand here and say loudly and clearly that; 'Enough is enough. This great nation and its government belong to all of the people, and not to a handful of billionaires, their Super-PACs and their lobbyists.' Brothers and sisters: Now is not the time for thinking small. Now is not the time for the same old–same old establishment politics and stale inside-the-beltway ideas. (Sanders 2015)

In that announcement speech, Sanders specifically targeted problems of income and wealth inequality, unemployment and the need for jobs, climate change, breaking up big banks and financial institutions, and the need for a living wage for Americans. Throughout his primary campaign, he continued to criticize wealth and income inequality and advocate for nothing short of "a political revolution" by voters. As a US Senator, in 2015, he introduced a bill regulating financial institutions, which he called the "Too Big to Fail, Too Big to Exist Act". This bill also would break up the biggest banks in the United States, avoid taxpayer bailouts, and restrict the banks' access to the Federal Reserve's discount facilities (Sanders 2016). With many of his proposals, he echoed some of the nineteenth-century populist criticism of establishment politics and the economy, while continuing to push the Democratic Party—and Hillary Clinton—farther to the left.

Early in the primary season, Sanders was battling more than the other primary contenders. In December 2015, Sanders filed a lawsuit against the DNC, claiming that the party had unfairly blocked his campaign's access to voter file information kept by the party on behalf of its candidates. In turn, the DNC had claimed that Sanders staffers had gained improper access to the Hillary Clinton campaign files. Sanders had admitted this occurred (although a private vendor operating the system was blamed for allowing this access), but had fired the staffers immediately. Although an agreement was worked out, and access to the files was allowed again, this early spat between the DNC and the Sanders campaign left some Sanders supporters feeling as though the DNC was showing favoritism toward Hillary Clinton (Wagner et al. 2015).

Sanders performed surprisingly well in the first three Democratic nominating contests. He narrowly lost the Iowa caucus by a 49.8% to 49.6% vote in the first contest of the primary season. About one week later, Sanders handily beat Hillary Clinton 60.4% to 38.0% in the New Hampshire primary, although many observers had expected the Vermont Senator to do well in his neighboring state. He lost by about five points in the Nevada caucus, 52.6% to 47.3%, but had been able to close a larger gap in the days prior to the caucus (Chozick and Healy 2016).

The populist message of Sanders, which some less-salient issues such as campaign finance reform—did not seem to make inroads into Hillary Clinton's base of supporters, especially in the South. He did not win a single primary in the Deep South, but did well in Upper Midwest, northern Plains, and Northwest states.

A total of nine Democratic debates were held beginning with an October 13, 2015, debate held in Las Vegas, Nevada, and the last held in Brooklyn, New York, on April 14, 2016. Sanders seemed to focus more on criticism of Donald Trump than Hillary Clinton in his campaign stump speeches, but in the debate held in Brooklyn, Sanders criticized Hillary Clinton specifically on several issues: Clinton's vote for the War in Iraq, her support of free trade agreements, and her acceptance of Super PAC money and her ties to Wall Street. He also argued that Clinton had not supported a national increase to a $15 per hour minimum wage, and she was too close to big banks and Wall Street to be able to effectively regulate those institutions.

While Bernie Sanders had some surprising success in a number of states, Hillary Clinton's more mainstream Democratic Party approach ultimately prevailed. In early June, with a handful of state primaries yet to be held, Clinton reached the minimum number of delegates to be nominated and she became the first woman ever to be nominated president by a major political party. The Sanders campaign continued to argue that super delegates (who were included in the number that put Clinton over the top) could switch their preference, so the nomination had not yet been sewn up (Dann 2016). Sanders supporters continued to complain that unfair nominating rules had put Sanders at a disadvantage.

The question of fairness returned several times during the primary campaign, with a blockbuster event that occurred in late July 2016. Just prior to the Democratic convention, thousands of hacked emails to and from DNC officials were publicly released. Much of the information from the emails was likely at least embarrassing to the DNC, as some of the emails were disrespectful of Democratic loyalists and large donors to the party (Blake 2016). For example, there was correspondence that fed into both Bernie Sanders' and the Republican Party's narratives that likely hurt Hillary Clinton's general election campaign. First, there appeared to be a lack of respect by DNC officials—who are supposed to remain neutral during primary season—of Sanders and his campaign. Favoritism of Clinton showed in the language of the emails, although it was less obvious that the DNC had acted overtly on behalf of Clinton. We would point out that such favoritism shown in private emails should not be too surprising, since Democratic Party loyalists did not regard Sanders as a true Democrat (after all, he had always run as an Independent prior to the presidential race). For Republicans and Donald Trump, this apparent favoritism toward Hillary Clinton allowed them to continue their narrative about Clinton conspiring behind the scenes to grab power, and that the political system was rigged on her behalf. The DNC chair, Debbie Wasserman Schultz, resigned in the wake of the leaked emails and subsequent fallout.

With his anti-party establishment strategy, Bernie Sanders found considerable support among younger and college-educated voters. Many of these voters shared his criticism of the current political and economic system. One interesting take-away from the Sanders campaign is that the ideas of (and even the label) socialism apparently have become more acceptable, at least within segments of the Democratic Party. In part, this might be due to the perceived limited prospects for young people, even those with a college degree. Wealth inequality and the issues raised by the Occupy Wall Street movement fit well with the Bernie Sanders view of the world. These issues have resonated with younger voters so much that a recent Pew Research poll found that 49% of millennials viewed socialism favorably (compared to 43% who were unfavorable).[3]

In the end, Bernie Sanders lost the popular vote to Hillary Clinton by 55% to 43% in the Democratic Party primaries. Sanders earned over 13 million votes to Clinton's almost 17 million, while winning 23 primary contests compared to Clinton's 34. These results were surprising, especially since Bernie Sanders was a democratic socialist candidate far to the left of the mainstream Democratic Party, who was not even a registered member of the party. While the Democrats experienced mostly a two-person contest for almost the entire primary season, the Republican primary saw many more candidates, with one candidate emerging as a clear anti-mainstream party candidate—Donald Trump.

3.4   TRUMP AGAINST THE ESTABLISHMENT

From the minute Donald Trump announced his candidacy for president of the United States at Trump Tower in New York City, it was clear that his campaign would be unconventional and outside of the Republican Party establishment. First, Trump was a candidate with no experience running for elective office. Trump had, however, either toyed with running or threatened to run for office in the past including in 1988, 2000, 2004, 2008, and 2012. In the 2004 and 2012 election cycles, Trump claimed he was "very seriously" considering running (Frizell 2015). Even during his prior flirtations with running for office, Trump's anti-establishment tendencies came out. In 2004, Trump clearly showed what could be called an aversion to the GOP when he said about his partisan leanings, "In many cases, I probably identify more as Democrat" (Moody 2015). In 2008, he called Republican President George W. Bush "the worst president in the history of the United States".[4] In the lead up to the 2012 cycle, Trump remarked, "A lot of people think I'm doing this for fun, they think it's good for my brand ... I'm not doing this for fun. I'm doing this because we have to take our country back", foreshadowing some of the rhetoric of his 2016 campaign.[5]

The closest Trump came to running for political office was in the 2000 election cycle when he stopped identifying with the Republican Party and participated in some nominating contests under the Reform Party banner.[6] At the time, Trump said, "I understand this stuff ... I understand good times and I understand bad times. I mean, why is a politician going to do a better job than I am?" (CNN 1999). Trump went so far as to form an exploratory committee with the Federal Election Commission which is short of a formal fundraising committee that candidates for federal office must create to run; the exploratory committee does not have the same kind of filing requirements as a formal candidate committee and permits candidates to "test the waters" of a run for office.[7] In 2000, Trump even won the Michigan and California Reform Party primaries (Federal Election Commission 2000). Trump had, however, already dropped out of the race before either contest took place.

Another aspect of Trump's unconventional and anti-establishment tendencies before becoming the 2016 GOP nominee was the range of his political contributions to candidates who were running for office. While he had not run for office before, Trump had been active in politics for many years, but mainly as a donor to other candidates' political campaigns. In many instances, he contributed to Democratic candidates' campaigns, including Hillary Clinton's previous campaigns, as well as the Clinton Foundation to which he donated $100,000 (Gass 2015). According to the Center for Responsive Politics, between 1990 and 2011, Trump made contributions to a total of 96 candidates running for office at the federal level (i.e., president, US House, and US Senate) but only half were to Republican candidates (Newkirk 2011). During the 2016 GOP primary process, Trump was asked about his pattern of contributions including those to Democrats, and he responded, "I support politicians. In 2008, I supported Hillary Clinton, I supported many other people, by the way, and that was because of the fact that I'm in business" (Gehrke 2016).

Some of the candidates to whom Trump contributed include, Clinton, then-Senator Edward Kennedy (D-MA), then-Senator John Kerry (D-MA), then-Senate Majority Leader Harry Reid (D-NV), and then-Senator Joe Biden (D-DE). Trump did contribute to Republicans, but many of those were not from the establishment wing of the party either and included former Florida Governor Charlie Crist and former Senator Arlen Specter (R-PA). Interestingly both of these individuals would at one point in their career leave the GOP and change their party affiliation to Independent and Democrat, respectively. Trump, however, also gave to Republicans like George W. Bush and Newt Gingrich, two elected officials who certainly fit the establishment Republican mold. Interestingly, after 2011, Trump began to give almost exclusively to Republican candidates (Kurtzleben 2015) .

Throughout the years, Trump had been circling around presidential politics. He occasionally made statements about his positions on issues, many of which seemed closer to what Democratic candidates and office holders might say. For example, the left-leaning online magazine *Salon* published a story in 2015 titled, "Let's all remember that time when Donald Trump sounded like Bernie Sanders on healthcare" (Tesfaye 2015). The story recounts some of Trump's previously announced issue positions including that "we need, as a nation, to reexamine the single-payer plan" and, in reference to Canada's single-payer, government-run system, his remark that the United States will "have to improve on the prototype" (Tesfaye 2015).

Moreover, Karl Rove, longtime Republican political consultant and "the architect" of George W. Bush's 2004 presidential victory, wrote an article in 2015 for the *Wall Street Journal* that methodically laid out Trump's previous positions that conflict with Republican policy tenets including on healthcare as noted above. Rove also pointed to statements that indicated Trump had, at one time at least, a pro-choice stance on abortion, been in favor of gun control, and favored "a one-time, 14.25 percent tax on individuals and trusts with a net worth over $10 million" to make Social Security solvent for a longer period of time (Rove 2015).

Other previous statements foreshadowed his bid for the presidency in 2016. For instance, according to *Time*, "Back in 1987, Trump took out full-page ads in several newspapers, criticizing the political establishment, then run by Ronald Reagan, for its coddling of the OPEC countries and Japan" (Scherer 2011). Ironies abound with this statement. First, President Reagan remains one of the icons in the Republican Party. Second, it hints at Trump's rhetoric and strategy for 2016. In addition, nearly 15 years later, Trump would make another unconventional and anti-establishment comment: "Nobody can do the job that I can do ... I can make this country great again. This country is not great. This country is a laughingstock for the rest of the world" (Scherer 2015). Of course, this mirrors Trump's popular slogan from 2016 "Make America Great Again", but it does so roughly four years before it connected with so many of his voters.

With Trump's prior hints at running for office and his varied contribution patterns behind him, Trump declared his intention to run for the Republican Party nomination for president on June 16, 2015. During his announcement speech, Trump hit on a variety of themes and issues. Some of these would sound familiar to those who had followed the previous instances Trump toyed with the idea of running for office. These included his ability to accomplish policy goals because he is not a politician, his criticism of current elected officials for creating gridlock, being a deal maker, and references to what would become his slogan during the campaign—calls to "make America great again". Others would be familiar because they hit on tenets of Republican Party orthodoxy, including calling for repeal of the Affordable Care Act (aka, Obamacare), a hard line on illegal immigration and ISIS, concern about the federal debt, strengthening the military, and a strong defense of Second Amendment rights. But others sounded strange coming from a GOP presidential candidate because they had what some would call a populist theme. Indeed, issues of trade and bringing back or creating manufacturing jobs were a central theme of the speech. Included in these statements were words that many in the state of Michigan would listen to carefully because they dealt with the automobile manufacturing sector and trade with other nations. In the speech, Trump said, "We need a leader that can bring back our jobs, can bring back our manufacturing … A lot of people … can't get jobs. They can't get jobs, because there are no jobs, because China has our jobs and Mexico has our jobs…" (Washington Post 2015). He continued, "I'll bring back our jobs from China, from Mexico, from Japan, from so many places. I'll bring back our jobs, and I'll bring back our money" (Washington Post 2015). And further, "I'm going to tell you a couple of stories about trade, because I'm totally against the trade bill [the Trans-Pacific Partnership] for a number of reasons" (Washington Post 2015). Then he noted an example that hit close to home for many in the Midwest:

> Now, Ford announces a few weeks ago that Ford is going to build a $2.5 billion car and truck and parts manufacturing plant in Mexico. $2.5 billion, it's going to be one of the largest in the world. Ford. Good company … I would call up the head of Ford, who I know. If I was president, I'd say, "Congratulations. I understand that you're building a nice $2.5 billion car factory in Mexico and that you're going to take your cars and sell them to the United States zero tax, just flow them across the border" … So I would say, "Congratulations. That's the good news. Let me give you the bad news. Every car and every truck and every part manufactured in this plant that comes across the border, we're going to charge you a 35 percent tax, and that tax is going to be paid simultaneously with the transaction, and that's it". (Washington Post 2015)

Statements like those above regarding trade and manufacturing clearly reflect a populist message. They simply are not what Republican voters are used to hearing more mainstream Republican candidates talk about. This combined with the fact that Trump had never gone as far in his pursuit of elective office as he did in 2016, his anti-establishment and anti-Republican statements and actions from previous years all beg the question: How did Donald Trump manage to win the GOP primary and the presidency?

Trump's victory in the primary phase of the campaign is beyond the scope of this chapter, but some factors are worth mentioning as they relate to the main themes of the chapter. First, Trump was not the only outsider in the race. The 2016 GOP primary featured neurosurgeon Ben Carson, and former CEO of Hewlett-Packard Carly Fiorina. The primary also featured other Republicans who could be considered outside of the party's main-stream including former New York Governor George Pataki, Kentucky Senator Rand Paul, and New Jersey Governor Chris Christie; each had, at some point in their careers, taken positions that could be construed as anti-establishment. Second, as the list of candidates above indicates, the 2016 primary field was incredibly large. At one point, there were 17 Republicans actively seeking the GOP nomination. Included here were Senators Marco Rubio (FL) and Ted Cruz (TX), Ohio Governor John Kasich, as well as former Florida Governor Jeb Bush and former Pennsylvania Senator Rick Santorum. This large field of candidates made it possible for Trump to secure the GOP nomination without winning a majority of the votes cast by those participating in nominating contests across the nation. Indeed, Trump won less than 45% of these votes (The Green Papers 2016). Simply put, the crowded field of GOP candidates that included those from across the party's spectrum—from a candidate like Santorum to one like Kasich—meant that the party's vote would be splintered in many of the primary con-tests. Even when excluding all the candidates who dropped out of the race before the final weeks of the primary campaign (all those except Trump, Kasich, Rubio and Cruz), Trump managed only 46.5% of the votes among these candidates (Real Clear Politics 2016a). In the end, however, these votes do not matter as the nomination is only won by winning a majority of delegates at the national convention, which Trump was able to do when the GOP met in August 2016. This brings about two other interesting points about Trump's nomination in 2016 and the party establishment. First, why was no party establishment candidate able to secure the nomina-tion? Second, how did the party establishment take Trump's nomination?

At the start of 2015, Jeb Bush was the consensus frontrunner for the 2016 GOP nomination. Bush was at roughly 17% in the polls, followed by Chris Christie at about 11%, Rand Paul at 8.6%, Ben Carson, Wisconsin Governor Scott Walker and former Arkansas Governor Mike Huckabee at 8%, and Ted Cruz and Marco Rubio around 5%, with other candidates registering even lower poll numbers (Real Clear Politics 2016b). This made some sense. Bush, a former successful governor from a very impor-tant general election state and brother of one former president and son of another, was a logical person to be out in front for his party's nomination. But Bush's status as a frontrunner did not last long. For about the first six months of 2015, these candidates traded positions in the polls, but for most of that time, Bush maintained a small lead. However, within roughly a month of Trump's announcement to seek the nomination, Bush's lead over Trump had all but disappeared, and after six weeks it was gone completely (Real Clear Politics 2016b). Trump led in the polls for the duration of the nomination battle, even if he had less than 25% support for most of this time. There was one exception; for a very brief period, Ben Carson was fractionally ahead of Trump in the early part of November 2015.

After Trump entered the race, Bush's poll numbers collapsed. So did those of Scott Walker and just about every other candidate from the establishment wing of the GOP. For the second half of 2015, the two candidates out in front were Trump and Carson, with Rubio and Cruz making some gains. By the end of 2015, Jeb Bush's campaign was effectively over, even though he did not formally drop out until late February 2016. This collapse of a candidacy is even more intriguing when we consider all the factors that political scientists consider that give candidates an advantage, including name recognition, success in previous runs for office, and possibly the most important—a fundraising advantage. During his campaign, Jeb Bush raised over $34 million. While in the end Bush was outraised by other candidates like Cruz, Carson, and Rubio, he dwarfed most other candidates with support from outside groups with a total of over $121 million (Center for Responsive Politics 2016). These kinds of advantages would make a candidate fitting Bush's profile a clear favorite to win a nomination battle, even one with such a crowded field.

The fact that Bush was not able to earn the nomination likely speaks to the anti-establishment dynamic that was present throughout the 2016 campaign. Another sign of this is the fact that no true establishment GOP candidate made a serious push for the nomination. Of those candidates who had a relatively strong presence in the polls for the last half of 2015 and the first half of 2016—Trump, Carson, Cruz, Rubio, and eventually Kasich—none could be considered part of the mainstream GOP establishment for their own reasons. Trump and Carson speak for themselves with their outsider status. Kasich is thought by many, and has shown in his actions as Ohio governor, to be more moderate than many mainstream Republicans. Even though Cruz was eventually the candidate of many GOP establishment types (Stokols 2016), he was not always considered among that group. A *Washington Post* headline nicely indicated this: "Ted Cruz is the Republican establishment candidate. That's absolutely insane" (Cillizza 2016). Even the more conservative *Washington Times* agreed with the headline: "No, Ted Cruz is not part of the establishment" (Riddell 2016). Marco Rubio was arguably the most establishment of these candidates, but was not described that way by the conservative publication, *National*

Review, which ran a headline: "If Marco Rubio Is 'Establishment' Then 'Establishment' Has Lost Its Meaning", and included the following: "For the most part, a fight between Rubio and Cruz is a fight over matters of tone and style, not substance. A fight between Rubio and Trump is a battle between a conservative and a populist. Unless something dramatic happens between now and the New Hampshire primary, the establishment has already lost this cycle. Only the insurgents remain" (French 2016).

In summary, Trump was able to secure the 2016 GOP nomination because of a very crowded field that allowed the votes to splinter to many candidates, especially early in the primary process, and because of the anti-establishment tone that dominated 2016, especially on the Republican side. As part of this, Trump, a clear outside-Washington, DC, candidate, was able to leverage his anti-establishment positions and rhetoric and take advantage of, as John Heilemann called it, "bipartisan, ecumenical populist rage". How Trump used this in the general election in key states is where we turn next.

3.5   Michigan 2016: A Case Study in Populist Messaging

A significant part of Trump's victory in the GOP primary was his victory in Michigan's primary. He carried a consistent message through the state with many of the same themes noted above. During a raucous debate held in Detroit at the historic Fox Theater that was more notable for the jabs the candidates traded, Trump promised in his closing statement that he would "bring jobs back to the United States" (Jackson 2016). The results of the primary in Michigan, in hindsight, foreshadowed what happened in the general election. Not only did Trump win the state by more than 10%, but he did well in areas that are home to key constituencies of his supporters. In addition, Bernie Sanders's victory in the Democratic primary should have been a hint to the Clinton team that her candidacy was not resonating well in the state. Some observers saw these signs. For instance, Republican strategist Ford O'Connell, noted after the Michigan primary, "Trump could make the map larger. Because of where he's standing with white voters right now, he would have the Democrats on their heels particularly in the industrial Midwest" (Liasson 2016). One key to this, according to O'Connell, was Trump's hardline stand on trade (Liasson 2016). An important group that seemed to be paying attention to this, and Trump's other messages, was the Reagan Democrats, a group of blue-collar, working-class individuals who had traditionally voted Democratic but voted for Ronald Reagan in 1980 and 1984. The term was coined by Democratic pollster Stan Greenberg, who later worked for President Bill Clinton, who wondered, "if the story of Trump could be called 'The Revenge of the Reagan Democrats'" (Liasson 2016). Greenberg noted after the primary, "The Reagan Democrats are alive with the angry white male who've made themselves felt in the Trump primaries" (Liasson 2016).

The results of the general election battle between Trump and Hillary Clinton turned on three states—Michigan, Wisconsin, and Pennsylvania. If the electoral votes of these states went for Clinton rather than Trump, Donald Trump might be no more than just another outsider candidate who failed to win office. But, the three states did go for Trump and they did so in part because of his populist message. These states also made up part of what some analysts termed Clinton's "Blue Wall"—states that had voted Democratic for some time and were thought to be "safe" for any Democratic candidate. Indeed, it had been since 1988 that Michigan and Pennsylvania had voted for a Republican presidential candidate (i.e., George H.W. Bush) and since 1984 that Wisconsin had done so (i.e., Ronald Reagan). After these elections, these states voted only for Democrats with their electoral votes.

We examine only one of these states here—Michigan. It is intriguing for many reasons as a case study in the 2016 election. It has a long history of relying on manufacturing jobs for a large segment of its job base with the automobile industry front and center in the state since the 1950s. Along with this comes a relatively strong labor union presence. This, in turn, has created a large number of voters who have been impacted by free trade agreements like the North American Free Trade Agreement (NAFTA). Many of these individuals (e.g., Reagan Democrats) in many parts of the state were attracted to Donald Trump's populist message and voted for him in 2016, changing the political landscape in Michigan, at least temporarily, and helped shake the political establishment. The dynamics in Michigan were largely repeated in both Wisconsin and Pennsylvania, making the "Blue Wall" crumble.

As Trump campaigned in Michigan throughout the general election season—he traveled to Michigan seven times between August 1 and Election Day[8]. He hit on the same themes noted above—jobs, trade, manufacturing, and his status as an anti-establishment candidate. Trump visited

Michigan twice in August. One was a speech to the Detroit Economic Club, where he hit on themes of tax and regulatory reform as well as trade and manufacturing jobs. During his speech, Trump referenced the "job-killing trade deal with South Korea ... the Trans-Pacific Partnership"; he continued: "This is a strike at the heart of Michigan, and our nation as a whole. According to the Bureau of Labor Statistics, before NAFTA went into effect, there were 285,000 auto workers in Michigan. Today, that number is only 160,000 ... According to the Economic Policy Institute, the U.S. trade deficit with the proposed TPP member countries cost over 1 million manufacturing jobs in 2015. By far the biggest losses occurred in motor vehicles and parts, which lost nearly 740,000 manufacturing jobs. Michigan ranks first for jobs lost as a share of state workforce due to the trade deficit with TPP members" (Charles 2016). In another visit to the state, this time to a more rural area outside of Lansing, the state capital, Trump hit on many of the same arguments and turned another populist theme—rebuilding the nation's infrastructure—and said after he was elected, "...millions of workers on the sidelines will be returned to the workforce. Crumbling roads, bridges and airports will be replaced with the infrastructure our country needs and deserves" (Politico 2016).

Trump also visited areas of the state that were home to large numbers of people in one of his target audiences—Reagan Democrats. Cities like Sterling Heights and Warren are both in Macomb County and include concentrations of individuals who work in the sectors that are at the heart of Trump's message—manufacturing and trade. For example, nearly 21% of all jobs in Macomb County are in the manufacturing sector (U.S. Census 2015). Indeed, Macomb was the birthplace of the Reagan Democrats when Greenberg first discovered and wrote about them in 1985 (Greenberg 1996).

Clinton also visited Macomb County, but less often than Trump. At the time, this was a signal to some in Michigan. "She's coming to Macomb County for one reason — because it's home of the Reagan Democrats", said state Sen. Jack Brandenburg, R-Harrison Township; "It tells me that Michigan's still in play" (Livengood 2016). In recent presidential elections, Macomb would have been considered safe territory for Democrats. But, according to Jamie Roe, a Republican consultant from the area, the voters there were ripe for the picking because of the populist message of Trump: "I think that she sees a vulnerability that she has in Macomb County, where a lot of voters are responding to Trump, particularly on trade..." (Livengood 2016).

Trump was able to win Michigan's electoral votes because of a combination of factors, but these all boil down to one—voter turnout. Voter turnout in the state was nearly 64%, up slightly from 2012. But it was turnout differences in key areas that led to Trump's victory and much of this turnout was tied to his populist message. In short, turnout in key rural areas—Trump's strength—was up while turnout in key urban areas—Clinton's strength—was flat or down slightly. For instance, in Wayne County—home of Detroit and a large concentration of African American voters—turnout was down by nearly a full percentage point. This is in contrast to some of the most rural areas of the state where turnout increased by roughly half of a percentage; for instance, in five of the seven counties with the smallest population, turnout was up by roughly 0.65% (there were two counties where turnout was slightly down from 2012). These percentages may not seem all that dramatic, but in Wayne County alone, it amounts to nearly 38,000 fewer voters. What is more, Clinton received nearly 80,000 fewer votes *in that one county* than President Obama did when he ran for reelection in 2012. One can draw from this that Democratic turnout was down significantly, but there were either more Republicans who turned out from parts of the county and/or there were some Democrats who voted for Obama in 2012 but voted for Trump in 2016.

Key, however, to the changes in turnout across the state were the messages that the candidates were delivering to voters. In short, Trump was able to energize voters in key parts of the state—those counties that are highly rural and with large proportions of voters in the manufacturing and trade sectors. Clinton, however, was not able to energize her base in urban areas, or in some places where people who were in those same economic sectors who had voted for President Obama four and eight years prior. Macomb county was the epicenter of the turnout and message battle in Michigan. Turnout in Macomb was up over a point from 2012 at 66.5%. It was also an area that helped deliver Michigan to Trump. After all the votes were counted, in Macomb County alone, Clinton received roughly 35,000 fewer votes than Obama did in 2012 while Trump earned roughly 35,000 more votes than Mitt Romney did four years prior. Why was turnout up and the shift in the county? To a large degree, it had to do with the message that Trump was communicating to voters in the county. They heard him promise to bring manufacturing jobs back and improve trade policy in ways that would benefit them.

Trump returned to Macomb County on the weekend before Election Day. He held a rally at Freedom Hill, an outdoor concert venue. "Trump spoke at length about trade, saying Democratic policies 'have decimated' the state's signature auto industry; seemingly ignoring that the domestic auto industry [was] coming off one of its best years ever, but winning wide applause from the large supportive crowd nonetheless because of the number of auto jobs that the state [had] clearly lost in recent decades" (Spangler 2016). In what was a final appeal to these voters, Trump also added, "We will stop the jobs from leaving your state" (Spangler 2016).

Once the votes were tallied, Trump won Michigan by less than 11,000 votes. As noted, keys to his victory were how his economic and populist message resonated with individuals in rural areas and those that are heavily dependent on manufacturing jobs and trade. This also impacted turnout. In short, many areas of Trump's strength saw increased turnout while many areas of Clinton's strength saw turnout that was very similar to or slightly down from 2012. In the eight counties that Clinton managed to win, turnout, on average, was slightly higher (0.34%) than four years before but in the ten counties where Trump got his highest percentages, turnout was up 1.67%. To put a finer point on this, there were 20 counties in Michigan that saw turnout of over 66%; seven of these were from the most rural parts of the state (i.e., each has less than 45,000 people); six are centers of manufacturing and trade jobs (i.e., the total number of jobs in the manufacturing sector is greater than 16,000, and the total number of trade-related jobs is greater than 2000); and five are counties where more than 20% of the total jobs in the county are in the manufacturing area or where 3% of the jobs are trade related (see Table 3.1). Nearly all (17 of 20) of the high turnout counties are captured when these factors are combined (i.e., they are either rural, high in trade or manufacturing jobs by number, or high in trade or manufacturing jobs by percent). Of those that were not in any of these categories, Hillary Clinton could garner no more than 40.8% of the vote.

Moreover, there were 12 counties across the state where turnout increased by more than 2%. Six were on the list of most rural counties while seven were on the list of those having 20% or more of all jobs in the manufacturing sector. Only two counties with turnout increases of more than 2% were *not* in one of these two categories. In one of these counties, Trump received almost 49% of the vote, and in the other, he earned over 62%.

One indicator of how Trump's message of populism resonated can be seen by examining the counties where he had his greatest success. Trump garnered 70% of the vote or more in 14 counties. Ten of these were the

Table 3.1 Counties with the highest turnout in Michigan and key indicators

County	2016 voter turnout (%)	Urban county[a]	Rural county[b]	County with concentration of trade-related jobs[c]	County with concentration of manufacturing jobs[d]	County with 20% or more manufacturing jobs[e]	County with 3% or more trade-related jobs[f]	Meets at least one condition
Leelanau	73.32		✓					✓
Keweenaw	73.28		✓					✓
Livingston	72.65	✓		✓			✓	✓
Ottawa	72.10	✓		✓	✓		✓	✓
Clinton	71.27					✓		
Grand Traverse	69.89				✓			
Oakland	69.42	✓		✓	✓			✓
Eaton	68.84			✓	✓			✓
Kent	68.02	✓					✓	✓
Benzie	67.79		✓					✓
Lapeer	67.60		✓			✓		✓
Missaukee	67.20		✓			✓	✓	✓
Barry	66.90			✓				✓
Antrim	66.50				✓			✓
Macomb	66.50	✓				✓		✓
Allegan	66.43					✓	✓	✓
Alcona	66.31		✓					✓
Presque Isle	66.26		✓					✓

(continued)

Table 3.1 (continued)

County	2016 voter turnout (%)	Urban county[a]	Rural county[b]	County with concentration of trade-related jobs[c]	County with concentration of manufacturing jobs[d]	County with 20% or more manufacturing jobs[e]	County with 3% or more trade-related jobs[f]	Meets at least one condition
Washtenaw	66.10	✓						
Bay	66.03			✓	✓			✓

[a]Qualifies if more than 15% of the county is urbanized according to the US Census, "2010 Percent Urban and Rural by County" (https://www.census.gov/geo/reference/ua/ualists_layout.html)

[b]Qualifies if the county has a population lower than 45,000, according to US Census American FactFinder, "Population, Housing Units, Area, and Density: 2010—State—County/County Equivalent 2010 Census Summary File 1" (https://factfinder.census.gov)

[c]Qualifies if the county is in the top ten statewide of total number of trade-related jobs, according to the US Census American FactFinder "Industry by Occupation for the Civilian Employed Population 16 Years and Over, 2011–2015 American Community Survey 5-Year Estimates" (https://factfinder.census.gov)

[d]Qualifies if the county is in the top ten statewide of total number of manufacturing jobs, according to the US Census American FactFinder "Industry by Occupation for the Civilian Employed Population 16 Years and Over, 2011–2015 American Community Survey 5-Year Estimates" (https://factfinder.census.gov)

[e]Based on calculations from the US Census American FactFinder "Industry by Occupation for the Civilian Employed Population 16 Years and Over, 2011–2015 American Community Survey 5-Year Estimates" (https://factfinder.census.gov)

most rural counties in the state and half are in the category of those with 20% or more of all jobs being in the manufacturing sector (one additional county has more than 3% of its total jobs in the trade sector). All of the counties where Trump received more than 70% of the vote fit into at least one of these categories and four are *both* highly rural *and* have 20% or more manufacturing jobs (see Table 3.2).

Obviously, another key to Trump's victory was his ability to do better than previous Republicans across the state. He would not have won had he not improved on other Republican performances all over Michigan. In 2016, there were 23 counties where Trump improved on Mitt Romney's two-party performance (i.e., percentage of the vote considering only the two major parties) by more than 12%. Sixteen of these counties are in the most rural category; and ten have 20% or more of all jobs in the man-ufacturing sector. Only two of these counties were in neither of those categories.

While President Obama won Michigan handily in 2008 (he beat John McCain by nearly 17%) and safely in 2012 (he beat Mitt Romney by nearly 10%), the state had shifted toward Republicans over those two election cycles. Donald Trump needed to keep that shift moving toward the GOP and did so. Another way to examine this is, again, by county. Barack Obama won 46 of Michigan's 83 counties in 2008; he won 20 in 2012. In 2016, Hillary Clinton only won 8. This means, of course, that there were 12 counties in Michigan that voted for Barack Obama twice and switched to Donald Trump in 2016 (see Table 3.3). Did these coun-ties shift because of Trump's appeal or because there was less interest in Clinton's candidacy? The answer is it was a bit of both. Only three of these counties are on the list of the most rural in the state and three others are in the category that have 20% or more of all jobs in the manufacturing sector. In 2012, Obama won these 12 counties, on average, with roughly 52.5% of the two-party vote, so it did not take much of a swing toward Trump; but he did manage to win them with an average of nearly 57%. Within these counties, however, there was some significant variation in Trump's support. Some counties he won narrowly (e.g., Saginaw with less than 51% of the two-party vote and Isabella with just shy of 52%) while others he won handily (e.g., Monroe with nearly 62%). Clearly in some places, Trump was able to attract significant support, while in others, he did just enough to win a majority of the two-party vote. Some individual counties are also instructive. Some counties, such as Gogebic, which is in the far

Table 3.2 Counties with the highest Trump voter percentages in 2016 with key indicators

County	Trump vote percent (%)	Urban county[a]	Rural county[b]	County with concentration of trade-related jobs[c]	County with concentration of manufacturing jobs[d]	County with 20% or more manufacturing jobs[e]	County with 3% or more trade-related jobs[f]	Meets at least one condition
Missaukee	77.49	✓						✓
Hillsdale	74.60		✓			✓		✓
Sanilac	73.40		✓			✓		✓
Oscoda	73.14		✓					✓
Montmorency	73.10		✓					✓
Osceola	73.06		✓			✓		✓
Kalkaska	72.84		✓					✓
Luce	72.06		✓					✓
Newaygo	70.95		✓			✓		✓
Alcona	70.81		✓					✓
Lapeer	70.23					✓		✓
Huron	70.02		✓			✓		✓
Branch	69.96					✓	✓	✓
Otsego	69.92							✓

[a]Qualifies if more than 15% of the county is urbanized according to the US Census, "2010 Percent Urban and Rural by County" (https://www.census.gov/geo/reference/ua/ualists_layout.html)

[b]Qualifies if the county has a population lower than 45,000, according to US Census American FactFinder, "Population, Housing Units, Area, and Density: 2010—State—County/County Equivalent 2010 Census Summary File 1" (https://factfinder.census.gov)

[c]Qualifies if the county is in the top ten statewide of total number of trade-related jobs, according to the US Census American FactFinder "Industry by Occupation for the Civilian Employed Population 16 Years and Over, 2011–2015 American Community Survey 5-Year Estimates" (https://factfinder.census.gov)

[d]Qualifies if the county is in the top ten statewide of total number of manufacturing jobs, according to the US Census American FactFinder "Industry by Occupation for the Civilian Employed Population 16 Years and Over, 2011–2015 American Community Survey 5-Year Estimates" (https://factfinder.census.gov)

[e]Based on calculations from the US Census American FactFinder "Industry by Occupation for the Civilian Employed Population 16 Years and Over, 2011–2015 American Community Survey 5-Year Estimates" (https://factfinder.census.gov)

Table 3.3 Counties that voted for Barack Obama in 2012 but voted for Donald Trump in 2016

County	Trump vote percent (two-party) (%)	Trump vote percent (all votes) (%)	Change in GOP two-party performance (2012–2016) (%)	Voter turnout (%)	Change in turnout (2012–2016) (%)	Percent voting for a third party (%)	Percent change in third-party votes (2012–2016) (%)
Bay	56.69	53.47	9.50	66.03	−0.41	5.68	4.57
Calhoun	56.59	53.47	7.40	58.51	0.69	5.52	4.27
Eaton	52.54	49.11	4.13	68.84	0.94	6.53	5.30
Gogebic	57.87	54.82	11.96	52.53	−4.04	5.27	4.29
Isabella	51.97	48.59	6.66	58.23	2.34	6.50	5.33
Lake	61.97	59.29	14.49	57.81	−0.91	4.32	3.41
Macomb	56.03	53.58	8.04	66.50	1.06	4.37	3.34
Manistee	58.14	54.89	11.15	63.89	0.87	5.60	4.05
Monroe	61.69	58.29	12.19	62.53	−0.97	5.52	4.21
Saginaw	50.60	48.21	6.60	62.87	−0.55	4.72	3.74
Shiawassee	60.52	56.37	12.38	64.63	0.66	6.85	5.30
Van Buren	57.44	53.77	7.67	60.12	0.71	6.39	5.15
Average	*56.84*	*53.65*	*9.35*	*61.87*	*0.03*	*5.60*	*4.41*
Statewide county average	**61.97**	**58.58**	**8.77**	**62.92**	**0.62**	**5.48**	**4.23**

Note: All data from Michigan Secretary of State; calculations by authors

western reaches of Michigan's Upper Peninsula, saw a dramatic increase in GOP performance (i.e., the GOP candidate's share of the two-party vote) (a 9.5% increase from 2012) *and* lower turnout (a decline of over 4% from 2012). Here many voters were not enthused enough to come out and vote and those that did went more heavily to Trump. Another story is Isabella County, which is almost in the geographic center of the Lower Peninsula, where there was a relatively small increase in GOP performance (6.66%) and a turnout increase of well over 2%. Here there was greater enthusiasm but because Trump only won that county by a narrow margin, it is still difficult to tell whether it was affinity for his candidacy or a lower enthusiasm for Clinton that was the reason.

One interesting component to the 2016 election that was felt across Michigan (and we presume other states as well) which also returns the discussion to party (or anti-party as it may be) is the large increase in the number of people who either skipped the presidential race or decided to vote for a candidate not represented by one of the two major parties. Across Michigan, over 250,000 voters chose someone other than Donald Trump or Hillary Clinton; another 75,000 skipped the presidential race all together. In other words, more than 5% of all voters picked a third-party candidate (e.g., Jill Stein (G) or Gary Johnson (L)) and 1.5% of all people who arrived at the polls decided to pass on the presidential contest. This is a dramatic increase compared to 2012 when just over 1% of all voters in Michigan cast a ballot for a third-party candidate and another 1% skipped the race between Obama and Romney. Clearly, the anti-party message continued in the general election as over 6% of all voters in Michigan registered a choice that indicated that they were not happy with either major party choice.

This was also a factor in the 12 counties that voted for Obama but Trump was able to turn to his column. In these counties, on average, 5.6% of all votes went to someone other than Trump or Clinton (the statewide average by county was 5.48%). In four counties, however, more than 6% of all votes went to third-party candidates. These 12 counties, on average, also slightly outpaced the county averages across the state in terms of increase in third-party vote choices (4.41% to 4.23%) and increase in GOP two-party performance (9.35% to 8.77%). However, these counties did not show much of a turnout increase (only 0.03%) compared to the county average statewide (0.62%).

3.6   CONCLUSION

Donald Trump's election caused both major parties to reflect on their immediate and long-term futures—and what path each should take. The Democrats had counted on blue-collar labor union members in blue states such as Pennsylvania, Wisconsin, and Michigan. But all three states voted for Trump, which helped give him his Electoral College victory. While it is true that Hillary Clinton gained almost three million more popular votes than Trump, the distribution of those votes left Democrats wondering how to win the next national election. Furthermore, Democrats had suffered continuing losses in Congress and at the state and local levels since 2010. The election of Tom Perez as the new DNC chair in early 2017, albeit in a relatively close vote, would seem to point to a party that is not entirely ready to abandon its moderate establishment approach given he was President Obama's secretary of labor from 2013 to 2017. His major opponent, U.S. Representative Keith Ellison (MN, 5), was endorsed by Bernie Sanders and was thought to represent the more progressive wing of the party that wanted to push the Democrats closer to a Sanders-like set of policies and positions. Ellison was quickly made deputy chair, although early on, it was unclear what his duties would be (Martin 2017).

Of particular concern among Democrats must be the switch by the blue-collar states of Pennsylvania, Wisconsin, and Michigan. As our Michigan data show, Trump successfully argued to Michigan voters, some of whom supported Democrats in prior elections, that they would be better off if he were elected. His views on North American Free Trade Agreement NAFTA and the Trans-Pacific Partnership (and free trade in general), along with his criticism that the political establishment hadn't accomplished anything, resonated with enough voters to elect him president.

While Democrats must face a reshuffling of some sort in order to find a way to electoral success, the Republican Party, too, will be dealing with its own challenges. Prior to 2016, the party already had experienced some internal conflicts regarding the direction of the party. Prominent elements of the party include fiscal conservatives (mostly through the Tea Party and in Congress, the Freedom Caucus), social conservatives, who are largely evangelical Christians, and traditional mainstream Republicans, who generally favored small government and free trade. The Trump victory, and his anti-free trade stance, had brought many supporters into the mix and further complicated the party's attempt to navigate its path to the future. The large number of Republican presidential candidates in 2016 illustrates some of the problems the party must address as it tries to bring its coalition of voters together.

By one measure, the Republican Party could be considered very successful, especially since the 2010 elections. The party controls the White House, has majorities in both chambers of Congress, and controls a majority of state governorships and state legislative chambers. Republicans have also taken away almost 1000 state legislative seats from Democrats since 2010 (Wilson 2016). But an emerging populist message in both the Democratic and Republican parties in 2016 suggests that each major party will likely need to confront its past positions on a variety of issues that voters feel have not been properly addressed.

NOTES

1. See, for example, Bart Bonikowski and Noam Gidron's "The Populist Style in American Politics: Presidential Campaign Discourse, 1952–1996", *Social Forces* 94 (4), 1593–1621.
2. See, for example, John Cassidy's "Bernie Sanders and the New Populism." *New Yorker*, February 3, 2016, http://www.newyorker.com/news/john-cassidy/bernie-sanders-and-the-new-populism. Accessed March 15, 2017; Michael Lind's "Donald Trump, the Perfect Populist." *Politico*, March 9, 2016, http://www.politico.com/magazine/story/2016/03/donald-trump-the-perfect-populist-213697. Accessed March 15, 2017; Brian Calle's, "Dynamic Duos Populism, Personalities Prevailing in Both Parties." *Orange County Register*, February 14, 2016, http://www.ocregister.com/articles/trump-703977-sanders-money.html. Accessed March 15, 2017; Chris Lehmann's "Donald Trump and the Long Tradition of American Populism." *Newsweek*, August 22, 2015, http://www.newsweek.com/donald-trump populism-365052. Accessed March 15, 2017. However, for contrary views, see Charles Postel's, "If Trump and Sanders are Both Populists, What Does Populist Mean?" *The American Historian*, February 2016, http://tah.oah.org/february-2016/if-trump-and-sanders-are-both-populists-what-does-populist-mean/. Accessed March 17, 2017; and Michael Kazin's "How Can Donald Trump and Bernie Sanders Both Be 'Populist'?" *New York Times*, March 22, 2016, https://www.nytimes.com/2016/03/27/magazine/how-can-donald-trump-and-bernie-sanders-both-be-populist.html?_r=0. Accessed March 17, 2017.
3. As reported in Cassidy (2016).
4. https://www.youtube.com/watch?v=j6N8l8DMu3M
5. https://www.youtube.com/watch?v=j6N8l8DMu3M

6. The Reform Party was made most famous by H. Ross Perot who ran for president in 1992 and 1996. He garnered nearly 20% of the popular vote in 1992. In addition, former WWE professional wrestler Jessie Ventura was elected as Minnesota's governor as a member of the Reform Party in 1998.
7. For more information, see, for example, Federal Election Commission, "Testing the Waters", http://www.fec.gov/rad/candidates/documents/CanGuideTestWater_000.pdf. Accessed March 15, 2017.
8. Trump's total is nearly twice as many trips as Clinton made to the state (4). These figures do not count appearances by candidates' surrogates other than vice presidential candidates. National Journal Travel Tracker, http://travel-tracker.nationaljournal.com. Accessed March 18, 2017.

REFERENCES

Blake, Aaron. 2016. Here Are the Latest, Most Damaging Things in the DNC's Leaked Emails. *Washington Post.* https://www.washingtonpost.com/news/the-fix/wp/2016/07/24/here-are-the-latest-most-damaging-things-in-the-dncs-leaked-emails/?utm_term=.c10096dd4f84. Accessed March 16, 2017.
Bonikowski, Bart, and Noam Gidron. 2016. The Populist Style in American Politics: Presidential Campaign Discourse, 1952–1996. *Social Forces* 94 (4): 1593–1621.
Calle, Brian. 2016. Dynamic Duos Populism, Personalities Prevailing in Both Parties. *Orange County Register.* http://www.ocregister.com/articles/trump-703977-sanders-money.html. Accessed March 15, 2017.
Cannon, Carl M. 2015. Immigration and the Rise and Fall of the "Know-Nothing" Party. *Real Clear Politics.* http://www.realclearpolitics.com/articles/2015/02/18/immigration_and_the_rise__fall_of_the_know-nothing_party_125649.html. Accessed March 17, 2017.
Cassidy, John. 2016. Bernie Sanders and the New Populism. *New Yorker.* http://www.newyorker.com/news/john-cassidy/bernie-sanders-and-the-new-populism. Accessed March 15, 2017.
Center for Responsive Politics. 2016. Also-Rans: 2016 Presidential Race. https://www.opensecrets.org/pres16/also-rans. Accessed March 15, 2017.
Charles, J. Brian 2016. Transcript of Donald Trump's Economic Policy Speech to Detroit Economic Club. *The Hill.* http://thehill.com/blogs/pundits-blog/campaign/290777-transcript-of-donald-trumps-economic-policy-speech-to-detroit. Accessed March 18, 2017.
Chozick, Amy, and Patrick Healy. 2016. Hillary Clinton Beats Bernie Sanders in Nevada Caucuses. *New York Times.* https://www.nytimes.com/2016/02/21/us/politics/nevada-caucus.html?_r=0. Accessed March 13, 2017.
Cillizza, Chris. 2016. Ted Cruz Is the Republican Establishment Candidate. That's Absolutely Insane. *Washington Post.* https://www.washingtonpost.

com/news/the-fix/wp/2016/03/23/ted-cruz-is-the-republican--establishment-candidate-thats-absolutely-insane/?utm_term=.9346b8793c7c. Accessed March 15, 2017.

Clinton, Hillary. 2015. Official 2016 Presidential Campaign Announcement. https://www.youtube.com/watch?v=N708P-A45D0. Accessed March 12, 2017.

CNN. 1999. Trump Officially Joins Reform Party. http://www.cnn.com/ALLPOLITICS/stories/1999/10/25/trump.cnn/index.html. Accessed March 15, 2017.

Dann, Carrie. 2016. Clinton Hits 'Magic Number' of Delegates to Clinch Nomination. *nbcnews.com*. http://www.nbcnews.com/politics/2016-election/clinton-hits-magic-number-delegates-clinch-nomination-n586181. Accessed March 16, 2017.

Federal Election Commission. 2000. 2000 Presidential Primary Election Results. http://www.fec.gov/pubrec/fe2000/2000presprim.htm. Accessed March 15, 2017.

French, David. 2016. If Marco Rubio Is 'Establishment' Then 'Establishment' Has Lost Its Meaning. http://www.nationalreview.com/article/429262/marco-rubio-establishment-tea-party-conservative. Accessed March 15, 2017.

Frizell, Sam. 2015. Trump Forming Exploratory Committee for 2016 Presidential Bid. *Time*. http://time.com/3748732/donald-trump-exploratory-committee-2016/. Accessed March 15, 2017.

Gass, Nick. 2015. Trump Has Spent Years Courting Hillary and Other Dems. *Politico*. http://www.politico.com/story/2015/06/donald-trump-donations-democrats-hillary-clinton-119071. Accessed March 15, 2017.

Gehrke, Joel. 2016. Trump on Why He Donated to Clinton: 'I'm in Business.' *Washington Examiner*. http://www.washingtonexaminer.com/trump-on-why-he-donated-to-clinton-im-in-business/article/2584918. Accessed March 15, 2017.

Greenberg, Stanley. 1996. *Middle Class Dreams: The Politics and Power of the New American Majority, Revised and Updated Edition*. New Haven: Yale University Press.

Jackson, David. 2016. 11th GOP Debate: Highlights from Detroit. *USA Today*. http://www.usatoday.com/story/news/politics/onpolitics/2016/03/03/live-republicans-detroit-debate-trump-cruz-rubio-kasich/81275106/. Accessed March 18, 2017.

Jacoby, Jeff. 2016. Does Hillary's Resume Really Make Her the 'Best Qualified' Presidential Candidate? *Boston Globe*. https://www.bostonglobe.com/opinion/2016/02/03/does-hillary-resume-really-make-her-best-qualified-presidentialcandidate/oVQRpgfUR5xvtmZylUYUbO/story.html. Accessed March 2, 2017.

Kazin, Michael. 2016. How Can Donald Trump and Bernie Sanders Both Be 'Populist'? *New York Times*. https://www.nytimes.com/2016/03/27/magazine/how-can-donald-trump-and-bernie-sanders-both-be-populist.html?_r=0. Accessed March 17, 2017.

Kurtzleben, Danielle. 2015. Most of Donald Trump's Political Money Went to Democrats—Until 5 Years Ago. *National Public Radio*. http://www.npr.org/sections/itsallpolitics/2015/07/28/426888268/donald-trumps-flipping-political-donations. Accessed March 15, 2017.

Lehmann, Chris. 2015. Donald Trump and the Long Tradition of American Populism. *Newsweek*. http://www.newsweek.com/donald-trump-populism-365052. Accessed March 8, 2017.

Liasson, Mara. 2016. Can Donald Trump Rewrite the Electoral Map for the GOP? *National Public Radio*. http://www.npr.org/2016/03/18/470911185/can-donald-trump-rewrite-the-electoral-map-for-the-gop. Accessed March 18, 2017.

Lind, Michael. 2016. Donald Trump, the Perfect Populist. *Politico*. http://www.politico.com/magazine/story/2016/03/donald-trump-the-perfect-populist-213697. Accessed March 15, 2017.

Livengood, Chad. 2016. Clinton Targets Trump Battleground of Macomb County. *Detroit News*. http://www.detroitnews.com/story/news/politics/2016/08/10/clinton-targets-trump-battleground-macomb--county/88546956/. Accessed March 18, 2017.

Martin, Jonathan. 2017. Democrats Elect Thomas Perez, Establishment Favorite, as Party Chairman. *New York Times*. https://www.nytimes.com/2017/02/25/us/politics/dnc-perez-ellison-chairman-election.html?_r=0. Accessed March 16, 2017.

Moody, Chris. 2015. Trump in '04: 'I probably identify more as Democrat.' *CNN*. http://www.cnn.com/2015/07/21/politics/donald-trump-election-democrat/. Accessed March 15, 2017.

Mudde, Cas, and Cristobal Rovira Kaltwasser. 2017. *Populism: A Very Short Introduction*. New York: Oxford University Press.

National Journal Travel Tracker. 2016. *National Journal*. http://traveltracker.nationaljournal.com. Accessed March 18, 2017.

Newkirk, Zachary. 2011. Donald Trump's Donations to Democrats, Club for Growth's Busy Day and More in Capital Eye Opener: February 17. *Center for Responsive Politics*. https://www.opensecrets.org/news/2011/02/donald-trumps-donations-to-democrats/#. Accessed March 15, 2017.

Politico. 2016. Full Transcript: Donald Trump Speaks in Michigan. *Politico*. http://www.politico.com/story/2016/08/donald-trump-michigan-speech-transcript-227221. Accessed March 18, 2017.

Postel, Charles. 2016. If Trump and Sanders Are Both Populists, What Does Populist Mean? *The American Historian*. http://tah.oah.org/february-2016/if-trump-and-sanders-are-both-populists-what-does-populist-mean/. Accessed March 17, 2017.

RealClearPolitics. 2016a. 2016 Republican Popular Vote. http://www.realclear-politics.com/epolls/2016/president/republican_vote_count.html. Accessed March 15, 2017.

———. 2016b. RCP Poll Average: 2016 Republican Presidential Nomination. http://www.realclearpolitics.com/epolls/2016/president/us/2016_republican_presidential_nomination-3823.html. Accessed March 15, 2017.

Riddell, Kelly. 2016. No, Ted Cruz Is Not Part of the Establishment. *Washington Times*. http://www.washingtontimes.com/news/2016/apr/22/no-ted-cruz-not-part-establishment/. Accessed March 15, 2017.

Rove, Karl. 2015. Which Donald Trump Will Debate? *Wall Street Journal*. https://www.wsj.com/articles/which-donald-trump-will-debate-1438813416. Accessed March 15, 2017.

Sanders, Bernie. 2015. Bernie Sanders Announces Bid for Democratic Presidential Nomination. https://berniesanders.com/bernies-announcement/. Accessed March 13, 2017.

———. 2016. Reforming Wall Street. https://berniesanders.com/issues/reforming-wall-street/. Accessed March 16, 2017.

Scherer, Michael. 2011. Trump's Political Reality Show: Will the Donald Really Run for President? *Time*. http://content.time.com/time/magazine/article/0,9171,2065235-1,00.html. Accessed March 15, 2017.

———. 2015. Forget the Past America, Donald Trump Could Run for President. *Time*. http://time.com/3722847/donald-trump-president/. Accessed March 15, 2017.

Smith, David. 2016. Most Americans Do Not Feel Represented by Democrats or Republicans – Survey. *The Guardian*. https://www.theguardian.com/us-news/2016/oct/25/american-political-parties-democrats-republicans--representation-survey. Accessed March 15, 2017.

Spangler, Todd. 2016. Donald Trump Makes Another Bid for Michigan at Macomb rally. *Detroit Free Press*. http://www.freep.com/story/news/politics/2016/11/06/trump-makes-another-bid-michigan-macomb-rally/93388574/. Accessed March 18, 2017.

Stokols, Eli. 2016. GOP Elites Line up Behind Ted Cruz: Establishment Is Increasingly Prepared to Lose with Cruz Than Hand the Party to Trump. *Politico*. http://www.politico.com/story/2016/03/ted-cruz-republican-establishment-elites-221174. Accessed March 15, 2017.

Tesfaye, Sophia. 2015. Let's All Remember That Time When Donald Trump Sounded Like Bernie Sanders on Healthcare. *Salon*. http://www.salon.com/2015/06/17/lets_all_remember_that_time_when_donald_trump_sounded_like_bernie_sanders_on_healthcare/. Accessed March 15, 2017.

The Green Papers. 2016. 2016 Presidential Primaries, Caucuses, and Conventions. http://www.thegreenpapers.com/P16/R. Accessed March 15, 2017.

U.S. Census. 2015. American Community Survey.

Wagner, John, Abby Phillip, and Rosalind S. Helderman. 2015. Accord Reached
    After Sanders Sues the DNC Over Suspended Access to Critical Voter List.
    Washington Post. https://www.washingtonpost.com/politics/sanders-threatens-
    to-sue-dnc-if-access-to-voter-list-isnt-restored/2015/12/18/fa8d6df8-a5a2-
    11e5-ad3f-991ce3374e23_story.html?utm_term=.014e19f00fa9.   Accessed
    March 15, 2017.
Washington Post. 2015. Full Text: Donald Trump Announces a Presidential Bid.
    https://www.washingtonpost.com/news/post-politics/wp/2015/06/16/
    full-text-donald-trump-announces-a-presidential-bid/?utm_term=.
    b887930a1bf0. Accessed March 15, 2017.
Wilson, Reid. 2016. Dems Hit New Low in State Legislatures. *The Hill*. http://
    thehill.com/homenews/campaign/306736-dems-hit-new-low-in-state-
    legislatures. Accessed March 21, 2017.

David A. Dulio is a professor and chair of the Political Science Department at Oakland University in Rochester, Michigan. His research and teaching interests are in areas including campaigns and elections, campaign strategy, Congress, and parties and interest groups, and he has published nine books on these topics.

John S. Klemanski is Professor of Political Science at Oakland University at Rochester, Michigan. He has co-authored six books and published numerous journal articles and book chapters on political campaigns and elections.

CHAPTER 4

From Consensus to Conflict: Political Polarization, the Culture War, and Gay Rights

Donald M. Gooch

My friends, this election is about much more than who gets what. It is about who we are. It is about what we believe. It is about what we stand for as Americans. There is a religious war going on in our country for the soul of America. It is a cultural war, as critical to the kind of nation we will one day be as was the Cold War itself.
—Patrick J. Buchanan, 1992 Republican National Convention

Pat Buchanan's martial call at the 1992 Republican National Convention is often cited as the opening salvo of the American culture war. In reality, the seeds of political polarization were sown much earlier, in the cultural transformations in the American public of the 1960s and 1970s. Political polarization flowered in the 1980s and 1990s, and it remains in full bloom in recent decades. The polarization thesis, of a burgeoning and widening cultural conflict in the United States, has engaged scholars, journalists, politicians, and activists alike. Political polarization as

D.M. Gooch (✉)
Department of Government, Stephen F. Austin State University, Nacogdoches, TX, USA

© The Author(s) 2018
C. Rackaway, L.L. Rice (eds.), *American Political Parties Under Pressure*, DOI 10.1007/978-3-319-60879-2_4

a shorthand explanation for divisive politics in the United States permeates media coverage of politics. It has become an iconic buzz word, and it has been used to explain a wide range of political phenomena, from the rise of alternative media to the results of national and local elections. Polarization underlies the tone of political debate from the halls of Congress to the barstools in local drinking establishments. "Not since the Civil War and post-Reconstruction period has the country been so divided" says John Kenneth White of Catholic University (O'Keefe 2004).

But what is polarization? There is much disagreement on the definition of polarization, the evidence on polarization, and the extent to which polarization exists and has an impact on American politics. Political polarization, at its core, is the emergence of and trends toward a bifurcated politics in America, evenly and deeply divided in an intense cultural civil conflict. There is substantial empirical evidence in favor of the polarization thesis, yet political polarization remains a controversial theory of American mass political behavior, and there is a strong counterfactual in the literature which suggests political polarization is oversold, ephemeral, and even mythical. In this chapter, I will review this literature, focusing on the theoretical and empirical points of agreement and disagreement in the study of political polarization. I will put forward a theoretically sound and empirically defensible definition of political polarization, attempting to bridge the theoretical and empirical gaps in our understanding of American public opinion and polarization in politics. I develop an empirical measure of polarization in polling responses, and use that measure to assess political polarization on gay rights issues in American public opinion from the 1970s through to 2016. Finally, I assess that evidence in the context of the literature on public opinion on gay rights, and I show that there was a consensus on gay rights in the 1970s, and that it has collapsed into significant opinion polarization in later decades. The emergence of salient and significant political cleavages on gay rights in public opinion in the later decades reflects the emergent and persistent polarization in the American public on gay rights.

4.1   The Study of Political Polarization and the Culture War: Myth or Reality?

The seminal article of the cannon on the culture war was penned a year in advance of Buchanan's clarion call. In *Culture War: The Struggle to Define America*, James David Hunter envisioned an emerging schism in society: the socially conservative "orthodox" in an uncompromising struggle against the socially liberal "progressives" on a number of hot-button cultural issues such as abortion and gay rights. Hunter feared that this cultural Balkanization would lead to a breakdown of American political institutions. Unable to traverse the gap and form acceptable compromises, this failure of politics could lead to political violence—a culture war in fact as well as in name (Hunter 1991).

Public opinion has sided with Hunter's thesis. In a poll taken in 2004, 72 percent of Americans assessed the country's division between fundamentally different views on gay marriage, abortion, and guns as an important or serious problem requiring moderate or major changes by presidents in the future. Only 25 percent of Americans identified the culture war as a small or moderate problem.[1] While not direct evidence of mass political polarization and whatever its merit as an extant political phenomenon, this is an indicator that the American public perceives that a cultural divide has emerged in recent years.

The polarization of elites—activists, politicians, government officials, organized interest groups, and opinion leaders—is well established in the literature (Conover et al. 1982; Poole and Rosenthal 1984; Hetherington 2001; Fleisher and Bond 2004; Brady and Han 2006; Fiorina and Levendusky 2006; Theriault 2008; Hill and Tausanovitch 2015). However, there remains considerable disagreement over whether the mass electorate has polarized on cultural issues. Culture war and polarization skeptics argue that only elites and activists, both diminishingly small segments of the American electorate, are polarized. Morris Fiorina went so far as to label mass polarization a "myth" in his seminal work on the culture wars, and polarization skeptics have argued that the mass public is relatively unmoved by elite polarization and remains consistently centrist and increasingly tolerant in its political disposition (Fiorina et al. 2004, 2008; Fiorina and Levendusky 2006; Fiorina and Abrams 2008; Hill and Tausanovitch 2015). Fiorina, along with other culture war skeptics, have argued that the rhetoric regarding the polarization of the American electorate over the last 10–15 years is apocryphal. They contend that Hunter and those who have accepted his thesis are wrong. There is no political polarization of the masses. "The simple truth is that there is no culture war in the United States—no battle for the soul of America rages" (Fiorina et al. 2004). The trend in public opinion over the last several decades on social issues is one of stability on the one hand or shifts toward a more centralized and moderate opinion distribution. The most comprehensive empirical analysis of mass political polarization to date examined decades of reported social issue attitudes from American National Election Study (ANES) and General Social Survey (GSS) surveys on a number of issue dimensions, but they found polarization only on abortion (DiMaggio et al. 1996). And their abortion polarization finding is itself disputed (Mouw and Sobel 2001).

On the other hand, there are a number of scholarly examinations of the culture war thesis that have found significant evidence of polarization in the mass public in issue, partisan, and ideological dimensions (Abramowitz and Saunders 2005; Abramowitz and Jacobson 2006; Bartels 2000; Hetherington 2001; Abramowitz and Saunders 1998; Jacobson 2000; Evans et al. 2001; Layman and Carsey 1999, 2002; Schier and Eberly 2016). These polarization scholars argue that the mass electorate has polarized on some social issues (i.e. abortion, social issues, and ideology), that ideologues have become more consistently partisan, and the public has become more ideologically polarized.[2] Layman finds considerable evidence in public opinion trends of political polarization. He traces the polarized cleavage in American politics, like Hunter, to the emergence of a divide between those that continue to accept the traditional religious and cultural teachings in America, and those that reject it (Layman 2001). Abramowitz and Saunders find increased ideological polarization in the electorate and that the "activist" segment of the populace is much larger than suggested by Fiorina and culture war skeptics (Abramowitz and Saunders 2005). Schier and Eberly (2016) find that both political parties have become more ideologically homogeneous and that politically active citizens have become more polarized on political issues. Like Abramowitz and Saunders (2005), they find a rise in the ideological orientation of citizens with a modicum of political activity, and that this group is proportionately large among the American electorate.

4.2   DEFINING AND ASSESSING POLARIZATION: AVERAGES, DENSITY, AND CONSENSUS VERSUS CONFLICT

As the struggle proceeds, "the whole society breaks up more and more into two hostile camps, two great, directly antagonistic classes: bourgeoisie and prole-tariat." The classes, polarize, so that they become internally more homogenous and more and more sharply distinguished from one another in wealth and power. (Deutsch 1971)

Justice Potter Stewart, tasked with imposing a definition of obscenity in order to rule on the constitutionality of a fine imposed on a filmmaker for showing the French film *The Lovers*, said of obscenity that he could not intelligibly define it but that "I know it when I see it" (1964, 197). It is tempting to do the same with polarization. Polarization is relatively easy to visualize but much more difficult to define. There is disagreement in the literature on how to define polarization and how to measure it. Some conceive it as increasing extremism in the electorate or among social groups on issues, ideology, partisan, and electoral choices. Others look to election results, though as Fiorina et al. (2004) make clear, polarized alternatives can lead to polarized choices between those alternatives, irrespective of the underlying distribution of opinion. Thus, contra-Stewart, knowing it when we see it is simply insufficient. A theoretically rooted conceptualization of polarization and a rigorous and valid empirical operationalization of polarization are imperative.

We start first with a population. At minimum, we must have at least two individuals in order to talk about positions relative to one another. While internal conflict for individuals is real, it is difficult to be polarized from one's self. Thus, we must have a population in order to talk about polarization. Whether it is two individuals on a desert island or the citizenry of the United States, a population greater than one is a pre-requisite of polarization. The American electorate is the conceptual population we are most often interested in when discussing political polarization. In 2016, the voting age population was roughly 231 million, certainly a sufficiently large population to satisfy the pre-requisite. Second, we need some attribute that is characteristic of a subset of the given population. By attribute I merely mean some characteristic (belief, position, identity, etc.) of an individual, institution, organization, or other subset, up to and including the entire population. The culture war literature has mostly dealt with social issues, however, any political attribute could potentially be a source of polarization. Foreign policy, government spending, taxes, welfare policies, and so on are all potential issues which can be attributes or components of attributes. The population of political issues is thus a subset of the population of possible attributes for our conceptual population of interest. Likewise, political attributes can be associated with any possible subset of the aggregate electorate, including the subset of the entire electorate.

With a population and a political attribute, we can then begin to conceptualize polarization. The first step is to identify a density of the population associated with different values of the political attribute. If the political attribute has only one value, then you have a density equal to one. Likewise, if all but one of the values of a political attribute is associated with the empty set of the conceptual population, the density would equal one. In all other cases, we can find a distribution of the population across the values of the attribute equivalent to the combination of all elements of the conceptual population and the possible values of the political attribute. Polarization is at its essence a *relative* concept. Much like one cannot define "larger" without reference to something "smaller" with which to compare, polarization must be conceived relative to either an absolute or an ideal distribution of the attribute in a population, or a different state of the distribution of the attribute in the population. Polarization suggests poles, and poles by definition must have separation. This observation has an important implication: the absence of polarization is the absence of a distribution. We can thus define the absence of polarization: consensus. When the density of a population on an attribute is equal to one, we have perfect consensus on that attribute in the population, and hence the absolute absence of polarization. Having thus defined polarization at its lower limit, we must define it at its upper bound. Absolute polarization at the limit is thus one half of the population located at the extreme point, or limit, of the attribute (i.e. upper bound), and 50 percent of the population located at the other limit (i.e. lower bound). Thus, other than the case of absolute consensus, there must be a distribution of the conceptual population at values of the attribute. Polarization is thus conceived as a departure from consensus. Thus, when we talk about a "polarized" opinion distribution in an absolute sense, we are contemplating the distribution of opinion relative to a "theoretical maximum" (DiMaggio et al. 1996). And in order to compare whether, of two distributions, one is the more polarized of the two, we assess it in terms of the density of the population located at the values of the attribute relative to consensus. This is relative polarization.

One of the problems that has plagued the scholarly debate over polarization is the vexing problem of how to validly and reliably define the concept of polarization for empirical testing in public opinion data (Hetherington 2009). We can see the importance of properly conceptualizing polarization in the empirical evidence often cited in the debate. Culture war skeptics have pointed to the relative stability of average issue positions in the American populace as evidence against the culture wars thesis. Average mass opinion on abortion as measured by the ANES, for example, has been relatively stable over the past three decades (Fiorina et al. 2004). Furthermore, culture war skeptics argue that, on politically salient social issues, the average of American mass opinion has moved in the direction of greater tolerance, which belies, in their minds, the polarization thesis. Some polarization skeptics point to the stability of centrist opinion on cultural issues, such as that in the ANES and GSS time series on mass public opinion. For example, Fiorina notes that abortion attitudes over the "polarization" time period of the last 30 years have been relatively stable (Fiorina et al. 2004). Second, polarization skeptics argue that uniform shifts in public opinion are not polarization. For example, both Fiorina et al. (2004) and Hill and Tausanovitch (2015) note that public opinion on homosexuals was unfavorable toward homosexuals in the 1970s, but became uniformly more tolerant in the present. According to these scholars, this is not evidence of polarization. If the average location changes, but the distribution remains consistent, then there is no change in the relative polarization of the mass public over time.

Unpacking the claims about the polarization of mass public opinion and change in that opinion over time is complicated. A stylized example may serve to elucidate the dynamic components of polarization. Table 4.1 reports six hypothetical distributions of opinions, ranked from 0 to 10, for a population of ten citizens. The location (mean, median, mode), dispersion (standard deviation), and density (average proportion of sample falling into a single category) statistics for each of the distributions are also reported. Note, four of the five hypothetical distributions depicted in Table 4.1 have exactly the same mean, and the fifth distribution is just a tenth of a point different from the means of those four distributions. If we imagine that Distributions 2–6 in Table 4.2 represent the change in the distribution of opinion on a cultural issue over time (i.e. abortion), then it is apparent that the distribution of opinion on abortion can radically change while the location of the mean and median of the distribution is stable—near constant—over the five hypothetical time periods. Distribution 1 versus Distribution 3 illustrates the point regarding location versus distribution made by polarization skeptics—that changes in opinion location may not involve changes in the characteristics of the distribution of opinion. While this is true, it also requires that the shift be accompanied by no change in the relative density of opinion as well. Note that the change from Distribution 2 to Distribution 3 is relatively small in terms of the absolute value shifts among the ten citizens' opinions, but result in rather large changes in the dispersion and density of the distribution. Consider also a hypothetical change from Distribution 1 to Distribution 5. If Distribution 1 reflects the anti-gay consensus of the 1970s, while

Table 4.1 Six hypothetical opinion distributions on a given issue in a population of ten citizens

Population (n = 10)	Extreme consensus distribution 1	Moderate consensus distribution 2	Centrist consensus distribution 3	Centrist polarization distribution 4	Moderate polarization distribution 5	Extreme polarization distribution 6
Citizen 1	1	5	5	1	4	0
Citizen 2	1	5	5	2	4	0
Citizen 3	1	5	5	3	4	0
Citizen 4	1	4	5	4	4	0
Citizen 5	1	5	5	5	4	0
Citizen 6	1	6	5	5	6	10
Citizen 7	1	5	5	5	6	10
Citizen 8	1	5	5	7	6	10
Citizen 9	1	5	5	8	6	10
Citizen 10	1	4	5	10	6	10
Mean	1.000	4.900	5.000	5.000	5.000	5.000
Median	1.000	5.000	5.000	5.000	5.000	5.000
Mode	1.000	5.000	5.000	5.000	6 | 4	0 | 10
Standard deviation	0.000	0.568	0.000	2.749	1.054	5.270
Mean density	1.000	0.333	1.000	0.125	0.500	0.500

Source: Compiled by the Author

Table 4.2 Dispersion and bimodality statistics for selected gay rights polls compared to hypothetical distribution

Poll question on gay rights		Year	Mean	Standard deviation	Kurtosis	Coefficient of variation
	Homosexual relationship	1974	0.979	0.143	43.186	14.591
Quaternary	Gay adoption	2004	2.783	1.232	−1.542	44.290
	Constitutional amendment	2004	2.467	1.323	−1.756	53.617
	Gay rights	2004	2.856	1.269	−1.508	44.423
	Gay marriage	2004	2.600	1.312	−1.743	50.492
Binary	Gay adoption	2004	0.565	0.496	−1.934	87.793
	Constitutional amendment	2004	0.299	0.458	−1.223	153.261
	Gay rights	2004	0.463	0.499	−1.980	107.752
	Gay marriage	2004	0.482	0.500	−1.997	103.783
	Hypothetical centralized distribution	–	2.5	0.807	−0.482	32.262

Distribution 5 reflects the state of opinion on gay rights today, then it is true, as the polarization skeptics argue, that opinion on the gay rights issue has become more liberal across the board. But it would not be true that there was no change in the distributional characteristics of opinion on gay rights from the 1970s to the present. Indeed, such would be a profound polarization of opinion. Is the change in opinion about gay rights in the public more like the change from Distribution 1 to Distribution 3, Distribution 2 to Distribution 3, or Distribution 1 to Distribution 6, or something else? Fundamentally, this is an empirical question that needs to be addressed with a rigorous empirical analysis using the conceptually valid measure of polarization.

What is apparent from the hypothetical distributions in Table 4.1 is that a complete conceptualization of polarization must take into account the range of the attribute, the density of the population across the range of the attribute, and the relative location of the sub-population masses at those points on the attribute. Certainly Fiorina and other polarization skeptics are correct to stress the importance of dispersion and relative mass, or density, of the population across the values of the attribute, but the location of those masses is important as well, and it is directly related to the magnitude of the dispersion to begin with. Distributions 5 and 6 illustrate this point clearly. While both of these distributions have the same population densities located at two points on the hypothesized attribute, in Distribution 6, they are each located at the opposite limits of the attribute, while in Distribution 5, both masses are located near the center of the values of the attribute. It cannot be that both Distribution 5 and Distribution 6 are equally polarized, yet that is precisely where a definition of polarization independent of location would lead us to.

Political polarization is where the distribution of opinion in the electorate on an issue is more concentrated in two or more separate densities relative to a past distribution of opinion in the electorate on the same issue, or one of the theoretical limits of polarization: absolute consensus or absolute polarization.

Esteban and Ray (1994) defined polarization similarly in their study of income inequality. They identified two components of polarization: identification and alienation. Polarization is characterized by increasing identification with those similar to oneself along some relevant attribute coupled with increasing alienation from those dissimilar to oneself along that same attribute. Identification is strongly correlated with density, that is the more individuals that share your opinion on a given attribute, the more likely you are to identify with those individuals as a coherent group. Stated explicitly, there are three features of polarization identified by Esteban and Ray: (1) there must be a high degree of homogeneity within each group, (2) there must be a high degree of heterogeneity across groups, and (3) there must be a small number of significantly sized groups (isolated small groups or individuals are irrelevant) across the values of the attribute (Esteban and Ray 1994; Esteban and Schneider 2008).

In politics, attributes which have a distribution of opinion at unanimity or near unanimity do not lend themselves well to the political process. This is especially so in the United States, where the bar for successful partisan competition is set by our first-past-the-post systems. There is little reason for a candidate or party to adopt a position in opposition to a unanimous or near-unanimous position, as doing so could carry with it a penalty of lost elections and sapped strength in American political institutions. Not coincidentally, individuals and groups with beliefs and positions that run counter to a unanimous or near-unanimous position have difficulty getting access to the policy process. Political parties tend to ignore them. Thus, political polarization is dependent on the magnitude of the density of the population located at values of the attribute, and the relative distance between the values of the attribute that these population masses are located at. Sometimes consensus positions—as a function of exogenous shocks, demographic and population shifts, or merely the vagaries of time—become non-consensus positions in the American electorate. This process of moving from consensus, where most people agree on an issue, to conflict, where a substantial portion of the public disagree on an issue, is at the heart of political polarization, and a key characteristic of polarization that has been overlooked by polarization skeptics. When the political dynamic on an issue changes such that there is a substantial portion of the American public in opposition to the rest of the citizenry, the conditions are ripe for political conflict, irrespective of whether it is accompanied by an overall shift in absolute location in one direction or the other. Density and dispersion are the primary characteristics of polarization, and their intersection with respect to political attributes can lead, over time, to more (or less) political polarization.

4.3   AN EMPIRICAL OPERATIONALIZATION OF POLARIZATION: CONSENSUS TO CONFLICT

Having thus defined polarization conceptually, in order to assess polarization in political attributes in the American electorate, it is necessary to create an empirical operationalization that measures polarization of a political attribute. The empirical operationalization needs to capture the fundamental factors of polarization. It needs to take into account the dispersion (extent of alienation between individuals on the attribute) and density (extent of identification on the attribute) of the conceptual population of interest on the political attribute. This empirical operationalization will also depend on the nature of the data on the political attribute. In this chapter, I examine polling data on gay rights from the 1970s to 2016 using the Public Opinion Consensus-Polarization (POCP) measure, which is a measure of the extent of consensus (in the maximum) and polarization (in the minimum) on a political attribute in polling data. Most of the public opinion question items have binary responses sets, giving respondents a dichotomous choice of, for example, "favor" or "oppose." Some of these questions do give respondents more than two substantive options from which to choose as their answer, the most common of these consistent with a four-point Likert scaling. In order to compare the polarization of gay rights public opinion across survey items, it is necessary to collapse all responses down to a dichotomy. While this does fix the range of dispersion in public opinion on gay rights on the political attribute, dispersion may still vary from item-to-item, dependent on the density of responses within the dichotomy.

After collapsing the polling item response sets to dichotomies, I order the response sets based on whether they are consistent with pro-gay rights attitudes and anti-gay rights attitudes across multiple questions that touch on multiple specific issues, such as the legality of gay marriage, that fall under the umbrella of LGBT political issues. While it is possible to work backward from the N and frequencies to produce means and standard deviations, it is ultimately unnecessary to assess polarization of political issues (i.e. gay rights). We can examine the trends in gay rights attitudes for the public in terms of consensus and polarization with a transformation of the binary densities in each of the categories for the available data. Figure 4.1 depicts the transformation of four binary and dichotomous-collapsed survey question responses with varying densities across the categories of the political attribute measured by the survey item to illustrate how the POCP is created. In order to conduct an analysis of the consensus and conflict trends in public attitudes on gay rights, it is useful to convert the categorical responses to a single statistic that realizes the theoretical features of polarization we have identified. Thus,

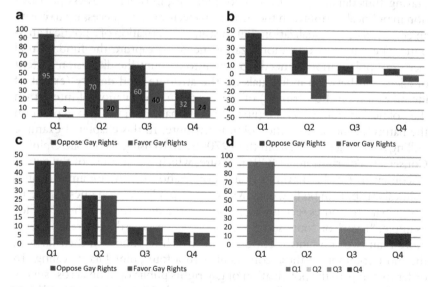

Fig. 4.1 Creating the Public Opinion Consensus-Polarization (POCP) measure. (a) Four hypothetical binary poll responses on gay rights; (b) proportional response deviations relative to 50 percent; (c) taking absolute value of response deviations; (d) absolute deviations added in consensus-polarization measure

the POCP measure consists of frequency percentages across the polling question categories, not the individual responses that make up those percentages. Necessarily, the observational unit for the POCP is the poll item itself and not the respondents who answered that item in the poll. Consistent with the conceptual definition of polarization we have identified, POCP's value for absolute conflict, that is maximum polarization, is a function of an even distribution of respondents across the anti-gay rights and pro-gay rights categories. In other words, where the densities for the two gay rights categories are equal (anti-gay rights density = ½; pro-gay rights density = ½), the consensus-polarization measure is at its minimum (zero). When the density of respondents to an item is equal to one in either of the categories, POCP is equal to one, reflecting maximum consensus. This measure of consensus-polarization provides a way of examining the dichotomous distribution of opinion on an issue relative to the 50/50 maximum polarization standard, and thus is an operationalization of polarization that captures the fundamental characteristics of polarization we have identified.

The three-step process of transforming the densities of the dichotomous gay rights categories into the single consensus-polarization statistic is depicted in Fig. 4.1. We start with the binary categories for the anti-gay rights and pro-gay rights attitudes in the American public. Figure 4.1a illustrates four hypothetical attitude distributions, ranging from near-absolutely consensus (95 to 3) to near-absolute conflict (32/24). We therefore see a hypothetical rendering of four sets of responses on four different aspects of the gay rights issue. These could be, for example, gays in the military, gay marriage, gay adoption, and gay inheritance. For illustrative purposes, the distributions are quite distinct: The first gay rights issue is near consensus, while the last is at near maximum polarization, that is conflict. The total densities across the categories of each of the questions shown in Fig. 4.1a show why one cannot simply choose one of the categories and use it as a proxy for consensus or polarization. In Q1, Q3, and Q4, the anti-gay rights and pro-gay rights categories do not sum to 100 percent. This is not an infrequent characteristic of the polling items in the data. These densities do not necessarily sum to 100 percent because respondents to poll items need not give substantive responses—they may respond that they do not know, have not thought about the issue, or refuse to answer. Furthermore, there are middle categories (neither approve nor disapprove) that may not be merged into one of the two categories. Only 31 of the 1404 gay rights poll survey items included in the analysis have binary categories that sum to 100 percent (2.21 percent). Importantly, the magnitude of POCP is independent of the total density for the two categories. Rather, it is dependent on the relative differential between the two densities. This fact is demonstrated in Fig. 4.1b–c.

The first step is to convert the category percentages to deviations from 50 percent (maximum polarization). In Fig. 4.1b, the anti-gay rights and pro-gay rights categories for each of the distinct questions on gay rights are represented in terms of their distance above and their distance below the 50 percent baseline. In a state of maximum polarization on gay rights, the American electorate is divided equally into the pro-gay rights and anti-gay rights camps on the specific gay rights issue the survey item addressed. If an issue is in a state of maximum consensus, then all of the respondents to the item who gave a substantive response fall into one, and only one, of the two possible camps. Once you have calculated deviations from 50 percent for both categories, the second step (Fig. 4.1c) is simply taking the absolute value of those deviations. This leads to the third and final step of combining the two deviations into a single, composite consensus-polarization measure (POCP). As can be seen in Fig. 4.1c, this consensus-polarization measure is a valid and reliable measure of the combined deviations from maximum polarization for the anti-gay rights and pro-gay rights categories. A consensus-polarization score of 100 represents maximum consensus, and a consensus-polarization score of zero represents maximum polarization. Relative changes in POCP over time and across items may thus be analyzed to assess trends in polarization.

One methodological criticism of the consensus-polarization dichotomy as a measure of polarization is that, through the combination of strong and less-strong respondents, it overstates the oppositional nature of public attitudes. In other words, binary response sets, or the collapse of multiple category response sets into a dichotomy, may overstate polarization by masking centrist attitudes within that dichotomy. There are five important ripostes to this legitimate concern. First, most of the included polling questions in this data set have binary response sets. Thus, the number of questions with collapsed categories is a fraction of the included items. In other words, to the extent this is a limitation, it is a limitation inherent to the data and not a methodological choice. Second, the fact that the use of a binary measure of public opinion (either through the original response set or collapsed categories) is *consistent* over the time period covered by the data set vitiates against a false positive in the polarization trend as a function of the response categories. The dichotomous structure of the responses is constant over the time period of the data set, and thus it cannot be the determinant of changes in the polarization measure over time. Third, the benefit in a maximally inclusive approach to substantive questions on gay rights helps ensure a more representative sample of public opinion on gay rights. Fourth, the binary measure accurately and consistently captures the distribution of opinion on gay rights as to conflict versus consensus. It permits the identification of conflict or consensus, the questions themselves permit variation in the centrality versus extremism of the gay rights issue (ranging from forbidding speech and job opportunities to permitting gay marriage and providing social security benefits), and the characterization of debate on these issues in terms of two opposing viewpoints is a good proxy for the actual distribution of opinion in the mass public. Last, as illustrated in Fig. 4.4, the binary response measures may actually understate the degree of polarization in the public attitudes toward gay rights, as the denser categories were the extreme categories, not the central categories. In other words, it can cut both ways. Given the number of poll items included, only a significant bias in the distribution of error would call into question the validity of the trend in gay rights identified in this analysis.

4.4   FROM CONSENSUS TO POLARIZATION: PUBLIC OPINION ON GAY RIGHTS IN AMERICA: 1970–2016

4.4.1   In to the Headwind: The Anti-Gay Rights Consensus, 1970–1988

Homosexuality is a taboo in many societies, but it is particularly so in countries with Judeo-Christian traditions. The United States is no exception, with nearly every state having had, at one time, sodomy laws outlawing homosexual relations. Until the 1960s, these laws were relatively uncontroversial. The 1960s witnessed the Civil Rights Movement and the sexual revolution, which led to both more expansive support for the rights of oppressed minorities and a transformation of social mores, an evolutionary process that continues in to the present. This revolution, however, had not encompassed homosexuals as of the 1970s. While some states had repealed their prohibitions on homosexual relations, and many such provisions still on the books went largely unenforced, there was little evidence that the taboo on homosexuality and the societal rejection of homosexuals would ever change, barring extraordinary legal action. Certainly the policy process, subject to popular opinion, seemed an unlikely avenue for change at that time.

The strong social norm proscribing homosexual identification and behavior in the 1970s, and their de facto second-class status as citizens is typified in the 1977 Harris Survey on public attitudes. A relative consensus did exist that homosexuals could hold certain jobs, should be permitted to make speeches, and be allowed to participate in civil society. A majority of Americans reported support for equal job opportunities for homosexuals.[3] But that was the extent of gay-friendly attitudes in the survey. In that survey, respondents were asked in what jobs it would be acceptable for homosexuals to openly hold in society (Fig. 4.2). The consensus limited homosexuals to blue-collar jobs and positions which required little contact with the public in authoritative or trusted positions. There was considerable opposition to homosexuals in positions of authority (congressman, policeman), positions of public trust (social worker), positions which require intimate contact with others (doctor, psychiatrist), religious positions (priest), and positions which involve contact with children (principal, teacher). We see strong evidence of the anti-gay rights consensual status quo in the Virginia Slims American Women's Poll in 1974, which asked 3880 respondents if they would find it acceptable if their grown daughter had a homosexual relationship (Fig. 4.3). Seventy-five percent of those respondents found it unacceptable, with an additional 19 percent who would accept it, but also reported they would both be unhappy about it and would have a strained relationship with that daughter as a result. Only 1 percent of respondents to the poll reported that they would find the relationship acceptable.[4] This is powerful evidence of a strong anti-gay rights consensus in the 1970s that perceived homosexuals as deviants, encouraged and endorsed intolerance toward gays, and opposed policy innovations on gay rights. Though the Harris survey demonstrates that the consensus on gays in the United States in the 1970s was not uniformly hostile, it also reveals, along with the VSAW poll, that homosexuals were generally perceived as morally suspect and, from the perspective of the consensus of the American electorate, rightfully relegated to the fringe of society. Well over half of the public endorsed outright discrimination against homosexuals in all but menial jobs or the arts.

The fact Americans were conflicted over the extension of basic civil rights to homosexuals illustrates that a powerful consensus marginalizing homosexuals existed in the 1970s, one that persisted well into the

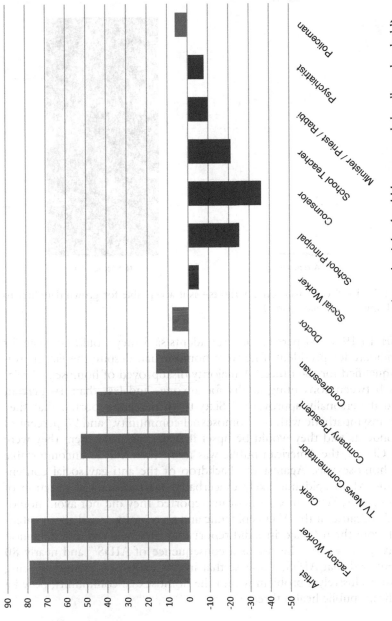

Fig. 4.2 Response differential for 1977 Harris survey question: what jobs should homosexuals be allowed to hold?

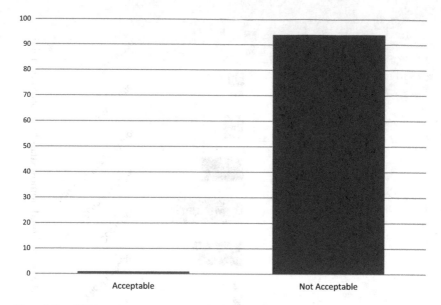

Fig. 4.3 1974 consensus on gay rights—is it acceptable for grown daughter to have homosexual relationship?

1980s. In 1983, 64 percent of respondents said they would not vote for a candidate for president if he were homosexual, despite the fact he was well-qualified for the office.[5] A majority disapproved of homosexual relations between consenting adults for anyone, and less than 10 percent found it personally approvable.[6] Sixty-three percent reported that they were unsympathetic with the homosexual community,[7] and 90 percent of respondents said they would be upset if their child told them they were gay.[8] Clearly, the American public was more than a little uncomfortable with homosexuals. Against the backdrop of the anti-gay social consensus, the AIDS epidemic likely exacerbated fears and social rejection of homosexuals. While most Americans reported they did not avoid homosexuals because of the AIDS epidemic and were not worried about catching it from them,[9] majorities did report that they believed discrimination against gays was on the rise as a consequence of AIDS[10] and nearly 80 percent said that AIDS, a disease that in the 1980s was viewed as being almost exclusively a problem within the homosexual community, posed a significant public health threat.[11]

4.4.2   Sowing the Wind: An Emergent Social Conflict on Gay Rights, 1988–1991

Whether a consequence of increasingly favorable representations in the movies and television, the organization of the gay rights movement into pressure groups like the Human Rights Campaign and ACT-UP, a reaction to the Supreme Court ruling in *Bowers v. Hardwick* that upheld the constitutionality of sodomy laws (only a bare majority reported approval), or some combination of these and other exogenous and endogenous shocks to the culture, the tide of public opinion began to turn in favor of homosexuals and gay rights in the late 1980s.[12] The consensus against homosexual identity and behavior was forever shattered, and a political conflict over gay rights began to emerge. One significant indicator of the radical change that was under way was in the number of respondents who reported they had friends or acquaintances who were gay. In 1985, 91 percent of respondents reported they had neither friends nor associates who were gay.[13] In 1986, 78 percent of respondents reported that they did not have a friend who was gay.[14] By 1992, nearly half of the American public reported knowing someone who was gay or lesbian.[15] A fourth reported having a close, personal friend who was gay.[16] While estimates of the homosexual population vary, there is no evidence that it experienced exponential growth over this time period. Rather, the more likely explanation for this trend is that, on the one hand, gays were more comfortable with being open about their sexual orientation with friends, family, and acquaintances, and on the other hand, more citizens were willing to acknowledge that they had gay friends and report this fact in surveys.

New gay rights issues, such as gay marriage[17] and gays in the military[18] began to emerge during this time period as well, indicating that the collapse of the anti-gay consensus had brought the panoply of gay rights issues in to the realm of policy, politics, and partisan competition. These issues thus became highly salient features of the public debates over politics, and it would embroil a president, Bill Clinton, in controversy early in his tenure. This period represents an inflection point in public attitudes toward homosexuals and the salience of gay rights as a cleavage in partisan politics.

4.4.3   Reaping the Whirlwind: The Culture War on Gay Rights, 1991–2016

The cultural conflict over gay rights would come to a head in the 1990s with the issue of gays in the military. President Clinton, just elected to office and thus ending 12 years of Republican rule in the White House, stumbled into a political briar patch by signaling he would end the ban on gays in the military. President Clinton (and Dick Morris) may have suspected this would be a relatively easy political win, given the consensus that had emerged supporting equal job opportunities for gays. They were wrong. Clinton's effort quickly became a political firestorm and, consequently, he adopted a "third way" compromise position of "Don't Ask, Don't Tell." While this was intended to end the controversy, the American public was as closely divided on DADT as they were gays in the military to begin with (54/47 against DADT).[19] The battle over gays in the military was merely a prelude to the war that would be waged over gay marriage. In 1996, the US Congress passed the Defense of Marriage Act, defining marriage as only between couples of the opposite sex at the federal level. The Supreme Court having paved the way with its ruling banning state sodomy laws in *Lawrence v. Texas*, a number of legislative, judicial, and state referendum efforts emerged in support of and opposed to gay marriage. Several state supreme courts ruled that allowing or recognizing gay marriage is required under their state constitutions, and many state legislatures moved to enact DOM-like provisions defining marriage as only between a man and a woman.

In the 2000s, the divide in the American electorate deepened. In the Pew Research time series on same-sex marriage, the 2000s began with a 60/40 split, with the majority of Americans opposed to same-sex marriage.[20] The trend lines for "favor" and "oppose" were on a trajectory toward convergence, with the first decade of the twenty-first century closing out near maximal polarization on gay marriage in the Pew series. Still, in 2003, a poll found the vast majority of respondents reported that their attitude toward gays and lesbians had "not changed," with 59 percent of respondents giving that answer. However, three times as many respondents reported that they had become "more accepting" (32 percent) as had become "less accepting" (8 percent).[21] This is the trend that Fiorina and other polarization skeptics have cited as non-polarization. But what this poll illustrates is that, in fact, liberalization has been uneven, mostly occurring with a subset of the American public. And that is a recipe for polarization. The substantial polarization on gay rights in the 2000s is illustrated in Fig. 4.4, which reports the results of four poll questions from 2004 with four-point response sets. On each of the four question items, the gay marriage constitutional amendment item (Fig. 4.4a), the legality of gay marriage item (Fig. 4.4b), the gay adoption item (Fig. 4.4c), and the general gay rights item (Fig. 4.4d), the two extreme categories have

Fig. 4.4 Polarized attitudes on gay rights, 2004. (a) Gay marriage constitutional amendment; (b) legality of gay marriage; (c) gay adoption; (d) gay rights

higher densities when compared to the two center categories. Further, if we collapse these items into dichotomies, there is a near even divide between the pro-gay rights and anti-gay rights groups.

Half way through the second decade of the twenty-first century, the even divide in the American electorate on gay rights gave way to a plurality in support of gay rights that sometimes has achieved majority status. More and more polls, including the Pew Research time series, showed majority support in the public for gay marriage. In that environment, the Supreme Court decided two cases with significant implications for gay rights. In *United States v. Windsor* (2013), the Court ruled the Defense of Marriage Act's federal definition of marriage to be unconstitutional, on the basis that it served no legitimate basis except to interfere with the prerogative of states to acknowledge same-sex marriage. Windsor did not reach the question of the constitutionality of gay marriage, resting its decision on federalism and the state prerogative to define marriage (2013b). In *Hollingsworth v. Perry* (2013), the Court considered the constitutionality of California Proposition 8, which was an amendment to the California state constitution banning same-sex marriage, because the parties bringing the appeal lacked standing—a right to sue. The Court avoided speaking to the efficacy of state bans on same-sex marriage in its decision, instead choosing to dismiss the case on standing, leaving the lower court ruling against California Proposition 8 in place (2013a). In June 26, 2015, in the case of *Obergefell v. Hodges*, the US Supreme Court ruled, in a 5–4 decision authored by Supreme Court Associate Justice Anthony Kennedy, that the US Constitution protects the fundamental right to marry, and that the right to marry for same-sex couples is guaranteed by both the Due Process Clause and the Equal Protection Clause of the Fourteenth Amendment to the US Constitution (2015). Public opinion in support of gay marriage and gay rights continued to grow in the wake of these landmark decisions.

More recently, transgender issues have become more salient in political debates. On March 23, 2016, North Carolina Governor Pat McCrory signed the Public Facilities Privacy & Security Act, a bill that overturned an LGBT anti-discrimination ordinance passed by Charlotte, North Carolina, that, among its provisions, permitted transsexuals to use public bathrooms consistent with their gender identity. It further forbade any other local governments in the state from adopting similar ordinances. The Obama Justice Department determined that the bill was in conflict with federal law, such as Title VII of the Civil Rights Act, and put the state on notice that it may lose billions of dollars of federal funding to the state (Shoichet 2016). In an independent move, the Obama Administration issued a transgender bathroom "guidance" to public schools that they must not treat transgender students differently from other students of the same gender identity, and that the school must provide equal access and provide accommodations to transsexual students, such as gender neutral bathrooms. Failure to comply may deprive a state or locality of significant federal education funds. Nine states sued in federal court challenging the Obama administration's policy, and the Trump administration withdrew the guidance (Trotta 2017). Public opinion on transgender bathrooms reflects the strong polarization on gay rights found in previous decades on other LGBT issues. In a Pew study, about half of US adults say transgender individuals should be allowed to use public restrooms, while just about the same proportion (46 percent) say transgender people should be required to use bathrooms that match their birth gender.[22]

With few exceptions, public opinion on contemporary gay rights issues is passionate and closely divided. While majorities are aligned in favor of gay marriage, those opposed to it are a substantial proportion of the

American public. Most respondents reported that they have a friend, family member, or colleague who is gay.[23] Strong majorities (around 70 percent) supported extending benefits, social security, and inheritance rights to homosexual couples.[24] But the consensus that has developed on benefits and job opportunities are the exception. The rule is close-quarters, evenly divided conflict, even on issues that have trended toward more tolerance of LGBT individuals. The American public is closely divided on whether there should be a constitutional amendment defining marriage as between a man and a woman.[25] Americans are evenly divided on the morality of homosexuality (49/49)[26] and gay adoption (40/52 against).[27] These individual polls confirm the trend toward liberalization of a substantial portion of the American public in their views of gay rights, but contrary to the view of polarization skeptics, that liberalization has been uneven. As such, it has wrought significant political polarization on gay rights. But to assess whether that polarization has increased, decreased, or stabilized over the past decades requires a comprehensive examination of the trend in the consensus-polarization measure. It is that analysis which follows.

4.5   Data

While a general discussion of the picture of public attitudes on gay rights painted by various and sundry opinion polls over the last 45 years provides a sense of the movement from consensus to conflict—from relative peace to cultural war on gay rights—it does not establish the trend in a rigorous and systematic manner. Are gay rights a burgeoning front in the culture war? Did we have a consensus on homosexuals that has since eroded into two camps—roughly balanced, passionate, and hostile? Has the entry of gay rights in to the continuum of potential vote-getting political issues affected the disposition of the parties on gay rights as well as the policy process? Given these are empirical questions, empirical data is necessary to strike at an answer.

The data for this analysis constitute 1615 polling questions on attitudes toward gays and gay rights compiled from 1971 to 2016. The poll questions and responses were culled from the IPOLL database developed by the Roper Center for Public Opinion Research and from reports by a variety of polling firms made publicly available.[28] The data were culled using constraints designed to elicit only those questions that go to substantive LGBT political issues. If a question was determined to be unrelated to public attitudes on gay rights, or what that attitude is was not clear, the question was excluded. For example, excluded from the data set were fact-based questions, such as "On a scale of one to seven, how would you rate your own personal risk of contracting 'AIDS'?"[29] Also excluded were questions that asked the respondent about the future, such as "In the future, do you think 'AIDS' (Acquired Immune Deficiency Syndrome) will affect more people who are homosexual, or gay, or do you think it will affect more people who are heterosexual, or straight?"[30] Some questions asked the respondent to rate how one of the political parties, government, or politicians have acted on gay rights. Since it was not clear from the question whether the respondent thought the performance on gay rights issues was good or bad, those questions were excluded as well. A few attitude-related questions were excluded from the 2004 polling items using the following criteria: (1) they were repetitive entries, that is they constituted the same question and response set, and had similar opinion proportions to items that are included in the data set, and (2) a sufficient number of questions on that attitude had been obtained for that year, with 40 questions on a specific issue chosen as the cut-off point for inclusion.[31]

As described previously, and in order to facilitate cross-poll comparisons, the response categories for each question were collapsed into a binary set, if the question did not already have a binary response set. The options were sorted into pro-gay rights and anti-gay rights groupings. Figure 4.5 reports the frequency of the poll questions per year in the Gay Rights Database (GRD). The minimum number of questions in the data base for each year is one polling question (i.e. 1971), the maximum number is 134 (2004) with an average of 39.39 questions per year. There are polling questions from 120 different polls in the database.[32] The most polling questions (153) in the database are from the Gallup Poll. Most, but not all, of the polls reported their sample sizes. Of the 1615 polls in the GRD, 1536 reported sample sizes (95.11 percent). Of the polls with reported sample sizes, the average number of respondents per poll was 1249 with a minimum of 466 respondents (CNN/Opinion Research Corp. Poll, 2005) and a maximum of 8769 respondents (CBS News Exit Poll, November 1978).

The GRD covers a larger variety of gay rights issues. The GRD allows for a more nuanced assessment of attitudes toward gay rights and LGBT issues, and thus it constitutes a comprehensive and valid assessment of the continuum of gay rights public opinion. It also has survey items on the same issue but with variant question wordings, thus decreasing the probability of an instrumental effect threatening the validity of the results.

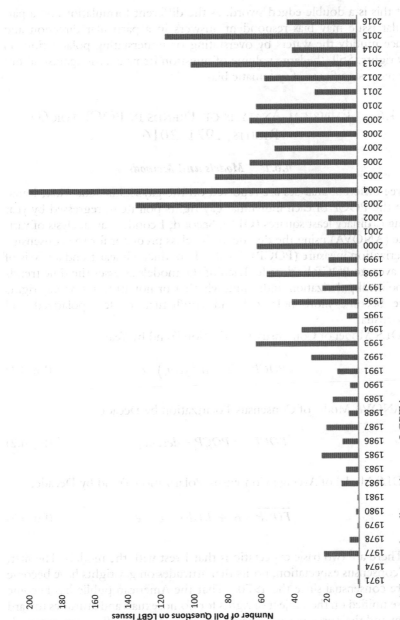

Fig. 4.5 Sample poll questions on LGBT issues

But this is a double-edged sword, as the different formulations on a particular issue may bias respondent answers in a particular direction and hence muddy the waters by overstating or understating polarization on gay rights. Still, the large volume of question items guards against all but the most significant of systematic bias.

4.6   EMPIRICAL ANALYSIS OF TRENDS IN POCP FOR GAY RIGHTS, 1971–2016

4.6.1   Models and Methods

Three different analyses are reported on the gay rights data. First, I analyze the POCP of each individual gay rights poll item, regressed by year using ordinary least squares (OLS). Second, I conduct an analysis of variance (ANOVA) using the decade as the class predictor for the consensus-polarization measure (POCP). Finally, I conduct a linear trend analysis of the average POCP by decade. Each of the models assesses the time trends in political polarization, indicating whether or not attitudes on gay rights have become more polarized and conflictual, or less polarized and consensual.

OLS Model of Consensus-PolarizationTrend by Year.

$$POCP_i = B_0 + B_1\left(year_i\right) + e_i \qquad \text{(Eq. 4.1)}$$

ANOVA Model of Consensus-Polarization by Decade.

$$POCP_{i,j} = POCP_i + decade_j \qquad \text{(Eq. 4.2)}$$

OLS Model of Average Consensus-Polarization Trend by Decade.

$$\overline{POCP} = B_0 + B_1\left(decade\right) + e \qquad \text{(Eq. 4.3)}$$

There are two basic expectations that I test with the models. The first, the consensus expectation, posits that attitudes on gay rights have become more consensual since the 1970s. That the American public has become more unified on the subject of rights for homosexuals and attitudes toward them and their presence in society. The second, the conflict expectation, is essentially the converse of the consensus expectation. The conflict expectation posits that the American public has become less consensual on the subject of gay rights. It asserts that the diversity of opinion on gay rights has increased, and that Americans have moved into opposing camps in their attitudes toward homosexuals and homosexuality.

4.6.2   Analysis: Exploring the Path from Consensus to Conflict on Gay Rights

America is a divided nation. This is an indisputable fact. We are split on the war, split on abortion, split on the unions, split on what the Constitution really means and split on the role of religion in this nation. (Cherry 2007)

As noted earlier, Fig. 4.4 reports four sets of responses to questions about contemporary gay rights issues from 2004: gay adoption, the legality of gay marriage, a constitutional amendment to define marriage as between a man and a woman (thus constitutionally barring gay marriage), and general attitudes toward gay rights. Substantively speaking, these polls, ranging the breadth of contemporary gay rights issues in the 2000s, demonstrate that the American public polarized on gay rights. All four of the distributions are bimodal or near-bimodal with more mass located in the extreme categories relative to the central categories (the extreme categories are also the two largest frequency categories for each of the issues). Contrasted with Figs. 4.2 and 4.3, which show the relative consensus that existed on gay rights attitudes in the 1970s, the trend from consensus to conflict and polarization on gay rights issues in the American electorate becomes apparent. For example, 90 percent of respondents to the Virginia Slims poll in 1974 reported that they would find their kid being gay unacceptable.[33] The difference between the consensus against homosexual relations in contrast to the near-evenly divided and highly polarized distributions (conflict) in 2004 is plain.

Table 4.2 reports the univariate statistics on the gay rights poll questions from 2004 reported in Fig. 4.3, both with their original four category response sets and as the collapsed dichotomies used in the consensus-polarization measure. Also reported is the 1974 poll on the acceptability of a homosexual relationship for the respondent's daughter depicted in Fig. 4.3. For a baseline comparison, a hypothetical centrist four category variable, with most of the mass of opinion located in the central categories (80 percent in center two categories and 20 percent in extreme categories), was created and the polarization statistics obtained for that distribution and reported in Table 4.2. These statistics capture two important aspects of polarization: dispersion (standard deviation, coefficient of variation) and a proxy for bimodality (kurtosis).[34] Table 4.2 points to the answers to several of the puzzles regarding polarization. It both illustrates the polarized nature of opinion on gay rights in the 2000s vis-à-vis that in the 1970s and provides a validity check for the consensus-polarization measure used in the trend analysis.[35] Comparing the standard deviations of the homosexual relationship (1974) distribution, that of the hypothetical centralized distribution, and then the four gay rights issues from 2004 (4 cat), the linear increase in dispersion on the attribute is apparent. The standard deviations for the binary, collapsed opinions on gay rights from 2004 (0.500, 0.499, 0.496, and 0.458) are substantially larger than that of the opinion from 1974 (0.143). It is also the case with the coefficient of variation (14.591 for the 1974 poll; 32.262 for the hypothetical centralized distribution; 48.21 average coefficient of variation for the four polls from 2004). The mean for the opinion on homosexual relationships from 1974 is near one, indicating the near maximal consensus of opinion at that time opposed to gay relationships for progeny, while the means for the opinions from 2004 approach the 0.50 maximal polarization limit, indicating a state of conflict.[36]

The measure of bimodality indicates a strong shift toward bimodality in gay rights public opinion in the 2000s when compared to the 1970s. The four measures of public attitudes toward gay rights in the 2000s, for either type of response set, are all bimodal, highly conflictual, and polarized distributions. This is true both from an absolute sense, compared to the hypothetical distribution, and in a relative sense, compared to the opinion on gay rights in the 1970s. Both the full and collapsed category measures of gay rights opinion in 2004 are platykurtic and hence indicate bimodality. The Virginia Slims poll on attitudes on homosexual relationships from 1974 reflects the consensus against homosexuals that existed at that time. The standard deviation for the 1974 poll is quite small (0.143) and small relative to the mean, as illustrated in the coefficient of variation (14.591). The kurtosis for this poll is extremely leptokurtic (43.186), reflective of the single-peaked distribution and the near-total mass of responses located at it (unimodal). Furthermore, note that the kurtosis of the distributions for both the binary and the quaternary responses sets are relatively similar. This tends to vie against Fiorina's argument that collapsing to binary categories artificially inflates polarization, at least with respect to bimodality in the public opinion data reported here.

If we compare the kurtosis of the hypothetical distribution relative to the other distributions, it illustrates the difference between a consensus position and a centralized distribution. An ordinal comparison of the kurtosis results for the hypothetical distribution is consistent with the consensus-to-conflict expectation. The normal (or near-normal) distribution is not, as some skeptics treat it, the ultimate expression of consensus or moderation. This is tangible evidence reinforcing the theoretical argument on polarization presented here: whether or not a shift to a normal distribution on an attribute is indicative of depolarization or polarization is dependent on the shape and dispersion of the prior state of the distribution. In the case of gay rights, the aggregate shift to an on average "moderate" position from the consensus position evident in the 1970s is *polarization*. Aggregate moderation, in this instance, is evidence of increasing conflict (i.e. polarization). As we can see from the distributions in 2004 relative to that in 1974, opinion on gay rights has shifted from one extreme (consensus and unimodality) to the other (conflict and bimodality).

While the analysis of a few representative polling items from the 1970s and 2000s is illustrative of the polarization trend in gay rights public opinion, a more systematic analysis is necessary to confirm this trend. Figure 4.6 depicts the fit plot for the linear trend model of consensus-polarization using ordinary least squares regression analysis. The slope of the line is clearly negative, indicating increased polarization per year as we move from the 1970s to the mid-2010s. The 95 percent confidence band around the trend line is larger earlier in the time series due to the fact that fewer polls undergird the point predictions in the 1970s and 1980s. However, the negative slope persists even if we compare the earliest point at the lower boundary line of the 95 percent confidence limit to the latest point at the upper boundary line. That said, there is clearly a great deal of within-year variation in the consensus-polarization measure. This is due to the variety of different issues and question items under the umbrella of gay rights that constitute the sample of polls included in the GRD. The relatively low proportional reduction in error relative to the mean model is consistent with this observation. However, even at the level of individual polls, we find a statistically significant polarizing trend in gay rights opinion. There is a quarter of a point increase in polarization for every year advanced in the time series (-0.262), and it is statistically significant at the

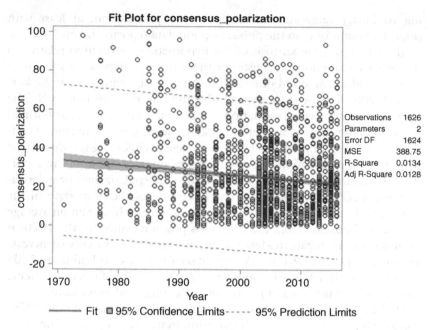

Fig. 4.6 Fit plot for OLS trend model of consensus-polarization on LGBT issues

0.0001 alpha level. This is strong, systematic evidence of polarization in gay rights public opinion over the four decades.

A more productive cut at the data is likely to be had by examining the consensus-polarization measure on a decade-by-decade basis. Doing so is likely to reduce the noise in the measure observable in the poll-level analysis shown in Fig. 4.6. Figure 4.7 reports the F-test from the ANOVA polarization analysis, assessing the empirical evidence against the null hypotheses that the decadal means of consensus-polarization are equal. Thus, this analysis assesses the differences between the decadal consensus-polarization means. The F-test critical value of 11.01 is strong statistical evidence that the decadal means are different, with the null hypothesis of equal means rejected at the 0.0001 alpha level. Two other features of the decadal change in consensus-polarization are apparent from Fig. 4.7. First, the interquartile range of consensus-polarization decreases significantly from the 1970s and 1980s to the later decades, which is consistent with a significant and substantial polarization trend from decade to decade in the time series. Second, the distribution of the consensus-polarization measure

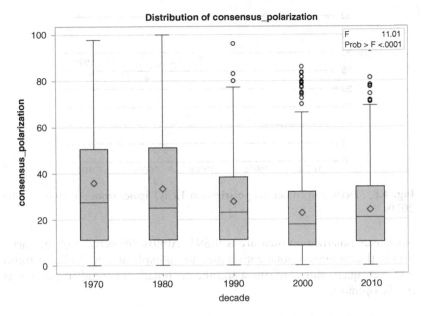

Fig. 4.7   Analysis of variance model of consensus-polarization by decade

is skewed to the right in each decade, indicating that the greater proportion of consensus-polarization scores are closer to absolute polarization
than they are to absolute consensus. Furthermore, high consensus items
constitute outliers in the later three decades of the time series, and the
threshold for consensual outliers declines in each decade except for the
2010s. Indeed, a consensus-polarization score greater than 67 in the
2000s was an outlier for that decade. All of this evidence is consistent with
that of the OLS year model: a significant polarizing trend in gay rights
public opinion.

Finally, Fig. 4.8 reports on the trend in the per-decade average of the
consensus-polarization measure (POCP) from the 1970s to the 2010s.
Through the 2000s, the decline in consensus (i.e. increase in polarization)
was 13 points, with a slight depolarizing uptick notable in the 2010s.
Still, even in the 2010s, the average consensus-polarization score is over
11 points below that of the 1970s, indicative of significant polarization
from decade to decade over this time series. The proportional reduction in
error measure shows that the negative sloping linear trend in the

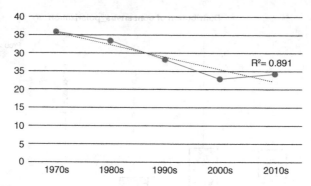

Fig. 4.8 Decline in consensus-polarization LGBT issues from the 1970s to the 2010s

consensus-polarization measure is 0.891. Almost 90 percent of the variation in the consensus-polarization measure is explained by the linear trend line. Yet again, this confirms a significant polarizing trend in gay rights public opinion.

4.7 From Consensus to Conflict: The Collapse of Consensus and Rise of Polarization on Gay Rights

Adults may choose to enter upon this relationship in the confines of their homes and their own private lives and still retain their dignity as free persons. When sexuality finds overt expression in intimate conduct with another person, the conduct can be but one element in a personal bond that is more enduring. The liberty protected by the constitution allows homosexual persons the right to make this choice.

—Justice Anthony Kennedy for the Majority, Lawrence v. Texas

Today's opinion is the product of a Court, which is the product of a law-profession culture, that has largely signed on to the so-called homosexual agenda, by which I mean the agenda promoted by some homosexual activists directed at eliminating the moral opprobrium that has traditionally attached to homosexual conduct. ... It is clear from this that the Court has taken sides in the culture war.

—Justice Antonin Scalia in Dissent, Lawrence v. Texas

In June, 2003, the Supreme Court issued an opinion in *Lawrence v. Texas*, striking down a Texas sodomy statute and overturning the precedent set in *Bowers v. Hardwick*, which had declined to find a constitutional right to private, consensual sexual relations a little over a decade prior. The divisive and charged argument between Justices Kennedy and Scalia illustrate the fact that gay rights and attitudes toward homosexuals are at the cutting edge of contemporary social conflict and that gay rights are a key front in the culture wars. However, it was not always so. In the not too distant past, there was a relative consensus in the American public on homosexuals and gay rights. There was a general attitude of distaste for homosexuals and their lifestyles and a bare tolerance for even fundamental civil rights for gays and lesbians, such as the right to hold a job. Homosexuals were not to be trusted in important positions like political office; they were not to be tolerated in jobs that required intimate contact with the public, nor permitted any position which might expose children to gays or the homosexual lifestyle.

While the gay rights movement hailed the decision in *Lawrence* and culture warriors decried it, one thing is certain irrespective of the constitutional questions: *Lawrence* was not out of step with the trend in public attitudes on gay rights in America. Gays had steadily gained traction in the public consciousness and attitudes toward gays have shifted significantly in favor of tolerance and normalcy for homosexuals and homosexual relations. The status quo on gay rights has clearly changed over the past four decades. One of the prime pieces of evidence against the culture wars thesis cited by polarization skeptics is this growing centrism on public attitudes toward homosexuals and gay rights. As scholars such as Morris Fiorina have noted, the American public has, on the whole, become more accepting of, tolerant of, and positive in its disposition toward LGBT individuals. Some culture war skeptics point to this as prima facie evidence against the culture wars thesis—that the aggregate decline in hostility toward gays and the slippage in opposition to gay rights is proof against an emergent divisive social conflict. They are wrong. The growing centrism on gay rights is powerful confirmatory evidence that the culture war has "gone hot." Contrary to what some polarization skeptics have argued, the liberalization trend has not uniformly manifested across the American electorate. Rather, a significant proportion of the American electorate has become substantially more liberal on gay rights and LGBT political issues, while a relatively equal proportion remains recalcitrant on gay rights and opposed to political innovations respecting LGBT rights. Nor has this trend proved to be transitory, as some culture war skeptics predicted (Fiorina et al. 2004). This loss of consensus on gay rights has produced a polarized divide in the American electorate that has persisted, even deepened, in public opinion trends from the 1970s to the mid-2010s. A strong shift from consensus to conflict and polarization on gay rights in the American public over four decades is hardly a fleeting political phenomenon.

In his seminal work on the culture wars, James Hunter (1991) argued that the social issues of the day were merely surface indicators of the deep cultural conflict between the orthodox, those who look to absolute sources of moral authority to structure their lives, and the progressives, those who rely more on reason and the spirit of the age to define moral boundaries. Gay rights have been precisely this sort of indicator—a touchstone of the culture wars and American social conflict. It is squarely on the public agenda in both legislative and legal environments. The parties have mobilized to provide alternative policy choices on gays and gay rights. Activists and political interest groups campaign for and against gay rights and hold officeholders to account on how they do or do not vote on gay rights measures. The mistake skeptics make in interpreting the data on attitudes toward gays and gay rights is to view centrism as commiserate with political moderation. While a normal distribution of attitudes is less polarized than a bimodal distribution, it is not the case when compared to a consensual distribution of opinion, where nearly everyone is in relative agreement on the issue at hand. In the latter case, a shift toward centrism is, in fact, polarization. It represents an increase in the probability of social conflict and an opening for political activism and mobilization in the policy process. Furthermore, the fact that certain issues come and go as salient features of the American political debate masks the deep cultural conflict that continues to churn up these issues in the collective social conscious of the American electorate and thus ignite political debates and partisan competition. While public opinions on gays in the military, and to a certain extent, gay marriage have become more consensual, the overall trend on this and other social issues is toward greater polarization and political conflict. New issues emerge along the same social issue dimension and break down along the same social and political cleavages that emerged in the 1970s and 1980s and continue to define American politics to the present.

Consensus positions rarely find their way onto the policy agenda, and if they do it is usually as a symbolic or affirmational gesture rather than real, substantive policy. Consensus positions present no incentive for political parties to diverge over related policy alternatives nor do they generate much activism against the consensus position oriented toward persuading electorate-responsive officials (given the small probability of success). When a consensus breaks down, with masses of the public attitude on the issue shifting away from the status quo, the issue becomes ripe for politics. In other words, the salience of issues is just as important as the distribution of public opinion on those issues, and in fact, one is dependent upon the other. As Hetherington notes, the very reason that gay rights became a salient political issue is because public opinion on gay rights moderated (Hetherington 2009). Now money and votes can be procured by appealing to one side or the other of the emergent divide. Policy alternatives can be generated that have some chance of successfully navigating the legislative process. Both sides seek political solutions: either through progressive change or successfully thwarting that effort at change. And as a consequence this issue becomes increasingly relevant to partisanship and electoral politics. The evidence presented here paints a very clear picture on political polarization and the culture wars within the issue domain of gay rights. The trend in gay rights is a perfect example of how the collapse in consensus, even when a function of large proportions of the citizenry becoming more tolerant toward a previously disfavored minority, leads to polarization. While the "myriad of self-contained cultural disputes," as Hunter termed them, may change, what does not change is the polarizing cultural conflict, shaped by fundamental disagreement over moral authority and competing moral visions, that underlies the social issue opinions of the mass public on gay rights and LGBT issues (Hunter 1991, 51). Polarization on gay rights typifies precisely the kind of political conflict that has characterized the culture wars since it emerged in the early 1970s, and it will likely continue to do so for the foreseeable future.

APPENDIX 4.1 FREQUENCY OF SAMPLE POLL QUESTIONS PER POLLING INSTITUTION

Polling institution	Count	Percent
1996 Survey of American Political Culture	4	0.25
2005 National Hispanic Survey	1	0.06
ABC News/Facebook Poll	7	0.43
ABC News/Washington Post Poll	105	6.46
ABC News Poll	13	0.8
AP National Constitution Center Poll	10	0.62
AP-GfK Poll	2	0.12

Polling institution	Count	Percent
Active Center Holds Survey	1	0.06
Adoption Survey	1	0.06
America's Evangelicals	1	0.06
American Public Opinion About Privacy at Home and at Work	10	0.62
American Values in the 1980s	1	0.06
Associated Press/IPSOS-Public Affairs Poll	2	0.12
Associated Press/Media General Poll	1	0.06
Associated Press Poll	18	1.11
Associated Press/AOL Poll	1	0.06
Attitudes Toward Smoking and the Tobacco Industry Survey	1	0.06
Barna Report 1993–1994 Absolute Confusion	2	0.12
Barna Report 1994–1995 Virtual America	1	0.06
Bloomberg	5	0.31
Boston Global Poll	24	1.48
CBS News	28	1.72
CBS News/New York Times Poll	116	7.13
CBS News Exit Poll	1	0.06
CBS News Poll	83	5.1
CBS News Polls	14	0.86
CNN/Opinion Research Corporation Poll	89	5.47
CNN/Time Poll	10	0.62
CNN/USA Today/Gallup Poll	11	0.68
Consumers in the Information Age	1	0.06
Defense of Marriage Act Poll	3	0.18
Democracy Corps Survey	39	2.4
Evangelical Christianity in the United States	1	0.06
Fair Juror Survey	1	0.06
Family Circle Ethics Poll	1	0.06
Family Research Council Survey	1	0.06
For Goodness Sake Survey	1	0.06
Fox News	21	1.29
Fox News/Opinion Dynamics Poll	21	1.29
Free Expression and the American Public	2	0.12
GSS	1	0.06
Gallup/CNN/USA Today Poll	38	2.34
Gallup/CNN Poll	1	0.06
Gallup/Newsweek Poll	12	0.74
Gallup/PDK Poll of Public Attitudes Toward the Public Schools	3	0.18
Gallup/USA Today Poll	3	0.18
Gallup Poll	153	9.41
Gallup Report	8	0.49
Garth Analysis Survey	1	0.06
General Social Survey	2	0.12
Gordon Black/USA Today Poll	1	0.06

Polling institution	Count	Percent
Great American TV Poll	5	0.31
Harris Poll	18	1.11
If Women Ran America	2	0.12
Judicial Confirmation Survey	2	0.12
Kaiser Family Foundation Survey on Americans and AIDS/HIV	1	0.06
Los Angeles Times Poll	63	3.87
McClatchy-Marist Poll	7	0.43
NBC News/Wall Street Journal Poll	57	3.51
NPR Poll	3	0.18
National Family Values	2	0.12
National Public Radio Poll	3	0.18
New Democratic Electorate Survey	3	0.18
New Models National Brand Poll	3	0.18
Newsweek Poll	23	1.41
PSRA/Newsweek Poll	74	4.55
Parents Magazine Poll	1	0.06
People & The Press—Mood of America Survey	1	0.06
People, The Press & Politics Poll	3	0.18
Pew Internet & American Life Project Poll	2	0.12
Pew News Interest Index/Believability Poll	1	0.06
Pew News Interest Index Poll	7	0.43
Pew News Interest Index Poll/Homosexuality Poll	6	0.37
Pew Research Center Political Survey	1	0.06
Pew Research Center for the People & the Press Political Typology Callback Poll	1	0.06
Pew Research Center for the People & the Press State of the Union Poll	1	0.06
Pew Research Center for the People & the Press Typology Poll	1	0.06
Pew Research Poll	149	9.16
Pew Social Trends Poll	1	0.06
Public Religion Institute	14	0.86
Quinnipiac University Poll	92	5.66
Reader's Digest Poll	1	0.06
Religion and Public Life	1	0.06
Roper/Ladies' Home Journal Poll	1	0.06
Roper/U.S. News & World Report Poll	3	0.18
Roper Commercial Survey	1	0.06
Roper Report 77-7	2	0.12
Roper Report 85-7	1	0.06
Roper Report 86-10	1	0.06
Roper Report 87-2	2	0.12
Roper Report 87-7	1	0.06
Suffolk University/USA Today Poll	5	0.31
TIPP/Investor's Business Daily/Christian Science Monitor Poll	4	0.25

Polling institution	Count	Percent
TV Poll	1	0.06
Taking America's Pulse III—Intergroup Relations Survey	3	0.18
Tarrance Group Poll	2	0.12
The Civic and Political Health of the Nation Survey	1	0.06
Time/CNN/Harris Interactive Poll	8	0.49
Time/CNN/Yankelovich, Clancy & Shulman Poll	40	2.46
Time/CNN Poll	17	1.05
Time/SRBI Poll	5	0.31
Time/Yankelovich, Skelly & White Poll	4	0.25
Time Poll	6	0.37
Times Mirror News Interest Index	1	0.06
U.S. News & World Report/Bozell Worldwide Poll	1	0.06
U.S. News & World Report Poll	15	0.92
USA Today	8	0.49
USA Today/Gallup	1	0.06
University of Pennsylvania	19	1.17
Views on Issues and Policies Related to Sexual Orientation Survey	25	1.54
Virginia Slims American Women's Poll	3	0.18
Voice of Mom Survey	2	0.12
Voter Attitudes on Political Campaigns Survey	1	0.06
Washington Post/Harvard/Kaiser Family Foundation American Values Survey	1	0.06
Washington Post/Harvard/Kaiser Family Foundation Race Relations Poll	2	0.12
Washington Post/Kaiser Family Foundation/Harvard Americans on Values Follow-up Survey	4	0.25
Washington Post/Kaiser Family Foundation/Harvard Political Independents Survey	1	0.06
Washington Post Poll	5	0.31
What Americans Expect from the Public Schools Survey	1	0.06
Women on Their Own in Unmarried America Survey	1	0.06

NOTES

1. Toward a Bold Politics Survey. Survey by Public Interest Project. Methodology: Conducted by Greenberg Quinlan Rosner Research, April 5–8, 2004, and based on telephone interviews with a national registered likely voters (see note) sample of 1000. National registered likely voters are registered voters who voted in the 2000 Presidential election/were ineligible/too young to vote or who did not vote in the 2000 election but did vote in the 2002 Congressional election. Respondents were asked to assess a list of issues presidents might face in the future, including the one

reported here: "The country divided into two Americas where people hold fundamentally different values about gay marriage, abortion and guns."

2. While Fiorina dismisses partisan "sorting" as a type of polarization, even assuming the underlying ideological dimension remains unchanged the ideological sorting of parties create more ideologically consistent and distinct parties. Whether you call it sorting or polarization, it is an important phenomenon.

3. Gallup Poll, June 1977. 2000 respondents. "In general, do you think homosexuals should or should not have equal rights in terms of job opportunities?"

4. Virginia Slims American Women's Poll conducted by Roper, April 1974. 3880 respondents. "For [a homosexual relationship], tell me for a daughter of yours who had just finished her schooling whether you would find it acceptable, or accept it but be unhappy about it, or not accept it and have the relationship very much strained as a result?"

5. Gallup Report, April 1983. 1517 respondents. "Between now and the political conventions in 1984 there will be discussion about the qualifications of presidential candidates. ... If your party nominated a generally well-qualified man for president and he happened to be homosexual, would you vote for him?"

6. Los Angeles Times Poll, September 1983. 1653 respondents. "What is your attitude toward homosexuality? Do you personally approve of homosexual relations between consenting adults ... or do you oppose it for everyone?"

7. Los Angeles Times Poll, September 1983. 1653 respondents. "Would you say you are very sympathetic, somewhat sympathetic, somewhat unsympathetic, or very unsympathetic to the homosexual community?"

8. Los Angeles Times Poll, September 1983. 1652 respondents. "If you had a child who told you he or she was a homosexual, what do you think your reaction would be? Would you be very upset, not very upset or not upset at all?"

9. ABC News/Washington Post Poll, March 1987. 1511 respondents. "Would you say that you are worried that [a homosexual] might give you AIDS (Acquired Immune Deficiency Syndrome)?"

10. CBS News Poll, October 1986. 823 respondents. "Do you think there has been more discrimination against homosexual men since AIDS became a serious problem, or don't you think the amount of discrimination against them is any different now than before?"

11. ABC News/Washington Post Poll, September 1985. "So far three-quarters of AIDS victims have been homosexual males. The rest of the victims have mainly been drug addicts or recipients of blood transfusions. Do you think that AIDS is spreading so that it is now a threat to the general public in the United States, or not?"

12. Gallup Report, July 1986. 1538 respondents. "The Supreme Court recently ruled that the Constitution does not give consenting adults the right to have private homosexual relations. Do you approve or disapprove of this ruling?"

13. ABC News Washington Post Poll, September, 1985. 1512 respondents. "Do you have a friend or someone you associate with on a regular basis who is a male homosexual?"

14. NBC News/Wall Street Journal Poll, January 1986. 1598 respondents. "Do you have any friends who are homosexual?"

15. CBS News/New York Times Poll, August 1992. 656 respondents. "Do you happen to personally know someone who is gay or lesbian?"

16. Harris Poll, October 1992. 1583 respondents. "Do you have any close personal friends who are gay or lesbian, or not?"

17. The first polling question in the IPOLL database on gay marriage was asked in the General Social Survey in February, 1988. "(Do you agree or disagree?). ... Homosexual couples should have the right to marry one another."

18. The first polling question in the IPOLL database on gays serving in the military was asked in a Los Angeles Times Poll in October, 1992. "Do you approve or disapprove of allowing openly homosexual men and women to serve in the armed forces of the United States? (If approve or disapprove, ask:) Do you (approve/disapprove) strongly or (approve/disapprove) somewhat?"

19. ABC News Washington Post Poll, January 1993. 549 respondents. "Do you think people who join the military should be asked if they are homosexual, or not?"

20. Pew Research Center Poll on Changing Attitudes on Gay Marriage, 2001–2016. http://www.pewforum.org/2016/05/12/changing-attitudes-on-gay-marriage/

21. CNN/USA Today/Gallup Poll, July 18–20, 2003. 1003 respondents. "Have you become more accepting of gays and lesbians, have your attitudes not changed, or have you become less accepting of gays and lesbians?"

22. CBS News/New York Times Poll, May 13–17, 2016. 1300 Respondents. "Do you think people who are transgender ... should be allowed to use the public bathrooms of the gender they identify with or should they have to use the public bathrooms of the gender they were born as?" https://www.scribd.com/doc/313143772/CBS-NYT-poll-toplines-Transgender-bathrooms-SCOTUS-Obama-approval

23. Princeton Survey Research Associates/Pew Research Center for the People & the Press Political Typology Callback Poll, March 2005. 1090 respondents. "Do you have a friend, colleague, or family member who is gay?"

24. Princeton Survey Research Associates/Henry J. Kaiser Family Foundation Views on Issues and Policies Related to Sexual Orientation Survey, February 2000. 2283 respondents. "(Next I'd like your opinion on some gay rights issues). ... Do you think there should or should not be ... health insurance and other employee benefits, Social Security, and inheritance rights for gay and lesbian domestic partners?"

25. Gallup/CNN/USA Today Poll, July 2003. 1003 respondents. "Would you favor or oppose a constitutional amendment that would define marriage as being between a man and a woman, thus barring marriages between gay or lesbian couples?"

26. CBS News/New York Times Poll, December 2003. 1057 respondents. "Do you think homosexual relations between adults are morally wrong, or are they okay, or don't you care much either way?"

27. Los Angeles Times Poll, March 2004. 1616 respondents. "Do you favor or oppose gay couples legally adopting children? (If Favor/Oppose, ask:) Do you strongly favor/oppose gay couples adopting children or only somewhat favor/oppose gay couples adopting children?"

28. IPOLL is a database of nearly half a million polling questions from 150 polling organizations cataloged since 1935. It includes data survey results from academic, commercial and media survey organizations such as Gallup Organization, Harris Interactive, Pew Research Associates, and many more. The data come from all the surveys in the Roper Center archive that have US national adult samples or samples of registered voters, women, African Americans, or any sub-population that constitutes a large segment of the national adult population.

29. Los Angeles Times Poll, December 1985. 2308 respondents.

30. Los Angeles Times Poll, December 1985. 2308 respondents.

31. Alternative cut-offs were tested, yielding no significant change in the results of the statistical analysis. The total sum of excluded repetitive questions represents a small fraction of the total poll items on LGBT issues included for 2004.

32. See Appendix A for a list of polls included in the GRD.

33. Virginia Slims American Women's Poll, April 1974.

34. The standard deviation is the second moment of the mean, and a measure of dispersion in the data. Kurtosis is the fourth moment of the mean, and serves as a proxy for bimodality: $kurtosis = [\sum(X - m^4 \div N)/S^4] - 3$. Bimodal distributions tended to be less "peaked" than normal distributions. Kurtosis = 0 is equivalent to the normal distribution—kurtosis scores which fall below zero are indicative of a more bimodal distribution than the normal distribution while higher values connote a unimodal or single-peaked distribution. The coefficient of variation is a ratio of the standard deviation to the mean.

35. Note that converting the polarized four category distributions to binary distributions does not affect the relative polarization comparisons of these distributions on conflict/consensus.

36. The difference in the means for the four polarized distributions and the hypothetical centralized distribution is negligible (2.67 vs. 2.5). You can have highly dispersed distributions with similar means to that of centralized distributions. While means can change as a consequence of polarization they do not necessarily do so. The direction of the change if it does change, and thus whether it indicates polarization or depolarization, is dependent on the change relative to the previous distribution. A significant mean shift to the center is polarization given a previous consensus position, while it is depolarization given a previous bimodal opinion distribution. Changes in means are not interpretable in terms of polarization/depolarization taken independent of the prior distribution.

References

1964. Jacobellis v. Ohio. In *United States Reports*. Supreme Court of the United States.

2013a. Hollingsworth v. Perry. In *United States Reports*. Supreme Court of the United States.

2013b. United States v. Windsor. In *United States Reports* Supreme Court of the United States.

2015. Obergefell v. Hodges. In *United States Reports*. Supreme Court of the United States.

Abramowitz, Alan I., and Gary C. Jacobson. 2006. Disconnected, or Joined at the Hip? In *Red and Blue Nation? Characteristics and Causes of America's Polarized Politics*, ed. Pietro S. Nivola and David W. Brady. Washington, DC: Brookings Institute Press.

Abramowitz, Alan I., and Kyle L. Saunders. 1998. Ideological Realignment in the U.S. Electorate. *Journal of Politics* 60 (3): 634–652.

———. 2005. Why Can't We All Just Get Along? The Reality of a Polarized America. *The Forum* 3 (2): 1–22.

Bartels, Larry M. 2000. Partisanship and Voting Behavior, 1952–1996. *American Journal of Political Science* 44 (1): 35–50.

Brady, David W., and Hahrie C. Han. 2006. Polarization Then and Now: A Historical Perspective. In *Red and Blue Nation? Characteristics and Causes of America's Polarized Politics*, ed. Pietro S. Nivola and David W. Brady. Washington, DC: Brookings Institute Press.

Cherry, Brian. 2007. The Great Divide. *USA Partisan*, June 28, 2007. https://usapartisan.wordpress.com/2007/06/28/the-great-divide-by-brian-cherry/

Conover, Pamela Johnson, Virginia Gray, and Steven Coombs. 1982. Single-Issue Voting: Elite-Mass Linkages. *Political Behavior* 4 (4): 309–331.

Deutsch, Max. 1971. Conflict and Its Resolution. In *Conflict Resolution: Contributions of the Behavioral Sciences*, ed. C.G. Smith. Notre Dame, IN: University of Notre Dame Press.

DiMaggio, Paul, John Evans, and Bethany Bryson. 1996. Have Americans' Social Attitudes Become More Polarized? *American Journal of Sociology* 102: 690–755.

Esteban, Joan-Maria, and Debraj Ray. 1994. On the Measurement of Polarization. *Econometrica* 62 (4): 819–851.

Esteban, Joan, and Gerald Schneider. 2008. Polarization and Conflict: Theoretical and Empirical Issues: Introduction. *Journal of Peace Research* 45 (2): 131–141.

Evans, John H., Bethany Bryson, and Paul DiMaggio. 2001. Opinion Polarization: Important Contributions, Necessary Limitations. *American Journal of Sociology* 106 (4): 944–959.

Fiorina, Morris P., and Samuel J. Abrams. 2008. Political Polarization in the American Public. *Annual Review of Political Science* 11: 563–588.

Fiorina, Morris P., Samuel J. Abrams, and Jeremy C. Pope. 2004. *Culture War? The Myth of a Polarized America, Great Questions in Politics Series*. New York, NY: Longman.

———. 2008. Polarization in the American Public: Misconceptions and Misreadings. *The Journal of Politics* 70 (2): 556–560.

Fiorina, Morris P., and Matthew S. Levendusky. 2006. Disconnected: The Political Class Versus the People. In *Red and Blue Nation? Characteristics and Causes of America's Polarized Politics*, ed. Pietro S. Nivola and David W. Brady. Washington, DC: Brookings Institute Press.

Fleisher, Richard, and John R. Bond. 2004. The Shrinking Middle in the US Congress. *British Journal of Political Science* 34 (3): 456–459.

Hetherington, Marc J. 2001. Resurgent Mass Partisanship: The Role of Elite Polarization. *American Political Science Review* 95 (3): 619–631.

———. 2009. Review Article: Putting Polarization in Perspective. *British Journal of Political Science* 39 (2): 413–448.

Hill, Seth J., and Chris Tausanovitch. 2015. A Disconnect in Representation? Comparison of Trends in Congressional and Public Polarization. *Journal of Politics* 77 (4): 1058–1075.

Hunter, James Davison. 1991. *Culture Wars: The Struggle to Define America*. New York, NY: Basic Books.

Jacobson, Gary C. 2000. The Electoral Basis of Partisan Polarization in Congress. Annual Meeting of the American Political Science Association, August 31–September 3, 2000.

Layman, Geoffrey C. 2001. *The Great Divide: Religious and Cultural Conflict in American Party Politics*. New York, NY: Columbia University Press.

Layman, Geoffrey C., and Thomas M. Carsey. 1999. Ideological Realignment in Contemporary American Politics: General Ideological Polarization Rather

Than Conflict Displacement. American Political Science Association, Atlanta, September.

———. 2002. Party Polarization and "Conflict Extension" in the American Electorate. *American Journal of Political Science* 46 (4): 786–802.

Mouw, T., and M.E. Sobel. 2001. Culture Wars and Opinion Polarization: The Case of Abortion. *American Journal of Sociology* 106 (4): 913–944.

O'Keefe, Mark. 2004. A Divide Forms When Politics Battles Religion. *Houston Chronicle*, Sat 02/14/2004, 1, 2 STAR.

Poole, Keith T., and Howard Rosenthal. 1984. The Polarization of American Politics. *Journal of Politics* 46 (4): 1061–1079.

Schier, Steven E., and Todd E. Eberly. 2016. *Polarized: The Rise of Ideology in American Politics*. New York, NY: Rowman & Littlefield.

Shoichet, Catherine E. 2016. North Carolina Transgender Law: Is It Discriminatory? *CNN*, April 5, 2016, Politics. http://www.cnn.com/2016/04/03/us/north-carolina-gender-bathrooms-law-opposing-views/

Theriault, Sean M. 2008. *Party Polarization in Congress*. Cambridge, MA: Cambridge University Press.

Trotta, Daniel. 2017. Trump Revokes Obama Guidelines on Transgender Bathrooms. *Reuters*, February 23, 2017, Politics. http://www.reuters.com/article/us-usa-trump-lgbt-idUSKBN161243

Donald M. Gooch is Assistant Professor of Political Science in the Department of Government at Stephen F. Austin State University (SFA). He received his M.A. in Political Science from the University of Arkansas, Fayetteville, in 2002 and his Ph.D. in Political Science from the University of Missouri-Columbia in 2009. He was appointed to the SFA faculty in August of 2012. Gooch studies civic education, public law, the federal court system, and American politics. His research agenda includes civic education, political polarization, campaign finance regulation, judicial behavior, and the spatial theory of voting. He is the SFA Pre-Law Program Coordinator and Co-Director of the SFA Pre-Law Academy.

CHAPTER 5

Ideology and the 2016 Election

Joseph Romance

One of the enduring questions in political science is the role of ideology in defining political parties. For much of US history, political scientists have lamented the seemingly non-ideological nature of our parties. Indeed, for much of US history, the relationship between the major parties and ideology was rather weak with geography playing as much of a role as anything else in explaining what the parties stood for. This caused such concern that by 1950 political scientists on the American Political Science Association's Committee on Political Parties were openly calling for the parties to assume clear and pronounced ideologies. The main idea was that by providing clear party programs that reflected distinct ideological views of politics and governing, democracy would be strengthened by giving voters clear political choices (American Political Science Association 1950). By the 1970s and early 1980s, for a variety of historical reasons, the parties had grown quite philosophically distinct. With the South gradually abandoning its traditional Democratic loyalties (probably the single most important factor, but there were others), the Democratic Party was the political home of liberals and the Republican Party completed its total embrace of conservatism. Yet, while this is an accurate summary of what happened, the actual story is much more complex. The ideologies

J. Romance (✉)
Department of Political Science, Fort Hays State University, Hays, KS, USA

C. Rackaway, L.L. Rice (eds.), *American Political Parties Under Pressure*, DOI 10.1007/978-3-319-60879-2_5

of the two major parties are more elaborate, even convoluted, than simply pronouncing that the Democrats are liberals and the Republicans are conservatives.

In recent years, scholarly research has delved into the issue of asymmetric polarization.[1] This is the idea the Republican Party is more uniformly conservative than the Democratic Party is united by liberalism. This appears to be true at the mass level and, to a significant degree, among elected officials. Furthermore, as Matt Grossmann and David Hopkins (2016) argue, party asymmetry explains a great deal about current politics—from elections to governing. They argue that:

> The Democratic Party's character as a social group coalition fosters a relatively pragmatic, results-oriented style of politics in which officeholders are rewarded for delivering concrete benefits to targeted groups in order to address specific social problems. Republicans, in contrast, are more likely to forge partisan ties based on common ideological beliefs, encouraging party officials to pursue broad rightward shifts in public policy. As a result, Republican voters and activists are more likely than their Democratic counterparts to prize symbolic demonstrations of ideological purity and to pressure their party leaders to reject moderation and compromise. (Grossmann and Hopkins 2016, p. 23)

The 2016 election gives us an opportunity to explore to what extent that is true. What does the rise of Donald Trump tell us about the role of ideology in the Republican Party? Furthermore, the most recent election showed the Democratic Party engaging in the most ideologically charged debates in recent memory. What is the state of ideology in both parties? What does the 2016 election add to the ongoing debates concerning polarization?

5.1   Ideology

Of course, ideology is a remarkably fluid, though central, concept in politics. As John Gerring (1997) writes,

> not only is ideology far-flung, it also encompasses a good many definitional traits which are directly at odds with one another. ... Indeed, it has become customary to begin any discussion of ideology with some observation concerning its semantic promiscuity. Few concepts in the social science lexicon have occasioned so much discussion, so much disagreement, and so much self-conscious discussion of the disagreement, as "ideology." (957–959)

Gerring's (1997) quite useful article, *"Ideology: A Definitional Analysis,"* then proceeds to investigate a number of approaches to the concept and settles on providing an overall framework that can be used when discussing ideology. Indeed, there are such striking differences in the way ideology has been defined, it is probably useless to forge a quite precise agreed upon definition. Thus, using this framework as a kind of menu, one can pick using certain traits, such as location (in thought or action or language), subject matter (politics or power or the world at large), function (explaining, repressing, motivating, among others), to employ the concept usefully (Gerring 1997). For the purposes of this chapter, I take ideology to mean political thoughts and ideas that strive to be internally consistent. These ideas seek to explain the world and motivate people to behavior in certain ways. Although, I do not see ideologies as necessarily rigid, they can become that way. And while the very concept of ideology is quite fluid, there is a sense that specific ideologies, such as conservative and liberal, are somewhat capacious as well, at least in the United States.

5.2   CONSERVATISM AND THE REPUBLICAN PARTY

The Republican Party has been sympathetic to conservatism for much of its history and, from an ideological point of view, the only institution to represent this ideology for well over 50 years. Indeed, increasingly since the 1970s, whatever conservatism is supposed to be the only area in which to battle that out is within the Republican Party. Along with the traditional party function of offering candidates and seeking power, one could say that one of the main functions of the Republican Party is to continually sort out just what conservatism is. However, just asserting that masks the diverse nature of American conservatism. While there are any number of ways to categorize conservatism, there are, I believe, three dominant schools of thought in the United States.

First, there are the social conservatives. This group is strongly anchored in a particular reading of Christianity, often identified as evangelical Christianity. On a host of issues, such as abortion, gay rights, the role of women in society, and law and order, social conservatives offer the Republican Party a definition of what it means to be conservative. Thus, to take just the issues mentioned, it means being prolife, opposed to the expansion of gays rights, championing traditional gender roles and a strong predilection to support the police and espouse a hostility toward protest and what is perceived as lawlessness. What should be emphasized is that particular policy positions reflect a deeper and coherent way of looking at the world, in general, and politics, in particular. This devotion to traditional values is founded on an ontological understanding of what God is and what human beings are and should be. Thus, the appeal to tradition is not a pragmatic one about what works and the nature of how societies function best. Rather, traditions are what is right. These traditional views of the family and the roles of people in the world are not some accident of history that reflects a particular culture. This is the way people are supposed to act based on their reading of Christian morality. This also means that at times Christian conservatives come close to a reactionary longing to return to some golden age. While social conservatives tend to be on the right when it comes to economic policies, this is not central to how they view the world. There is a general skepticism of government and of the taxes needed to support that government; however this skepticism toward government is rooted in the perception that liberal, secular elites have captured Washington, no matter who actually occupies the White House. As Trump's key advisor Steve Bannon argued, after the election, there was a "deep state" of bureaucrats loyal to Obama who are working to smear Trump and thwart his political agenda. This is a kind of variation on a theme that resonates with many Christian conservatives (Abramson 2017).

A second, and quite different, conservatism is libertarian conservatism. Libertarianism sits uneasily in both the conservative camp and among many Republicans. Yet, nonetheless, many who identify as conservative are so for libertarian reasons. Libertarianism is grounded in a strong belief in individual freedom. Indeed, freedom, protected by rights (granted by the state but usually believed to be natural), is fundamental to what politics is all about. People are by nature free and should remain that way. The state is viewed skeptically as a necessary evil that is always in danger of limiting individual freedom. Thus, this freedom is seen, to use Isaiah Berlin's famous formulation, as negative freedom:

> I am normally said to be free to the degree to which no man or body of men interferes with my activity. Political liberty in this sense is simply the area within which man can act unobstructed by others. If I am prevented by others from doing what I could otherwise do, I am to that degree unfree. (Berlin 1969, 122)

While there are many ways in which my freedom can be limited, the state is probably the most dangerous institution. At times, libertarianism can almost verge into a kind of political anarchism given its deep suspicion of government. Indeed, probably the most important American philosopher of libertarianism, Robert Nozick (1974) asks, in his book *Anarchy, State, and Utopia*, "Why not anarchy" (p. 4). Yet, libertarians, such as Nozick accept that government is necessary but it must be viewed by constant and critical eyes. As he writes,

> Our main conclusions about the state are that a minimal state, limited to the narrow functions of protection against force, theft, fraud, and enforcement of contracts, and so on is justified; that any more extensive state will violate persons' rights not to be forced to do certain things, and is unjustified; and that the minimal state is inspiring as well as right. (Nozick 1974, ix)

Many libertarians find both major parties impure and thus their skepticism of government is often matched by their skepticism of the Republicans and Democrats. However, for those most devoted to economic issues, the Republican Party's desire to lower taxes and loosen economic regulations is quite appealing. Economists such as F. A. Hayek and Milton Friedman champion a kind of libertarianism, though in the former case, it is rather a pragmatic one and not anchored in a pure devotion to natural freedom.

Finally, there is what we might identify as Burkean conservatism so named for the eighteenth-century British parliamentarian and writer Edmund Burke. Burke is often seen as the father of modern conservatism in the English speaking world; however, there are many who doubt that Burke exerts much influence on American politics. Nonetheless, thinkers such as Russell Kirk and pundits like William Buckley and George Will all looked to Burke to explain how politics should be. In the academy, Harvard Politics Professor Harvey Mansfield is something of a Burkean. In many ways, Burkean conservatives, as with Burke himself, are sympathetic to libertarianism and usually champion the free market and capitalism. Furthermore, Burke himself was quite sympathetic to traditional values and the role of Christianity in western civilization. And, his most important work, *Reflections on the Revolution in France*, is energized by his belief that the French revolutionaries were overthrowing the very traditions necessary to make life prosper. Yet, while Burkean conservatives often agree with the specific policies of other conservatives, it is usually for quite different reasons. In the *Reflections*, Burke defends the important role of religion in society. Yet, as contemporary Burkean George Will admits,

I'm an amiable, low voltage atheist. ... I deeply respect religions and religious people. The great religions reflect something constant and noble in
the human character defensible and admirable yearnings. (Weinstein 2014)

At its heart, Burkean conservatism is rather pragmatic and always skep-
tical of anyone who is too rigid in their beliefs. Indeed, this conservatism is deeply uncomfortable with the unyielding certainty that the other
two conservatisms display. And, in the name of social stability, Burkeans
will often make peace with liberals and, after a time, come to accept liberal policies and institutions, assuming these have been successfully inte-
grated into society or government. In effect, once policies have become
entrenched and accepted by people they are usually worthy of defending in the name of tradition and political stability. There is, for instance,
nothing inconsistent about a Burkean decrying Social Security in 1935
and defending it in 2017. And this defense would be, in the Burkean
eyes, a conservative defense. As the twentieth-century conservative philosopher Michael Oakeshott argued, the conservative disposition is "to
enjoy what is available rather than to look for something else; to delight
in what is present rather than what was or what may be" (1991, p. 408).
He adds, "[R]eflection may bring to light an appropriate gratefulness for
what is available, and consequently the acknowledgment of a gift or an
inheritance from the past; but there is no mere idolizing of that is past
and gone. What is esteemed is the present" (Oakeshott 1991, 408).[2] This
is a far different take from the typical view of many American conservatives that there is something deeply wrong with the present—that the
world has fallen away from God (the view of social conservatives) or that
the present government is dangerously close to becoming a repressive
socialist nightmare (the view of many libertarians). It also is emphatically
not reflected in Trump's signature call to "Make American Great Again."
And, Trump's constant harping on just how bad things are today makes
the present unworthy of esteem. In fact, this conservative disposition, as
Oakeshott (1991) calls it, delights in the present and seeks to prefer the,
"limited to the unbounded, the near to the distance, the sufficient to the
superabundant, the convenient to the perfect, present laughter to utopian
bliss" (408). One could hardly expect Trump to share any of those beliefs.
But that is true not just of Trump. Many conservatives today delight not
in the present but rage against the failings of the present.

Each election cycle, in recent years, has witnessed, to varying degrees,
the Republicans struggle to make these three approaches to politics

cohere. And, it is usually the case that Republicans can only win by appealing to voters who consciously or unconsciously fit into these three camps. Yet whatever peace the Republicans can find among these three groups is a temporary one subject to renewed fighting as the next election nears. And it is usually the case that candidates will try to prove their bona fides to each of these factions.

Of course along with these three distinctive camps, there is also the sense in which candidates are more extreme and pure in their devotion to conservatism or more moderate and willing to compromise to achieve conservative goals. Thus, along with the specific kinds of ideas favored by these three camps, there is also an ideological tone, if you will, that marks some candidates as more extreme or moderate. To many conservatives, to compromise is itself a sign of being something other than conservative. Hence, the birth of RINO (Republican in name only) as a pejorative word to describe conservative apostates.

5.3   THE REPUBLICANS IN 2016

The Republicans approached the 2016 election with a fair amount of confidence. In some ways, this is quite understandable. In an era where the two parties are rather evenly matched, it is simply hard for one party to win three straight elections. Whether there are scandals, failings to achieve policies and fulfill promises, or just a general fatigue with the president's party and the attendant desire for change, the out party should be cautiously confident.

Thus, as the election season dawned, a remarkable number of Republicans saw their opportunity. And, the race initially looked to be a familiar one ideologically. The moderate and more conservative wings of the party seemed set to do battle. On the one hand, Ted Cruz was set to carry the "true" conservative legacy. Cruz's positions from abortion, to gay rights and immigration aligned quite nicely with the further right wing of the party—particularly those of conservative Christians. Of course, suggesting that Cruz represents the more conservative wing of the party simplifies a more complicated picture ideologically. The Republicans have always maintained social and economic divides and we should not lose sight of the libertarian strains of the party. Thus, Cruz does believe in a kind of libertarianism and, when younger, talked a great deal about Friedrich Hayek and Ludwig von Mises (another economist favored by libertarians). Yet, just as important is his belief in conservative Christian values. Hence, he proposed a Constitutional amendment to allow states to outlaw gay marriage (Flegenheimer 2016). And, we should not forget that Cruz was influenced by his father, a very conservative Christian pastor.[3] Throughout his campaign, he was apt to speak about the crisis America was in and that the solution was found in a spiritual awakening. As he said while campaigning in Iowa, using cadences familiar to Christians, "I'm here this morning with a word of hope and encouragement and exhortation. All across the state of Iowa and this country, people are waking up. There is a spirit of revival that is sweeping this country" (Draper 2016). Thus, it is not surprising that after winning the Iowa Caucus, the first thing he said was "To God be the glory" (Buncombe 2016).

In a different way, Rand Paul has consistently championed the more libertarian elements of the Republican universe, which Cruz rather hoped to fuse with a strong defense of conservative Christianity. As different as Paul and Cruz are, they nonetheless represent a kind of ideological purity and conservatism with which the Republican Party is familiar and comfortable with. Paul's libertarianism led him to support marijuana legalization, made him a constant critic of government spending (he supported cutting defense spending a very un-Republican and un-conservative stance to many), and a defender of individual privacy. On the latter point, Senator Paul remained a skeptic of many of the government's surveillance programs as too intrusive and a threat to personal freedom (Topaz 2015). When the Senator began his campaign, he urged "a return to a government restrained by the Constitution. A return to privacy, opportunity, liberty. Too often when Republicans have won we have squandered our victory by becoming part of the Washington machine" (Beckwith 2015). This does not mean Paul is against the Christian conservatives; rather, his beliefs grow out of his libertarian roots.

On the other side were a number of candidates such as Jeb Bush, Carly Fiorina, John Kasich, and Chris Christie who, while certainly on the political right, were seen as moderates. Whether this was due to the tone of their language or specific policies, they reflected a cautious conservatism that seemed less extreme than the one offered by Cruz and Paul. In the case of Bush, Kasich, and Christie, we should not ignore the fact that their primary political experience is being a governor. The day-to-day running of state, none of which is completely dominated by Republicans, forced a kind of pragmatism upon them. Indeed, in the case of Christie, New Jersey is predominately a Democratic leaning state and one of his supposed appeals was his ability to work with Democrats. With regards to Bush, Florida is a more conservative state and Republicans arguably dominate state government; however, it is also a swing state in presidential elections and does elect Democrats to the US Senate.

Finally, we must consider Marco Rubio. In some ways, he represented someone with a logical appeal to all three aspects of conservatism that I mentioned earlier. On social issues, he opposes abortion, even in the cases of rape and incest. He favored a stronger national defense, the repeal of Obamacare and lower taxes, and the repeal of many economic regulations. As the Senator from Florida, he also had a strong following in that swing state. However, he was hampered by an attempt, early in his Senate career, to find some compromise on immigration that allowed undocumented immigrants a path to citizenship. Such a view is an anathema to a great many Republican voters. These efforts failed and, while he later changed his views to align more closely with the stricter Republican orthodoxy on the issue of immigration, he was never quite able to shake the view that he was soft on the matter. Nonetheless, he was one of the more important candidates, won primaries, and lasted longer than most in the very crowded field.

The parameters of this chapter limit our ability to systematically investigate and summarize each Republican candidate's resume and ideological beliefs. Furthermore, as the campaign progressed, all the candidates modified their views in an effort to win over voters and appeal to different groups of people. This is, obviously, what they must do as they compete in a crowded field and trek across the country seeking to win primaries and accumulate delegates. The main point I wish to make, though, is that in discussing these candidates, 2016 looked like a normal election for Republicans. The various subcategories of conservatism were reflected in these candidates. And, as the campaign began, the eventual nominee appeared to be someone who could balance those categories in the right way for general election in the fall.

But, as we all know, 2016 was anything but a customary election. Into this familiar ideological mix Donald Trump thrust himself. And, Trump not only challenged the Republican establishment, he called into question just what conservatism means. This is an important point to underline. There have been many insurgent candidates over the years who challenge party leaders. One could look back to Wendell Willkie who stormed the 1940 Republican convention and won the party nomination. And, in a superficial way, Willkie and Trump might seem alike. They were both lacking in political experience, both were businessmen, and both had some association with the opposing Democrats in their past. Yet, at a deeper and more important level, they are nothing alike because Willkie did not fundamentally upset the Republican Party's understanding of its ideology. Insurgencies are not necessarily ideological (though they can be). For Trump, though, his ideology is, to say the least, a confusing one that mixed in new ideas that seemed ambiguously conservative, if conservative at all. While, Trump bandied the word conservative around and claimed to be one—his ideas do not fit neatly into any traditional understanding of what the ideology means. In so doing, the question that must be asked is whether Trump is changing what it means to be conservative or is he something else who was able to capture the Republican Party—the traditional institutional home of conservatives? And, this question leads us to ask just how conservative is the party?

The word that is often employed to describe Trump is populist. But, much like the word ideology, populist is open to a myriad of interpretations resulting in a number of distinct definitions. So, what does populism mean, is Trump a populist and how well does populism align with conservatism are questions that need to be addressed. According to Jan Werner Muller populism is by its very nature anti-pluralist. "Populists claim that they, and they alone, represent the people" (Muller 2016, 3). Trump's position on immigration speaks to that position exactly. This one signature issue of Trump became a symbol for all that he believes. If there was one image that is associated with Trump, it was the young Mexican coming over the border. In announcing his candidacy, he famously said, "When Mexico sends its people, they're not sending their best. They're not sending you. They're not sending you. They're sending people that have lots of problems, and they're bringing those problems with us. They're bringing drugs. They're bringing crime. They're rapists" (Time Staff 2015). This is not a principled stand of any kind of conservative (or liberal for that matter). It is the stand of someone who speaks for the "people." It may be just his style of speaking but in the passage just quoted, he repeated the phrase, "They're not sending you. They're not sending you." This "you" spoke directly to the people and represented a form of populist rhetoric. However, the various strands of what are considered conservative in this country do not support this. For libertarians, immigration is almost a right—the free flow of people to new markets, new jobs, and new lives. For social conservatives, the imperative of the Christian ideal of charity and love demands that we be kind to the stranger, the new comer to our community. Only the Burkean might be perceived as agreeing with

Trump. But this is not the case because the Burkean belief in customs, traditions, and community is never based on hate or exclusion for exclusion's sake. For Trump speaking for the "true American" is at the heart of his message. But this is not conservatism in any traditional sense.

The other issue that was central to his message was his isolationism and his opposition to recent US free-trade policy—hence this underlies his call for "America first." Almost all American politicians believe in the uniqueness and greatness of America. Democrats make the same pledge. However, for most Democratic and Republican leaders, this cannot be achieved through an aggressive isolationism. Trump's "America first" is again a highly populistic and nationalistic message. This, however, is not conservatism. Most Republican leaders are pro-trade to various degrees. (There are a few exceptions.) Trump's opposition to Trans Pacific Partnership (TPP) and North Atlantic Free Trade Agreement (NAFTA) are not consistent with most Republican free-trade ideals. This ideal of America first, as defined by Trump, is inconsistent with traditional left and right beliefs that the United States is an integral player in world politics—indeed, the central player in the world order post World War II.

Many of the so-called neo-conservatives believe the only way to protect America is through nation building, the exact opposite of Trump's isolationist rhetoric. Although, American conservatism may embrace pro-nationalism this is not fundamental to the various strands of conservatism that I have identified. Libertarians believe America is great for its devotion to capitalism. Social conservatives believe that America is a Christian nation. Finally, Burkeans believe that America has an exemplary founding that set it on the right path. But none of these versions would align with Trump's assertion of "America First." For many conservatives, American greatness can only be achieved with a true understanding of Christianity or the correct interpretation of the Constitution. For other conservatives, isolationism would be detrimental to the safety and well-being of the nation. Although many people who call themselves conservative would lean toward isolationism, such isolationism is not central to any of the strands of conservatism I have identified.

Thus, Trump's candidacy and eventual success revealed a crisis in American conservatism and a challenge to the Republican establishment. While many of his ideas were championed by various Republicans and conservatives (then Senator Jeff Sessions' views on immigration aligned quite closely with Trump's, for instance, and he became an important advisor to candidate Trump and eventually the Attorney General in the Trump administration) he in no way offered anything approaching a coherent ideology. Of course, it is quite common for candidates to lack sophisticated and complete ideologies. However, Trump's populist and nationalist rhetoric posed a significant challenge to the standard views of social conservatives, libertarians (Trump, during the campaign, was officially in favor of protecting social security and providing healthcare for all), and to Burkeans.

5.4 Democrats and Liberalism

As the election neared, Hillary Clinton was the presumptive nominee of the Democratic Party and probably the closest any non-incumbent ever was to a coronation. However, she was challenged on ideological grounds by the rather uncharismatic Vermont Senator Bernie Sanders. Yet, this battle between the "traditional" Hillary Clinton and the unconventional, socialist Bernie Sanders reflected a profound schism in an understanding of liberalism.

The real conflict of 2016 on the Democratic side was about the definition of liberalism. More so than in many elections, 2016 included a profound debate about the ideological beliefs of the Democratic Party. Most people saw Hillary Clinton as part of the liberal establishment and its philosophy. Indeed, in some sense she clearly was. How could that not be the case as a former First Lady, Senator, and Secretary of State? Yet, her candidacy and career invite us to ask what does liberalism mean? To her critics, including Senator Sanders, her philosophical understanding of politics was deficient. As a deeper philosophical question, liberalism is open to many interpretations. Liberalism is clearly part of a philosophic tradition starting with John Locke, moving forward to J. S. Mill and reaching to it best American expression in John Dewey. At its most basic level, though, liberals believe that human beings should be free and not oppressed. However, the complexity of modern life makes our understanding of the role of government open to interpretation and the means government uses to help people more complex. To contemporary liberals what can oppress people moves beyond simply government. (This contrasts with libertarians who simply maintain a constant skepticism of any government activity.) Liberalism, to Clinton, is about human empowerment. Government has the role of providing the resources (be they financial or otherwise) for people to flourish. In the simplistic minds of too many pundits that meant that she was some sort of interest group liberal. They thought she was beholden to different individual interest groups essential to her effort to win the nomination. Yet, that was clearly not the case as exemplified by her entire career starting with her early devotion to childhood issues. This was later reinforced by her efforts on healthcare and most notably her statement in China that women's rights were human rights.

These were all part and parcel of the same belief that humans cannot flourish when oppressed whether that takes the form of government (in China and human rights) or a defective economy as in the United States (with regards to healthcare and the lack of access for so many). This was consistent with her belief that it "takes a village." To her critics, this sounded like socialism, but in reality, this was about human empowerment supported by government. This was necessitated by the changing dynamics of the family in the twentieth to twenty-first century. But nothing was inconsistent about her beliefs. To Hillary Clinton government was a power for good—but good to help all people. There was nothing particularistic about it. Furthermore, there was nothing about "paying" off different groups—Clinton was about how government enabled people to better themselves in a challenging world. This makes her a contributor to an American liberal tradition that runs from Franklin Roosevelt to Lyndon Johnson; however, she brought their beliefs about government to a different and new complex level for a new and different century. To her critics (and to some defenders), she might only be about female empowerment, a symbol for people as a potential first female president—in reality, her entire career was about human empowerment—full stop.

Secretary of State Clinton was challenged by Senator Sanders who offered a different perspective on politics—one more closely associated with what he identified as democratic socialism. Senator Sanders' beliefs about a living wage, single payer health insurance, and free college education were all part of that vision. But this begs the question what is social ism and how does that ideology exist in the American political context? Strict socialism is rooted in the beliefs of Karl Marx and his views that workers should own the means of production. In Marxist theory, this is also tied to his understanding of history and how this very notion of economic ownership would become obsolete. Since history is about class conflict eventually we will reach a classless society in Marx's opinion. As all people became part of one big class, there would be the end of history and the end of all class conflict. This is confusing to many people as they cannot grasp the idea of history ending. Yet, to a strict Marxist, history is only about class conflict and when this conflict is done history is done. Yet, Senator Sanders offered what might be called "socialism light" that reduced all the big ideas of Marxism down to a few policy positions and a deep distrust of inequality. In a speech about Wall Street, he opened with the observation that, "The American people are catching on. They understand that something is profoundly wrong when, in our country today, the top one-tenth of 1 percent own almost as much wealth as the bottom 90 percent and when the 20 richest people own more wealth than the bottom 150 million Americans—half of our population" (Marketwatch 2016). Indeed, Senator Sanders' career in supporting small time family businesses and his time as the mayor of Burlington reveal his practical and non-doctrinal appreciation of day-to-day politics. Clearly Sanders was on the left, influenced by socialist ideas, but also in the broad stream of American political life. His socialism was a homegrown variety and not true Marxism.

Traditionally, Americans have been distrustful of socialism. The language of class is somehow repellent to the American belief in self-governance and self-reliance. Indeed, there is a powerful belief that people, and most centrally families, should be self-sufficient. This notion of self-independence might be called an American ethos—*the American ideology* if you will. However, the changing nature of economics, the power of capitalism, calls this faith into question. Socialism is back in vogue in some circles. As Julia Mead, of the Nation Magazine, recently argued,

> Socialism, the redistribution of wealth, providing vital benefits and social service through the mechanism of the state—people were talking about this in the 1960s. And in the 1930s. And in the 19-*teens*. And now Sanders and Corbyn are recycling those hoary ideas (or so the argument goes), their only concession to the 21st century being the incorporation of racial-, queer-, and climate-justice rhetoric. (We can argue about how earnest they are and how successful that's been.) (Mead 2017)

The success of the socialistic programs in the Nordic countries is no longer to be ignored, at least for many Americans. The intense nature of the Cold War, with its attendant economic restrictions on what Americans found acceptable, was over. Thus, Senator Sanders' message was no longer considered out of bounds. Indeed, it was more than inbounds—it resonated with what many Americans on the left (and even some on the right) believed. His appeal to so many was based on the intense inequalities created by capitalism and the reality that too many people were no longer part of the American success story. This was true regardless of whether they were part of the young and educated or older workers displaced by new economic realities.

Senator Sanders was not simply a creature of "blue states." Indeed, he made striking inroads in finding political supporters in traditional Republican states. His message reached beyond the economics. His appeal was surprisingly diverse spanning across the ideological spectrum and not limited to the traditional left. His appeal was grounded on three foundations. Younger people who were fearful of the seeming lack of concern with economic opportunity were drawn to him. Added to that was a deep concern by many with global warming—an issue of particular and profound interest especially to those under 30. And there were many who saw this as something central to the challenges that defined the twenty-first century. The elitist capitalist system ignored the health of the planet for their own self-interest. Young and old, right or left, man or woman, citizens felt that the economic system is rigged against them. Older workers, many white, saw an establishment figure fighting an economic system that no longer cared about them. Finally, there was a general population that felt disenfranchised by a distant political state that was ruled by economic elites. Senator Sanders' entire career was built on attacking these concerns. Although these three concerns were not part of fully developed socialism—indeed his so called socialism was never fully developed—they provided an underlying philosophy of politics.

Yet, Senator Sanders' world view was largely defined by economics. Each issue ultimately dissolved into an economic question. To Secretary of State Clinton, the complex demands of modern life required a more holistic response. As Wilson Carey McWilliams, in a different context, argued:

> Self rule requires, then, that I be free to do what is according to nature. No barrier in my environment or in me must stand in the way. To help me toward self-rule, democracy must provide me with an environment that has resource enough to permit me to live in a fully human way. (McWilliams 2011b, 13)

But Secretary of State Clinton's perspective was based on the McWilliams belief in self-governance and his profound observations about self-rule. To both Clinton and McWilliams, self-rule could not be distinguished from self-fulfillment and this could not be separated from a commitment to the community that included all the disenfranchised. These groups included, but are not limited to, people of color, the LGBT community, and women struggling to fulfill themselves in a world that denied them choices. To her critics she was pandering to interest groups but it was clear she saw an overall commitment to the greater good. The greater good was about all people working to help themselves and their community. To help themselves meant helping their families in a challenging economic world—Senator Clinton was devoted to this process. Democracy demands that all people be recognized as part of the greater community. Senator Clinton saw these distinct groups as struggling to achieve recognition as part of that overall community.

Senator Sanders was all about resources and Secretary Clinton was all about a deeper understanding of self-rule—to use McWilliams' terminology. In one sense, the candidates were in agreement—money and government programs matter. But in a deeper sense, Senator Clinton was asking a more profound question about self-rule and democracy. It was not that she ignored the economic question, it was that she saw them as integral to questions of human empowerment. In 1995, as First Lady, Clinton famously said that "human rights are women's rights and women's rights are human rights, once and for all" (Wagner 2016). Many see this speech as a key moment in her political career. She added in that speech that, "What we are learning around the world is that if women are healthy and educated, their families will flourish. If women are free from violence, their families will flourish. If women have a chance to work and earn as full and equal partners in society, their families will flourish. And when families flourish, communities and nations do as well" (Clinton 1995). To some critics, this may seem like special pleading for a particular group but notice that she equated women's rights and human rights—they are part of a greater whole. She was urging her listeners to see how people excluded from community must be included to make their communities complete. The themes of that 1995 speech resonated throughout the 2016 campaign. For instance, in September of 2016, she proposed the creation of a National Service Reserve in many ways similar to President Kennedy's Peace Corp (Wagner 2016). This National Service Reserve was all about connecting people to their communities and making service to others an important part of life.

To Senator Sanders, economics was virtually the only way of understanding human freedom. Thus, it is not surprising that when he spoke to The Pontifical Academy of Social Sciences, his remarks were entitled "The Urgency of a Moral Economy" (Sanders 2016). To Secretary of State Clinton, economics was only part of a more complex and nuanced understanding of reality. To be a free and active member of society required not only resources, it required recognition. Hence, this explains Secretary Clinton's ongoing rhetoric about being a member of society. It is not surprising that the great Congressman John Lewis said, in reference to the civil rights movement, "she was there with us from the beginning." She saw standing on healthcare and standing on civil rights as part of the same endeavor to make people free and this made us full standing members of society. To add that she spent an entire career devoted to children is as intellectually redundant as it is significant. All of these matters cohere in a profound sense of self-development and, to use McWilliams' words, self-rule. Senator Clinton knew that people are only free when they have government resources to better themselves and the acknowledgment from society that they were welcomed. Politicians have an extraordinary role in making all members of society free and they are part of the collective democratic process. It is not that Senator Sanders ignored this, it was that he did not see this in the profound way Senator Clinton did. When she was recognizing groups, she was not only about just seeing groups of voters she was about seeing integral members of society. She was not about "throwing a shout out" for instance to gays, she was about bringing them into the community. This goes back to her learning at the footsteps of Martin Luther King in the 1960s. His vision of America recognized disempowered groups as much as he saw the struggling individual. And it is well known that Senator's Clinton's exposure to King's ideas was not some sort of abstraction—she met and was influenced by the minister (Merica 2014).

5.5   American Ideology in the Twenty-First Century

As different as Donald Trump, Senator Sanders, and Secretary of State Clinton were, they all spoke to a complex economic world that made people feel disempowered. Each of the main candidates spoke to a sense of loss. But that sense of loss was vastly different in each case. To Trump, that loss was about a world where primarily white men felt a loss of privileges. To Senator Sanders, this was a world of economic disempowerment of most people. To Secretary of State Clinton, this was a world of lost promises that was never fully realized for large segments of our society. To return to professor McWilliams, "civic equality ... does not in the first instance mean equal treatment but rather equal feeling and sympathy, a conviction of equal dignity and common destiny" (McWilliams 2011b, 7). And only Secretary Clinton addressed the deeply felt lack of democracy. (Although Senator Sanders did frequently decry the way the wealthy were able to manipulate the political system and he was a constant advocate of campaign finance reform.)

What these candidates also revealed was that the ideological state of the major parties was in a great deal of flux. The parties remain as intensely polarized as ever but the philosophical underpinnings of what the parties assert is now an open question. The common assumption that the Republicans, while having some ideological diversity, were the more ideologically pure and conservative party was challenged by the ascendency of Donald Trump. His strong appeal to nationalism seemed to be the only common thread tying together his stands on the issues—at least rhetorically. And, while nationalism has always held an appeal to American conservatives, it was never the *only and central* foundation of conservatism that bound Republicans together for decades. It remains to be seen whether Trump is sui generis or a sign of the transformation of the Republican Party into a strictly nationalist party with a great deal of issue flexibility.

On the Democratic side, the party engaged in one of its most sustained ideological debates in recent memory. Both Secretary Clinton and Senator Sanders strove to offer reasonably coherent ideologies. The main question for the future is whether the Democrats will focus more strictly on economics as a main key to understanding the political problems of our times (Sanders) or seek to balance economics with the demands of community and inclusion (Clinton). The Democrats are largely in agreement about the main components of their collective ideological identity. (Senator Sanders did not completely ignore community and Secretary Clinton was hardly uninterested in economic concerns.) But the relative degree of emphasis on these ideas remains to be seen and will probably continue to generate debate within the party for quite some time to come.

NOTES

1. Matt Grossmann and David A. Hopkins, *Asymmetric Politics: Ideological Republicans and Group Interest Democrats.* Oxford: Oxford University Press, 2016. For a slightly different version of this argument, see Thomas Mann and Norman Ornstein, *It's Even Worse Than It Looks: How the American Constitutional System Collided with the New Politics of Extremism.* New York: Basic Books, 2016.

2. I would add, though, that Oakeshott was not a great admirer of Burke.
3. For a general discussion of Senator Cruz's religious and political beliefs and his father's influence, see Jenkins, Jack (2016). "The Story Behind Ted Cruz's Religious Beliefs." *Think Progress.* https://thinkprogress.org/the-story-behind-ted-cruzs-religious-beliefs-b21ada9ca2c9. Accessed April 19, 2017.

References

Abramson, Alana. 2017. President Trump's Allies Keep Talking About the 'Deep State.' What's That? *Time.* http://time.com/4692178/donald-trump-deep-state-breitbart-barack-obama/. Accessed April 19, 2017.

American Political Science Association. 1950. A Report of the Committee on Political Parties: Toward a More Responsible Two-Party System. *American Political Science Review* 44 (3).

Beckwith, Ryan Teague. 2015. Transcript: Read Full Text of Sen. Rand Paul's Campaign Launch. *Time.* http://time.com/3773964/rand-paul-presidential-campaign-launch-speech-transcript/. Accessed April 19, 2017.

Berlin, Isaiah. 1969. *Two Concepts of Liberty, in Four Essays on Liberty.* Oxford: Oxford University Press.

Buncombe, Andrew. 2016. Ted Cruz Thanks God and Claims His Win Is Victory for 'Judeo-Christian Values.' *Independent.* http://www.independent.co.uk/news/world/americas/us-elections/ted-cruz-thanks-god-and-claims-his-win-is-victory-for-judeo-christian-values-a6848971.html. Accessed April 19, 2017.

Burke, Edmund. 2015. *Reflections on the Revolution in France and Other Writings,* ed. Jesse Norman. New York: Alfred A. Knopf.

Clinton, Hillary Rodham. 1995. Remarks to the U.N. 4th World Conference on Women Plenary Session. *American Rhetoric.* http://www.americanrhetoric.com/speeches/hillaryclintonbeijingspeech.htm. Accessed April 19, 2017.

Draper, Robert. 2016. Ted Cruz's Evangelical Gamble. *The New York Times Magazine.* https://www.nytimes.com/2016/01/31/magazine/ted-cruzs-evangelical-gamble.html. Accessed April 19, 2017.

Flegenheimer, Matt. 2016. Ted Cruz's Conservatism: The Pendulum Swings Consistently Right. *The New York Times.* https://www.nytimes.com/2016/04/18/us/politics/ted-cruz-conservative.html. Accessed April 19, 2017.

Gerring, John. 1997. Ideology: A Definitional Analysis. *Political Science Quarterly* 50 (4): 957–959.

Grossmann, Matt, and David A. Hopkins. 2016. *Asymmetric Politics: Ideological Republicans and Group Interest Democrats.* Oxford: Oxford University Press.

Jenkins, Jack. 2016. The Story Behind Ted Cruz's Religious Beliefs. *Think Progress.* https://thinkprogress.org/the-story-behind-ted-cruzs-religious-beliefs-b21ada9ca2c9. Accessed April 19, 2017.

Mann, Thomas, and Norman Ornstein. 2016. *It's Even Worse Than It Looks: How the American Constitutional System Collided with the New Politics of Extremism.* New York: Basic Books.

Marketwatch. 2016. Text of Bernie Sanders' Wall Street and Economy Speech. *MarketWatch.* http://www.marketwatch.com/story/text-of-bernie-sanders-wall-street-and-economy-speech-2016-01-05. Accessed April 19, 2017.

McWilliams, Wilson Carey. 2011a. *Redeeming Democracy in America,* ed. Patrick J. Deneen and Susan J. McWilliams. Kansas: University of Press of Kansas.

——— 2011b. *The Democratic Soul: A Wilson Carey McWilliams Reader,* ed. Patrick J. Deneen and Susan J. McWilliams. Kentucky: University Press of Kentucky.

Mead, Julia. 2017. Why Millenials Aren't Afraid of Socialism. *The Nation.* https://www.thenation.com/article/why-millennials-arent-afraid-of-the-s-word/. Accessed April 19, 2017.

Merica, Dan. 2014. From Park Ridge to Washington: The Youth Minister Who Mentored Hillary Clinton. *CNN.* http://www.cnn.com/2014/04/25/politics/clinton-methodist-minister/. Accessed April 19, 2017.

Muller, Jan-Werner. 2016. *What Is Populism?* Philadelphia: University of Pennsylvania Press.

Nozick, Robert. 1974. *Anarchy, State, and Utopia.* New York: Basic Books.

Oakeshott, Michael. 1991. On Being Conservative. In *Rationalism and Politics and Other Essays.* Indianapolis: Liberty Press.

Sanders, Bernie. 2016. The Urgency of a Moral Economy: Reflections on the 25th Anniversary of Centesimus Annus. https://berniesanders.com/urgency-moral-economy-reflections-anniversary-centesimus-annus/. Accessed April 19, 2017.

Time Staff. 2015. Here's Donald Trump's Presidential Announcement Speech. *Time.* http://time.com/3923128/donald-trump-announcement-speech/. Accessed April 19, 2017.

Topaz, Jonathan. 2015. Rand Paul's Policy Views Set Him Apart from Republican Field. *Politico.* http://www.politico.com/story/2015/04/rand-pauls-policy-views-2016-116716. Accessed April 19, 2017.

Wagner, John. 2016. Clinton Calls for New National Service Reserve During Florida Swing. *The Washington Post.* https://www.washingtonpost.com/news/post-politics/wp/2016/09/30/clinton-to-offer-national-service-initiative-during-florida-swing/?utm_term=.7959af5aa142. Accessed April 19, 2017.

Weinstein, Jamie. 2014. George Will: 'I'm an Amiable, Low Voltage Atheist.' *The Daily Caller.* http://dailycaller.com/2014/05/03/george-will-im-an-amiable-low-voltage-atheist/#ixzz4cJKwUzjy. Accessed April 19, 2017.

Joseph Romance is Associate Professor of Political Science at Fort Hays State University. His main interests include American politics, political theory, and public policy. He is the co-author of the textbook *The Challenge of Politics* and the co-editor of and contributor to *Democracy's Literature*, *A Republic of Parties?* and *Democracy and Excellence*.

CHAPTER 6

Campaign Visits, Party Ties, and Challenges to the Party Establishment in Presidential Nominating Contests

Laurie L. Rice

As the 2016 primaries unfolded and victories began to stack up in his favor, Donald Trump repeatedly boasted about how he was drawing in new people to the Republican Party.

> We're up by 50 percent and even more than that. You're talking about millions of people. So I actually think it's the biggest story in politics today. And I hope that the Republicans will embrace it. We have—don't forget, we have Democrats coming over, very importantly. We have independents coming over and they haven't done that ever, probably ever. And with all of these people coming over, we're going to have something very, very special. (Trump 2016)

I am grateful for the support of the Southern Illinois University Edwardsville's Undergraduate Research and Creative Activities (URCA) program and the talented URCA research assistants I have worked with over the years who have diligently contributed to the collection of data employed in this chapter: Samuel Borders, Kayleigh Brummett, Paige Cooper, Taylor Day, Thad Marshall, T. J. Pearson, Robert Wann, and Sharon Whitaker.

L.L. Rice (✉)
Department of Political Science, Southern Illinois University Edwardsville, Edwardsville, IL, USA

C. Rackaway, L.L. Rice (eds.), *American Political Parties Under Pressure*, DOI 10.1007/978-3-319-60879-2_6

He continued on in his March 8 election night news conference, "We had people come over here who have never voted Republican, who have never even thought about it, and they came and they voted Republican" (Trump 2016). Were these statements about expanding the party another unsubstantiated boast or was there some truth to his claims?

As Trump hinted, the battle for the 2016 Republican presidential nomination was not politics as usual. As Trump began to rack up victories, some members of the Republican establishment watched in disbelief as their party was co-opted by the brash outsider who showed little apparent respect for some of the ideals they held dear and whose rhetoric seemed to erode any progress they had hoped to make in their recent attempts to improve the party's reputation with women and members of racial and ethnic minority groups. Some like former Republican presidential nominee Mitt Romney attempted to stop Trump. Others, like Speaker of the House Paul Ryan, somewhat tepidly endorsed him once it was clear he could win the votes to secure the nomination, while making it clear they did not agree with his position on banning Muslims from entering the country. Some prominent Republican leaders refused to attend the Republican National Convention (RNC) in Ohio. The notably absent included former Presidents George H. Bush and George W. Bush and some of those who ran against Trump, including Ohio Governor John Kasich. Also missing were a number of prominent members of Congress like Senator John McCain, another former Republican presidential nominee. While some Republican Senators and Representatives scheduled events in their districts and states as excuses for not attending, Senator Jeff Flake of Arizona said he would be at home in the Arizona desert because "I've got to mow my lawn" and a spokesman for Senator Ben Sasse of Nebraska said Sasse and his kids would be watching "some dumpster fires" instead of attending the convention (Ornitz 2016).

How did the Republican Party get to this place? Donald Trump may have drawn the largest number of votes in 37 states, but his candidacy also helped create or expose clear rifts in the Republican Party. In this chapter, I test several potential explanations for Donald Trump's success in securing the Republican presidential nomination, each with important implications for party organization and party strategy. If Trump's path to victory involved drawing in a sizable number of Independents and Democrats, as he claimed, then establishment Republicans can blame voters outside their party for helping to produce this outcome and look to close their ability to participate in future Republican presidential primaries, as some already tried but failed to do at the 2016 RNC (Cheney 2016a, b). If, instead, Trump secured his victory through appealing to Republicans who do not normally participate in Republican nominating contests, then party leaders need to look within the party to place blame and find solutions. Since both of these potential explanations tie back in some way to the decisions of party leaders, the analysis presented here has implications that stretch beyond the 2016 election.

The chapter begins with a preliminary assessment of Trump's claims about expanding the base of the Republican Party through drawing in many Independents and even Democrats to vote for him. It then turns to develop a theory in support of an alternate potential contributor to Trump's success—areas ignored by previous candidates for the Republican presidential nomination—that receives much stronger preliminary support. After making a case for why candidates' previous patterns of visits matter, I estimate a multivariate model of Trump's county-level vote share that pits these alternate explanations against each other, while controlling for other factors likely to influence Trump's vote share such as the county's unemployment rate and candidates' 2016 visits to the county. These results are then compared to those of a similar model of Bernie Sanders' county-level vote share. The chapter concludes with a discussion of the implications of these findings for political parties as they seek to move beyond 2016.

6.1 Who Turned Out for Trump? Assessing Trump's Claims

There is no question turnout in the primaries was up. The Pew Research Center found that Republican primary turnout was at its highest since at least 1980 (Desilver 2016). However, while the Republican nominating contests drew high turnout, the reason for this increase was not as clear cut as Trump made it seem. Close, highly competitive primaries can draw higher levels of turnout, as may more protracted battles for the nomination since voters in states with later contests have more incentive to participate than normal (Rothenberg and Brody 1988).[1] The race for the 2016 Republican presidential nomination also drew a large number of candidates, another factor that may increase turnout (Norrander and Smith 1985; Moran and Fenster 1982). As more and more candidates dropped out and Trump's delegate lead mounted, voter turnout began to drop. After Trump's May 3 victory in Indiana pushed his last main opponents out of the race for the nomination, the average turnout for the remaining Republican contests dropped in half to just over 8% (Desilver 2016).

Still, over the course of the nominating contests, a number of voters went to the polls and cast their ballot for Donald Trump, and establishment efforts to stop Trump failed in their tracks. Did Independents and Democrats join Republicans in bringing him victory as he claimed? This was not possible everywhere as not all states gave candidates for the Republican presidential nomination a chance to win votes from Independents or Democrats. In 2016, about 40% of counties were in states with closed contests limited to those voters already registered as Republicans.[2] If some party leaders and candidates had their way, this number might be 100%. Party leaders have pushed for closed contests in the past, even going so far as attempting to ban open contests (Geer 1986; Manatt 1982). Some candidates for their party's presidential nomination have also pushed for closed contests to block the success of a likely opponent with more Independent appeal.

However, there are also reasons why party leadership might favor open contests. Strategic party leaders can employ open contests in an effort to dilute the ideological extremity of voter participation in primaries in the hopes of producing more moderate candidates with increased chances of winning the general election (Geer 1986; Kaufmann et al. 2003). In addition, any desire to limit candidate decision-making to the party faithful must be balanced against the growing trend of voters rejecting a partisan affiliation. Disenfranchising such a large and growing segment of the American public in the primary elections may prove increasingly dangerous for the party's general election chances. In the face of these considerations, a number of state legislatures have decided to either make their primaries or caucuses open to Independents or to change voter party affiliations to reflect whatever ballot voters ask for at the polls or whichever caucus they attend that year. If Donald Trump's claim about drawing many Independents and Democrats to vote for him in the primaries is correct, then, all else equal, he should have received higher shares of the vote in states that allow them to participate.

Figure 6.1 displays Donald Trump's mean county-level vote share based on whether or not counties are located in states with contests open to Independents or Democrats.[3] In counties with closed contests that are limited to voters already registered as Republicans, Trump averaged

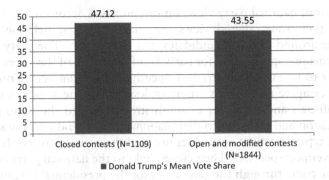

Fig. 6.1 Donald Trump's mean vote share based on contest type.
Note: Difference in means test: $t = 5.357$, $p < 0.0000$

47.12% of the vote while in those with open or modified contests, he only averaged 43.55% of the vote. This difference in vote share of just over 3.5% is statistically significant. While there may be other factors contributing to this difference that will be explored and controlled for later in the chapter, on first examination it appears he did worse, rather than better, in those areas that allowed Independents and/or Democrats an opportunity to vote for him. Alternative explanations, resting within the Republican Party and previous elections, need to be explored. The next section considers how the past pattern of campaign visits by candidates for the Republican nomination may have helped pave the way for a Trump victory.

6.2   Ignored Areas and Support for Donald Trump

Trump's path to victory exposed clear rifts within the Republican Party. In this section I consider how the previous decisions of party leaders and candidates for the nomination could be partially to blame. Political parties in the United States have often been characterized as "catch-all parties", or "big tents". They tend to be more candidate-centered and fairly decentralized (see, e.g., Hetherington and Keefe 2007) and they allow for a certain level of diverse views at the state or local level, in response to the ideological makeup of the state and its specific concerns. Presidential elections help link these state-level party organizations together around a common goal of winning the presidency (Cox 1997). As a result, while candidates for office with local or state-level electorates are still allowed to depart from national party views on certain issues according to the inter-ests of their state, shared views are established that help unite them together around not just candidates, but causes, too. The party conven-tions provide opportunities for party faithful from all of the states to come together to be inspired by rousing speeches while hammering out a plat-form they agree to abide by (more or less) for the next four years. State party officials and delegates establish strong links to the national party organization and their ties to their national party brand become stronger. Yet, the typical partisan voter does not read these platforms nor hear all of the convention speeches. Their closest links to the national party organiza-tion may come through the candidates for the presidential nomination.

Some counties like Polk County in Iowa and Hillsborough County in New Hampshire, routinely draw visits by a number of prospective Republican presidential nominees, election year after election year. Voters in these counties have the opportunity to hear from the range of candi-dates contesting for their party's presidential nomination. They can attend speeches or debates that expose them to a range of competing ideas, views, and ideological perspectives within the Republican Party. They have the opportunity, if they desire, to ask questions of candidates at town hall meetings and at diners, and get the assurance that candidates are aware of and listening to their concerns and views. While these voters' preferred candidate might lose, they are reassured that they are an active part of the process. This may make it easier to support the eventual nominee and retain strong party ties. Candidates, in turn, become aware of area voters' views and concerns as they visit. They meet with state party representatives in their quest for endorsements and build links between different levels of party organization. Through campaign visits, links are strengthened between candidates and voters, voters and the national party, and the national candidate and state-level party organizations. Yet, candidates can-not visit everywhere and each presidential election year, a number of coun-ties go unvisited by candidates for their party's nomination for president. This inattention from candidates leaves ample room for voters in unvisited areas to drift apart from the views of the national party establishment. They may more easily become disengaged and disaffected and more vul-nerable to an outsider's appeals.

Figure 6.2 displays the counties visited by candidates for the Republican presidential nomination in 2012. Shaded counties were visited by at least one candidate for the 2012 Republican presidential nomination, while counties without shading went unvisited. As can be seen, the vast majority

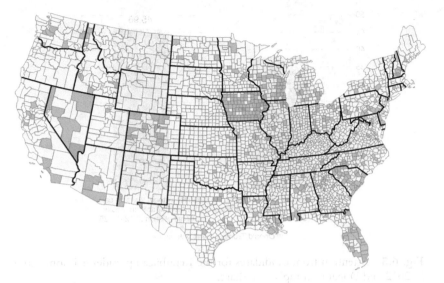

Fig. 6.2 Counties visited by 2012 candidates for the Republican presidential nomination.
Note: Filled and shaded counties were visited by at least one candidate for the 2012 Republican party nomination. The remaining counties went unvisited

of counties did not have a presidential candidate seeking the Republican nomination visit them in 2012.

This past inattention from candidates for the Republican presidential nomination leaves more room for Trump to prey on voter dissatisfaction with establishment Republicans. I theorize that Trump will do better in these unvisited areas because they more easily allow area voters to feel distanced from and disillusioned with the Republican Party. As a first test of this argument, Fig. 6.3 displays the difference between Donald Trump's vote share in counties that were visited by at least one candidate for the Republican presidential nomination in 2012 and his vote share in counties that went unvisited.[4] While he did well in both considering the crowded field, he clearly did far better in counties that were not visited by a candidate for the Republican nomination in 2012. The difference in mean vote share of 8.26 is statistically significant at the 0.0000 level.

Repeated inattention from candidates for their party's presidential nomination leaves voters from an area even more space to grow distanced from and feel ignored by their national party leaders. Voters in counties

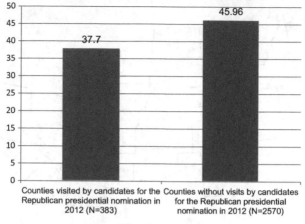

Fig. 6.3 Attention from candidates for the Republican presidential nomination in 2012 and Donald Trump's vote share.

Note: Difference in means test: $t = 8.703$, $p < 0.0000$

that have gone multiple election cycles without a visit from a candidate for the Republican presidential nomination have even more time and freedom to drift away from Republican establishment views (or be left behind by them). Meanwhile, those areas that have received more attention from prospective Republican presidential nominees over time should be more in line with the Republican establishment and less amenable to Trump's appeals. If so, then there should be evidence that the pattern of Republican presidential candidate visits dating back to the battle between George W. Bush and John McCain for the nomination in 2000, the last time a Republican became president, shapes Trump support. Since candidates have a tendency to visit some of the same counties year after year, thanks in part to contest timing or how fertile of grounds for campaign fundraising they provide, including visits back to 2000 only increases the number of visited counties by just over 100. This leaves a vast number of counties that have gone unvisited by candidates for the presidential nomination for multiple election cycles.

Figure 6.4 compares Donald Trump's mean vote share in those counties that have been visited by a candidate for the Republican presidential nomination at least once between 2000 and 2012 to those that were never visited during that time. Once again, while Trump drew relatively high

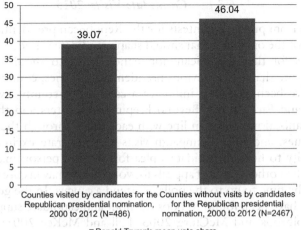

Fig. 6.4 Previous attention from candidates for the Republican presidential nomination and Donald Trump's vote share.
Note: Difference in means test: $t = 8.029$, $p < 0.0000$

average vote shares in both, his support was significantly higher in areas that have been repeatedly ignored by prospective Republican presidential nominees. The difference in vote share of nearly seven points is statistically significant at the 0.0000 level.

6.3   OTHER POTENTIAL INFLUENCES ON COUNTY-LEVEL VOTE SHARES

While these comparisons of mean vote shares based on whether or not candidates for the Republican nomination have visited a county lend support that Trump did better in areas previously ignored by potential Republican candidates for the country's only nationwide office, there are a number of other factors that could account for these differences, such as campaign visits being more likely to occur in states with earlier contests and in counties with larger populations. Fully testing whether previous candidates' past pattern of visits helped open the door for Trump, as well as Trump's claims about expanding the Republican Party, requires considering additional factors that may influence vote shares and then conducting multivariate analysis.

6.3.1   Candidate Visits: 2016

The visits from previous contests for the Republican presidential nomination are not the only ones that should shape candidate support. Visits from candidates for the Republican nomination in 2016 should also shape Trump's vote shares. In previous presidential primaries, county-level vote shares have been found to influence a candidate's county-level support (Prengel and Rice 2009). Beyond keeping area voters and the national party organization's views in line with each other through the sharing of views, issues, and ideas, campaign visits also generate excitement. The opportunity to hear a candidate's plea for votes in person may be more effective than other forms of appeals for votes. They may inspire supporters to make the time to go to the polls or attend a caucus. In the general election, they have been found to boost turnout and candidate support (Shaw 1999; Holbrook and McClurg 2005; Hill and McKee 2005; Hill et al. 2010). Given the more difficult choice faced by primary voters, visits may have an even greater impact in the primaries. If Donald Trump's in person bids for support at campaign rallies were effective above and beyond other mechanisms of building support, one would expect him to win higher vote shares in the counties he visited.

Candidates' visits should also affect each other. Visits may enable some candidates to win support away from a competitor while other candidates' visits may instead backfire and boost support for an opponent. The visits of at least some of Trump's competitors should have also influenced his vote shares. For example, a visit from a fellow outsider, like Ben Carson, might sway disaffected Republicans to support Carson over Trump. Other candidates may find their visits unintentionally boosting Trump support by emphasizing issues like job creation, foreign trade, or religious liberty that area voters might think Trump would more forcefully advocate or defend than the candidate emphasizing them. Further, some of these candidates visited areas but dropped out of the race before the area went to the polls, and voters concerned about these issues might see Trump as a good second choice.

6.3.2   Other Contest Variations

Winning a caucus requires different strategies than winning a primary (Gurian 1990; Davis 1997). Getting voters to attend caucuses and advocate for candidates typically requires strong on the ground organization

(Davis 1997), something the Trump campaign was criticized for lacking (Gabriel 2016). In Iowa and some of the other caucus states, his principal opponents' ground games far outmatched his. In fact, 8 of the 13 states where Trump failed to obtain a first place finish employed caucuses or conventions. Meanwhile, in most primary states, where ground games are less critical, Trump did well. Thus, all else equal, Trump should have done better in counties located in states that employ primary elections.

It is important to also control for contest timing. Candidates gain or lose momentum as the nominating contests unfold (Aldrich 1980). This momentum can help guide vote choices (Bartels 1988). Norrander (2006) characterizes the nominating contest season as a "game of attrition", driven in part by money, poll standings, early contest results, and the frontloading of contests. In 2016, Trump was the last one standing as the field of candidates winnowed further and further. He should have gained momentum, and votes, as the contest season unfolded. Further, states with earlier contests are likely to have more candidate visits (Gurian 1993), thus to separate out the role of candidate visits from contest timing, both need to be considered in the same model. As Trump's number of victories increased and the Republican field of opponents winnowed, Trump should have increased his vote shares.

6.3.3   County-Level Variations

Several county-level variations may also shape Trump's county-level vote share. While county-level unemployment averaged just under 6%, residents of some counties had far greater job prospects than others. At the extremes, Baca County and Summit County in Colorado had unemployment rates of only 1.6%, while Magoffin County, Kentucky, had an unemployment rate of 21.2%, Colusa County, California, had an unemployment rate of 22.3%, and Issaquena County in Mississippi had an unemployment rate of 23%. Donald Trump repeatedly touted his credentials as a businessman during the campaign. He promised job creation and better negotiations of trade deals that would protect American jobs. In his announcement speech, he declared, "I will be the greatest jobs president that God ever created. I tell you that. I'll bring back our jobs from China, from Mexico, from Japan, from so many places. I'll bring back our jobs, and I'll bring back our money" (Trump 2015). These themes and promises are likely to resonate more where there is higher unemployment. Further, his campaign slogan itself, to "make America great again", should work best in areas facing economic struggle that enjoyed better days in the past. Thus, all else equal, he should win higher vote shares in counties with higher levels of unemployment.

Finally, I control for county-level population. Voters in rural counties with smaller populations may be more likely to feel left behind by globalization and a changing economy. If so, Donald Trump's vote shares should be higher in those locales. Also, all else equal, campaign visits may be less likely in less populous areas. Thus, voters in less populous areas may also be less likely to be in tune with Republican establishment ideals and more likely to feel left behind by them, also making them more likely to support Donald Trump. To make sure the campaign visits measure is not also capturing trends in support by population size, county-level population needs to be included in the analysis.

6.4   Data and Methods

The dependent variable is Donald Trump's county-level share of the vote. In most cases, this is the county-level results released by the Associated Press and reported by most major news organizations. For those states for which the county-level data was missing, additional searches for alternate data sources were employed.[5]

The independent variable of primary interest is the number of visits to the county by candidates for the Republican presidential nomination in previous presidential election years. The first measure, employed in Model One, is of visits to counties by candidates for the Republican presidential nomination in 2012. To create this variable, the four main Republican candidates' (Mitt Romney, Rick Santorum, Newt Gingrich, and Ron Paul) daily schedule of campaign visits was obtained from the PBS News Hour 2012 Political Calendar, the county for each visit was identified, and then a count was made of the number of total visits to each county. The second measure, employed in Model Two, also includes the number of visits made by candidates for the Republican presidential nomination in 2000 and 2008.[6] In 2008, the campaign visits schedule for the four main candidates for the Republican nomination (John McCain, Mitt Romney, Mike Huckabee, and Ron Paul) was obtained from *The Washington Post*'s Campaign Tracker and the Democracy in Action website (Appleman 2008). In 2000, a campaign tracker was not available so LexisNexis was used to search campaign coverage in *The New York Times* and *The Associated Press* and assemble the campaign visits schedule of George

W. Bush, John McCain, and Steve Forbes. After the visit locations were collected for each year, the counties where the visits were made were identified and a count was created of the total number of visits by candidates for the Republican presidential nomination from 2000 to 2012.

The other key independent variable helps test Trump's claim about expanding the Republican Party. It measures whether the contest was open to those not already registered as Republicans. If Trump drew in Independents or caused voters to cross party lines in the primary, he should have done better in areas that employed open or modified contests that allowed these voters to participate. Voter eligibility was determined through the state by state contest information available on the website *The Green Papers* (Berg-Andersson 2016). This measure was coded 1 if the contest was open to either Independents, Democrats, or both, and 0 if participation was limited to those previously registered as Republicans.

Other contest details were coded as follows. Contest type—primary or caucus—was also determined from the state by state contest details provided on the website *The Green Papers* (Berg-Andersson 2016). This variable is coded 1 for states that held a primary for their Republican contest and 0 for those that employed a caucus or convention. The dates for these contests were also identified through these listings. This information was then used to create a measure of the number of days into the nominating contest the state's contest occurred, with the first contest in the nation, Iowa, coded as 0, and each subsequent contest coded as the number of days after Iowa the state's contest was held.

Since visits by candidates for the Republican nomination in 2016 should also shape vote totals, I also include the number of visits to each county by each Republican primary candidates who qualified for the main debate stage for three or more Republican debates: Jeb Bush, Ben Carson, Chris Christie, Ted Cruz, Carly Fiorina, Mike Huckabee, John Kasich, Rand Paul, Marco Rubio, and, of course, Donald Trump. The candidates' daily schedule of campaign visits were compiled from National Journal's 2016 Travel Tracker app, an interactive database based on campaign press releases and news articles (Isenstein et al. 2016). Each visit was then matched to the county where it occurred. Finally, this information was consolidated to create a count of the number of visits made per county for each of the ten candidates.

The county-level unemployment data comes from the Bureau of Labor Statistics' "Labor force data by county, not seasonally adjusted" and is for January 2016, just before the nominating contests began. Finally, for county population, I used data from the US Census for 2012, as county populations may have influenced campaign visits decisions in 2012 as well as 2016.[7]

6.5   RESULTS

Table 6.1 presents the results of these OLS regression models.[8] Model One considers the role of visits to counties by candidates for the Republican presidential nomination in 2012 while Model Two expands this measure to include visits to counties by candidates for the Republican presidential nomination from 2000 through 2012. I begin with a discussion of the results for the control variables and then turn to the independent variables of primary theoretical interest.

The results clearly indicate that Donald Trump did far better in states with primaries than in those with caucuses. Both Models One and Two show that, all else equal, Donald Trump could expect an increase in vote share of 14.5 in counties in states with primaries as opposed to those in states with caucuses or conventions. Also, as expected, momentum was clearly on his side. Holding other potential influences on his vote share constant, he could expect to gain just over a third of a percentage in vote shares as each day passed in the nominating contest calendar.

As the results show, Donald Trump also clearly did better in areas left behind by economic growth. All else equal, for each percentage point increase in county-level unemployment, Trump could anticipate an additional vote share of 2.09. However, there is little evidence that, holding other factors constant, Trump did better in counties with smaller population size. While the sign is negative, county population is quite far from standard levels of statistical significance.

There was no indication Trump did significantly better in the counties that he visited. While the sign for his visits was positive, they were nowhere near standard levels of statistical significance. However, the results show that the visits of five of Trump's opponents to counties influenced his county-level vote total, albeit not always in the direction his opponents would have hoped. Based on the results of Models One and Two, only two of his opponents successfully steered votes away from Donald Trump through their visits: Ben Carson and John Kasich. For each time Ben Carson visited a county, all else equal, Donald Trump could expect a drop in county-level vote share of a little under 2%, while for each time John Kasich visited a county, Trump could expect a drop in vote share of 2.17.

Table 6.1 Influences on Donald Trump's county-level vote share during the 2016 contests for the Republican nomination

	Model one	Model two
State contest open beyond those already registered Republican	−1.06** (0.44)	−1.05** (0.44)
Number of visits made to the county by candidates for the Republican presidential nomination in 2012	−0.44** (0.21)	–
Number of visits made to the county by candidates for the Republican presidential nomination from 2000 to 2012	–	−0.31** (0.13)
Donald Trump's visits to the county	0.46 (0.64)	0.32 (0.63)
Jeb Bush's visits to the county	0.03 (0.53)	−0.01 (0.53)
Ben Carson's visits to the county	−1.76*** (0.51)	−1.77*** (0.51)
Chris Christie's visits to the county	−0.41 (0.54)	−0.38 (0.54)
Ted Cruz's visits to the county	0.30 (0.42)	0.42 (0.42)
Carly Fiorina's visits to the county	1.96*** (0.71)	2.09*** (0.72)
Mike Huckabee's visits to the county	3.33*** (0.49)	3.31*** (0.48)
John Kasich's visits to the county	−2.17*** (0.57)	−2.08*** (0.57)
Rand Paul's visits to the county	1.18* (0.64)	1.40** (0.66)
Marco Rubio's visits to the county	0.17 (0.43)	0.22 (0.43)
Number of days into the nominating contest season the state's contest occurs	0.35*** (0.01)	0.35*** (0.01)
State holds a primary	14.50*** (0.59)	14.54*** (0.60)
County-level population	−9.64e-07 (6.71e-07)	−7.60e-07 (6.89e-07)
County-level unemployment	2.09*** (0.08)	2.09*** (0.08)
Constant	3.03*** (0.72)	2.97*** (0.72)
N	2953	2953
R^2	0.7018	0.7020
Adj. R^2	0.7002	0.7003

***$p < 0.01$, **$p < 0.05$, *$p < 0.10$

Meanwhile, the results suggest that three of his opponents' visits actually helped steer more votes to Trump—Rand Paul by a little over 1% per visit to a county, Carly Fiorina by roughly 2%, and Mike Huckabee by 3 and 1/3%. While Senator Rand Paul was not an outsider, he also advocated positions outside those of the traditional Republican establishment, which may have helped Trump, especially after Paul left the race. Voters drawn to isolationist foreign policy views might see Trump as a natural substitute for Paul. Meanwhile, Fiorina's visits may have encouraged voters to evaluate candidates on the basis of business backgrounds and job creation, only some judged Trump as superior on this measure, and others switched their support to Trump once Fiorina left the race. Finally, when Huckabee stirred up concerns about religious liberty, perhaps some voters in areas he visited came to believe Trump, who repeatedly showed he had no concern for political correctness, would be a more forceful defender of their concerns, while others settled on Trump once Huckabee abandoned the campaign trail.

6.5.1   Expanding the Party

What about Trump's claim of bringing in Democrats and Independents to the Republican Party during the primaries? If correct, especially on a widespread basis, then, all else equal, he should have done better in those states that allowed them to vote in the Republican contest. Instead, the results at the county level show his vote share was just over 1% lower in counties located in these states. While it is still possible he attracted the vote of some Independents or Democrats, on net, at the county level their ability to participate in the Republican contests hurt him, rather than helped him. Contrary to his claims, the results would suggest that of those Independents or Democrats who were motivated to vote in a Republican nominating contest in 2016, more voted against him than for him. Perhaps Trump did bring "millions of people" to the polls to vote for him, but they were overwhelmingly Republicans.

There is, however, strong evidence in support of the argument that Trump did better in areas previously ignored by candidates for the Republican presidential nomination. Both measures are statistically significant. Model One shows that all else equal, he lost 0.44% in county-level vote share for each visit made to a county by a candidate for the Republican presidential nomination in 2012. Meanwhile, in Model Two, Trump lost 0.31% in county-level vote share, all else equal, for each visit made to a county for the Republican presidential nomination from 2000 through 2012. While these changes per visit may be relatively small, they can add up. In 2012, while 2706 counties were never visited by candidates for the Republican presidential nomination and another 224 counties were only visited once (and by a single candidate), the remaining 181 counties had multiple candidate visits, with visits to Polk County, Iowa and Hillsborough County, New Hampshire numbering in the dozens. When visits back through 2000 are included, there were 269 counties visited multiple times, with 45 counties attracting ten or more visits. Republican presidential candidates' past pattern of visits were by no means solely responsible for helping Trump win the nomination, but they did contribute. Areas that were ignored by candidates in previous years were clearly more vulnerable to Trump's appeals.

6.5.2   Comparison to the Democratic Party in 2016

To help place these results in context, Table 6.2 provides a similar model for the county-level vote of Vermont Senator and 2016 challenger for the Democratic nomination, Bernie Sanders. His challenge to establishment favorite Hillary Clinton lasted clear through the end of the last Democratic nominating contest in June until he finally endorsed her on July 12, 2016 (Chozick et al. 2016).

There are several reasons to expect the results in Table 6.2 to be different. The last battle for the Democratic nomination, between Barack Obama and Hillary Clinton, also lasted until June, which brought them to more counties than their Republican counterparts. In 2008, candidates for the Republican nomination visited only 208 counties, while candidates for the Democratic nomination visited 438. With a Democrat in the White House for the last two terms, Democrats were less likely to be disillusioned with the status quo. Leading into the primaries and caucuses in January 2016, 67% of Republicans reported being very dissatisfied with the direction of the country compared to 21% of Democrats (McCarthy 2016). Also, while Bernie Sanders represented a different ideological wing of the Democratic Party, he was not an outsider like Donald Trump. He served in the House of Representatives for 16 years before being elected to the Senate in 2012. While he was officially an Independent for much of his time in office, and not an official part of the Democratic Party, he did caucus with the Democrats. His campaign pushed for a more progressive

Table 6.2 Influences on Bernie Sanders' county-level vote share during the 2016 contests for the Democratic nomination

	Model one	Model two
State contest open beyond those already registered as Democrats	2.80*** (0.60)	2.82*** (0.60)
Number of visits made to the county by candidates for the Democratic presidential nomination in 2008	−0.12 (0.21)	–
Number of visits made to the county by candidates for the Democratic presidential nomination from 2000 to 2008	–	−0.01 (0.17)
Bernie Sanders' visits to the county	2.25*** (0.64)	2.16*** (0.64)
Hillary Clinton's visits to the county	−0.98 (0.70)	−1.05 (0.70)
Martin O'Malley's visits to the county	−0.56 (0.86)	−0.62 (0.87)
Number of days into the nominating contest season the state's contest occurs	0.21*** (0.01)	0.21*** (0.01)
State holds a primary	−21.87*** (0.71)	−21.86*** (0.71)
County-level population	−2.49e-06** (9.84e-07)	−2.48e-06** (1.00e-06)
County-level unemployment	−0.74*** (0.11)	−0.74*** (0.11)
Constant	53.77*** (0.94)	53.72*** (0.94)
N	2934	2934
R^2	0.3328	0.3327
Adj. R^2	0.3308	0.3307

***$p < 0.01$, **$p < 0.05$, *$p < 0.10$

Democratic agenda, hoping to bring some of the ideals of democratic socialism into a more prominent place in the mainstream of the party.

The results in Table 6.2 suggest that at the county level it was Bernie Sanders, not Donald Trump, who was successfully drawing in new people to his party. His vote share in counties located in states with open or modified contests that allow participation by Independents and/or Republicans, increased by about 2.8%, all else equal. However, while the sign suggests he may have done worse in areas that received more prior attention from candidates for the Democratic presidential nomination, neither measure comes anywhere close to achieving standard levels of statistical significance when controlling for other influences on the vote.[9] There is no compelling evidence that he did better in areas that were ignored by past candidates for the Democratic presidential nomination.

Unlike Trump, Sanders' stops on the campaign trail brought him added support. Bernie Sanders did far better in the counties he visited, gaining, all else equal, a little over two percentage points in vote share. Also unlike Trump, Sanders did far worse in states that employed primaries than in those that employed caucuses. Sanders had more organization on the ground and his campaign used it to mobilize his passionate group of supporters to devote the time and effort to attend caucus meetings and advocate for him. Of the 22 states where he came in first in vote shares, 12 employed caucuses. Sanders also gained momentum as his challenge to Clinton continued, picking up, all else equal, 0.2% with each additional day into the nominating contest season. Meanwhile, all else equal, he did worse in counties with larger populations (compared to more rural areas) and worse in areas with higher unemployment rates. Finally, the models in Table 6.2 do far worse at predicting Bernie Sanders' county-level vote share than the similar models in Table 6.1 did for Donald Trump's county-level vote share. While the adjusted R^2 in Table 6.1 indicated that the models accounted for roughly 70% of the variance in Trump's county-level vote share, the models in Table 6.2 only explain 33% of the variance in Sanders' support. It is clear from the results that some different processes were at work shaping the support of Bernie Sanders compared to that of Donald Trump. Both of these have important implications for political parties moving forward.

6.6   MOVING BEYOND 2016

The results of the 2016 presidential nominating contests for both parties have already led to a flurry of discussions among party leaders and party activists about how best to reform the system to prevent similar outcomes. On the Republican side, efforts were made at the 2016 Convention Rules Committee by delegates supporting Ted Cruz, who did better in states with closed contests, to change party rules to entice states to choose closed contests, a move also supported by Republican National Committee (RNC) Chairman Reince Priebus (Cheney 2016a). This move to award states choosing closed contests with extra delegates failed in the Convention Rules Committee (Cheney 2016b). Had it succeeded, it might have actually opened the door wider for another candidate like Trump in the future.

The results presented here suggest that if that were in place during the 2016 nominating contests, that actually would have helped Trump's vote shares at the county level rather than hurt them. While Trump may have done better in states with open contests, once one looks at votes at the county-level and controls for other factors, Trump did worse where Independents and Democrats could more easily participate in Republican contests.

Republican Party leaders seeking to stop the possibility of another candidate like Trump do not need to close their contests so that participation in them is limited to those already registered as Republicans. Instead, the results presented here suggest they would be better served by paying more attention to the circumstances that leave party members particularly open to an outsider's appeal. Inattention, and repeated inattention, from candidates leaves room for partisans to drift from the views of the national party establishment. When areas have gone ignored by their party's candidates for the presidential nomination in previous election cycles and there is high geographic variation in unemployment, voters in unvisited counties and those with higher unemployment rates may be particularly vulnerable. In addition, although the results for one election cycle alone cannot confirm it, voters may be most vulnerable to outsiders' appeal when the party does not hold the presidency. When a party has been out of the presidency for eight years, a large swathe of the country has gone ignored by its candidates for the presidential nomination for multiple election cycles, and unemployment, while it may be generally low, has wide regional variations, the ingredients are ripe for a candidate like Donald Trump to do quite well, and even win the presidency. Establishment candidates, or the party establishment itself, may need to engage in specific outreach to these areas or face serious challenge from outsiders.

Further, the results presented in this chapter suggest that reforms that lead to more presidential candidates visiting more areas would also help keep voters more closely tied to the party mainstream. The laws governing primaries and caucuses, put in place by state legislators, and influenced by party rules and policies at the national level, shape incentives for where candidates visit. The most important of these is contest timing (Gurian 1993), with candidates targeting their visits to those states most likely to matter. The RNC has implemented rules in the past to try to discourage frontloading by awarding an increasing number of bonus delegates with each month later states placed their contest on the calendar but most states chose to forego these bonuses (Busch 2000). Geer (1986) suggested that a move to awarding delegates through proportional representation would also help prolong the race for the nomination. Democratic National Committee (DNC) rules require that all contests allocate delegates proportionally (Kamarck 2009) and both the 2008 and 2016 races for the Democratic nomination illustrate how proportional representation can lengthen the time it takes to amass enough delegates to secure the nomination. In 1972, the RNC considered and rejected mandating that states employ proportional representation to award delegates, with some party leaders expressing a preference for winner take all allocation (Kamarck 2009). However, Republican Party leaders could find that reconsidering a rule that would either require or incentivize states to allocate delegates by proportional representation would be helpful in leaving less area unvisited by candidates for their presidential nomination. After all, the longer it takes for a candidate to secure enough delegates for the nomination, the more states get visited, and the more voters get the opportunity to hear from a candidate in person, play an active role in choosing the nominee, and feel a more valued part of the party.

While the results on the Democratic side told a different story, they were also met with calls for reform. Bernie Sanders and his supporters pushed for more open contests and an end to superdelegates. Although his supporters lacked the votes to pass these changes in the DNC Rules Committee, a compromise was reached and the convention voted to establish a "unity reform commission" to explore more limited changes to the superdelegate system and to caucus participation that does not seem to include a switch to all open contests (Parks 2016). Had Sanders' supporters succeeded at their push for open contests, the move could have helped a candidate like Sanders in the future. The results presented here show that all else equal, Sanders did significantly better in those counties located in states with open contests. However, this move would not help all candidates on the more liberal end of the Democratic Party. Kaufmann et al. (2003) found that, "Through the adoption of open primaries, Republicans' primary electorates often wind up less conservative than their party following and Democratic primaries less liberal than theirs" (Kaufmann et al. 2003: 471). Sanders' high support from Independents, as indicated in exit polls and borne out in his better showing in states with open contests, may be due primarily to his attack on the harmful role of money in politics and its impact on the American people (Brownstein 2016).

The year 2016 was unusual in some respects. In the year leading into the election, trust in government was at all-time lows (Pew Research Center 2015). A number of voters were fed up with politics as usual and looking for change. During the primaries and caucuses, a number of disillusioned and disconnected Republicans thought this would come through Donald Trump, while a number of Independents and young Democrats thought it would come through Bernie Sanders. Yet, there were other factors in play that helped or hindered their candidacies that hold implications for party strategy that extend beyond 2016. The combination of past candidate activity, current candidate activity, party rules, and economic conditions advantaged some candidates and disadvantaged others, and not always in the direction party leaders think. The results presented in this chapter help identify some of the circumstances that make parties and their voters vulnerable to the challenges of outsiders. Most notably, it identifies a contributor to Trump's victory that has been missing from pundits and party leaders' deconstruction of the election—areas ignored previously by candidates for the Republican presidential nomination. While the party establishment may have failed in its efforts to stop Trump, this finding also suggests that through candidates persisting in their efforts to oppose Trump, they also may have helped close the door a little tighter to the possibility of another candidate like Trump winning the nomination in the near future. This finding also adds to the literature on the impacts of primary campaign visits. The results presented here demonstrate that their effects linger beyond a single election. Further research is needed on the broader impacts of being visited or ignored by candidates during the presidential nominating contest season.

NOTES

1. While Rothenberg and Brody (1988) do not find support for the latter in their statistical model they make an argument for why it should hold true that the results of recent elections would seem to support.
2. Independents or Democrats wishing to vote for Trump in the primaries in these states would have to change their party affiliation in advance, a much higher barrier than that faced by Independents and Democrats in states with open contests.
3. More information on the construction of these measures can be found in the data and methods section.

4. A description of how this data was collected can be found in the data and methods section.

5. County-level results for Maine came from the Maine Republican Party's website, county-level results for Minnesota came from Minnesota's Secretary of State's website, and county-level results from Kansas came from Dave Leip's Atlas of U.S. Presidential Elections. Alaska, Colorado, and North Dakota were excluded from the analysis due to lack of comparable data.

6. George W. Bush faced no serious challenger for the nomination in 2004.

7. While undoubtedly counties experienced population changes between 2012 and 2016, in most cases, population levels in 2012 and 2016 should highly correlate with each other, and any population changes should not be massive or widespread enough to necessitate different measures.

8. Since OLS regression models are not constrained to values between 0 and 100 as vote shares are, I also estimated a series of Tobit models bounded between 0 and 100, an approach recommended by Long (1997). These resulted in no changes in conclusions about significance and only relatively small changes to coefficients. Since there is some debate over whether Tobit models should be used in this circumstance (see Sigelman and Zeng 1999), the Tobit models produce no substantive changes in conclusions, and the OLS models are more readily interpretable, I have chosen to report the OLS results. The results of the Tobit models are available upon request.

9. Simpler difference of means tests, like those shown for Donald Trump in Figs. 6.3 and 6.4, showed that Sanders actually did better in areas that candidates for the Democratic nomination had previously visited, although the difference was small (less than 1.5), and only significant for the visits from 2000 to 2008.

REFERENCES

Aldrich, John H. 1980. *Before the Convention: Strategies and Choice in Presidential Nominating Campaigns.* Chicago: University of Chicago Press.

Appleman, Eric M. 2008. Democracy in Action: P2008 Race for the White House. http://www.gwu.edu/~action/P2008.html. Accessed August 11, 2016.

Berg-Andersson, Richard E. 2016. *The Green Papers.* http://www.thegreenpapers.com/. Accessed August 11, 2016.

Bartels, Larry M. 1988. *Presidential Primaries and the Dynamics of Public Choice.* Princeton: Princeton University Press.

Brownstein, Ronald. 2016. A Primary that Pitted Democrats Against Independents. *The Atlantic.* http://www.theatlantic.com/politics/archive/2016/06/the-partisan-gap/485795/. Accessed August 11, 2016.

Busch, Andrew E. 2000. New Features of the 2000 Presidential Nominating Process: Republican Reforms, Early Voting, and Frontloading's Second Wind. In *Pursuit of the White House 2000: How We Choose Our Nominees*, ed. William G. Mayer. New York, NY: Chatham House Publishers.

Cheney, Kyle. 2016a. 'Never (Again) Trump' Sets Sights on 2020. Grass-Roots Conservatives and Party Leadership Are Finding a Common Cause: Limiting Republican Primaries to Registered Republican Voters. *Politico*. http://www.politico.com/story/2016/05/republican-primary-rules-donald-trump--223136#ixzz4Gm7WixlX. Accessed August 11, 2016.

———. 2016b. GOP Panel Rejects Plan to Push Closed Primaries. *Politico*. http://www.politico.com/story/2016/07/gop-panel-rejects-plan-to-push-closed-primaries-225575#ixzz4Gm7s2egY. Accessed August 11, 2016.

Chozick, Amy, Patrick Healy, and Yamiche Alcindor. 2016. Bernie Sanders Endorses Hillary Clinton, Hoping to Unify Democrats. *The New York Times*. http://www.nytimes.com/2016/07/13/us/politics/bernie-sanders-hillary-clinton.html. Accessed August 11, 2016.

Cox, Gary W. 1997. *Making Votes Count: Strategic Coordination in the World's Electoral Systems*. New York, NY: Cambridge University Press.

Davis, James W. 1997. *U.S. Presidential Primaries and the Caucus-Convention System: A Sourcebook*. Westport, CT: Greenwood Press.

Desilver, Drew. 2016. Turnout Was High in the 2016 Primary Season, but Just Short of 2008 Record. Pew Research Center's Fact Tank: News in the Numbers. http://www.pewresearch.org/fact-tank/2016/06/10/turnout-was-high-in-the-2016-primary-season-but-just-short-of-2008-record/. Accessed August 11, 2016.

Gabriel, Trip. 2016. Donald Trump's Iowa Ground Game Seems to Be Missing a Coach. *The New York Times*. http://www.nytimes.com/2016/01/14/us/politics/donald-trumps-iowa-ground-game-seems-to-be-missing-a-coach.html?_r=0. Accessed August 11, 2016.

Geer, John G. 1986. Rules Governing Presidential Primaries. *The Journal of Politics* 48 (4): 1006–1025.

Gurian, Paul-Henri. 1990. The Influence of Nomination Rules on the Financial Allocations of Presidential Candidates. *Western Political Quarterly* 43 (3): 661–687.

———. 1993. Candidate Behavior in Presidential Nomination Campaigns: A Dynamic Model. *The Journal of Politics* 55 (1): 115–139.

Hetherington, Marc J., and William J. Keefe. 2007. *Parties, Politics, and Public Policy in America*. 10th ed. CQ Press.

Hill, David, and Seth C. McKee. 2005. The Electoral College, Mobilization, and Turnout in the 2000 Presidential Election. *American Politics Research* 33 (5): 700–725.

Hill, Jeffrey S., Elaine Rodriquez, and Amanda E. Wooden. 2010. Stump Speeches and Road Trips: The Impact of State Campaign Appearances in Presidential Elections. *PS: Political Science and Politics* 43 (2): 243–254.

Holbrook, Thomas M., and Scott D. McClurg. 2005. The Mobilization of Core Supporters: Campaigns, Turnout, and Electoral Composition in United States Presidential Elections. *American Journal of Political Science* 49 (4): 689–703.

Isenstein, Libby, Andrew McGill, Kimberly Railer, and Adam Wallner. 2016. Travel Tracker. *The National Journal*. http://nj-travel-tracker.herokuapp.com/. Accessed August 11, 2016.

Kamarck, Elaine C. 2009. *Primary Politics: How Presidential Candidates Have Shaped the Modern Nominating System*. Washington, DC: Brookings Institution Press.

Kaufmann, Karen M., James G. Gimpel, and Adam H. Hoffman. 2003. A Promise Fulfilled? Open Primaries and Representation. *The Journal of Politics* 65 (2): 457–476.

Leip, David. *Dave Leip's Atlas of U.S. Presidential Elections*. http://www.uselectionatlas.org. Accessed August 11, 2016.

Long, J. Scott. 1997. *Regression Models for Categorical and Limited Dependent Variables*. Thousand Oaks, CA: Sage Publishing.

Manatt, Charles T. 1982. *Commission on Presidential Nomination. The Report of the Commission on Presidential Nomination*. Washington, DC: Democratic National Committee.

McCarthy, Justin. 2016. As Obama Delivers SOTU, 23% Satisfied with Direction of U.S. *Gallup*. January 12. http://www.gallup.com/poll/188141/obama-delivers-sotu-satisfied-direction.aspx. Accessed August 11, 2016.

Moran, Jack, and Mark Fenster. 1982. Voter Turnout in Presidential Primaries: A Diachronic Analysis. *American Politics Quarterly* 10 (October): 453–476.

Norrander, Barbara. 2006. The Attrition Game: Initial Resources, Initial Contests and the Exit of Candidates During the US Presidential Primary Season. *British Journal of Political Science* 36 (3): 487–507.

Norrander, Barbara, and Gregg W. Smith. 1985. Type of Contest, Candidate Strategy and Turnout in Presidential Primaries. *American Politics Quarterly* 13 (January): 28–50.

Ornitz, Jill. 2016. 'I've Got to Mow My Lawn': Here Are the Prominent Republicans Skipping the Convention and Why. *Los Angeles Times*. http://www.latimes.com/politics/la-na-pol-republicans-skipping-convention-20160718-snap-htmlstory.html. Accessed August 11, 2016.

Parks, Maryalice. 2016. DNC Rules Committee Passes 'Unity' Resolution Calling for Commission on Super Delegates and Caucuses. *ABC News*. http://abcnews.go.com/Politics/dnc-rules-committee-passes-unity-resolution-calling-commission/story?id=40827997. Accessed August 11, 2016.

PBS News Hour. 2012. 2012 Political Calendar. http://www.pbs.org/newshour/vote2012/calendar.html. Accessed August 11, 2016.

Pew Research Center. 2015. Trust in Government: 1958–2015. November 23. http://www.people-press.org/2015/11/23/1-trust-in-government-1958-2015/. Accessed August 11, 2016.

Prengel, Dan, and Laurie L. Rice. 2009. Visits and Votes: The Geographic Spread of Campaign Visit Effects in the 2008 Presidential Primaries. *Illinois Political Science Review* 13: 60–107.

Rothenberg, Lawrence S., and Richard A. Brody. 1988. Participation in Presidential Primaries. *Western Political Quarterly* 41 (June): 253–271.

Shaw, Daron R. 1999. The Effect of TV Ads and Candidate Appearances on Statewide Presidential Votes, 1988–1996. *The American Political Science Review* 93 (2): 345–361.

Sigelman, Lee, and Langche Zeng. 1999. Analyzing Censored and Sample-Selected Data with Tobit and Heckit Models. *Political Analysis* 8 (2): 167–182.

Trump, Donald. 2015. Presidential Announcement Speech. http://time.com/3923128/donald-trump-announcement-speech/. Accessed August 11, 2016.

———. 2016. Primary Night News Conference. Federal News Service Transcript March 8. https://www.c-span.org/video/?406174-1/donald-trump-primary-night-news-conference

Washington Post. Candidate Tracker. http://projects.washingtonpost.com/2008-presidential-candidates/tracker/dates/

Laurie L. Rice is associate professor of Political Science at Southern Illinois University Edwardsville where she teaches classes in American politics including the presidency, presidential campaigns, and political parties and interest groups. She received her Ph.D. in political science from the University of California, San Diego. Her research appears in journals such as *Congress & the Presidency*, *Presidential Studies Quarterly*, *Social Science Computer Review*, and *Social Science Quarterly*. Rice is a co-author of the book *Web 2.0 and the Political Mobilization of College Students* and a contributor to *Technology and Civic Engagement in the College Classroom*. Rice has also written pieces for *The Hill* and *The Huffington Post* and provides expertise on elections, social media, and the presidency to regional, national, and international media.

CHAPTER 7

Weak Parties and Strong Partisans

Chapman Rackaway

Primary elections are complex and intricate methods of selecting party nominees in the American context. Rules governing the primary calendar, type of primary conducted, and subsequent allocation of delegates alter the strategic calculus of candidates and the influence political party organizations have over their eventual nominees. The 2016 presidential election showed that both parties' nomination processes were manipulated according to the rules of each primary system.

Both strategically successful candidates effectively engaged in hostile takeover attempts of each party's nomination. One was not completely successful, where Vermont Democratic Socialist candidate Bernard Sanders challenged eventual nominee Hillary Clinton through a strategy focused on caucuses. While Sanders was able to win a number of states, his caucus strategy also restricted his ability to compete to the end for the nomination.

Much more successful was Donald Trump's hostile takeover attempt of the Republican Party. Using a combination of a divided field (itself stemming from changes to Republican Party rules for 2016) and support

C. Rackaway (✉)
Department of Political Science, University of West Georgia,
Carrollton, GA, USA

© The Author(s) 2018   169
C. Rackaway, L.L. Rice (eds.), *American Political Parties Under Pressure*, DOI 10.1007/978-3-319-60879-2_7

from non-Republicans, Trump was able to successfully secure the GOP nomination and subsequently be elected president of the United States.

While Sanders may not have been as successful as Trump, both experiences are as important because of what they tell us about political party organization strength in 2016. In times of weak party organizations and strong partisanship, candidates like Sanders and Trump can be expected to become much more common. Political party organizations had managed to revive their influence over candidates prior to 2010, but in the last decade, parties have seen their power shrink significantly. Candidates like Trump and Sanders suggest that the party organization is a subsidiary general election campaign support entity and little more.

The nomination and election of Donald Trump as the 45th president of the United States was the most surprising federal election in decades, and thus significant effort from political scientists and pundits alike will be devoted to understanding why Trump won despite so many predictive indicators to the contrary. Was Trump's appeal to marginal groups vital? Did Trump's ability to self-fund give him advantages over other candidates? Did Trump's fame from the worlds of business and reality television give him name recognition among voters with which no other candidates could compete? The above reasons may contribute to why Trump won the GOP nomination and subsequent general election, but another important element contributed to Trump's success through the primary election: the primary election rules of delegate allocation. By changing the rules of delegate allocation, the Republican Party unwittingly created a condition amenable to Trump's nomination.

Sanders' competitive primary season was less due to strategically responding to a new set of rules and more from focusing on one type of primary: the party caucus. Sanders' campaign used the highly polarized electorate to maximum advantage, activating a high-interest cadre of voters and mobilizing them where they could to best effect: in the lowest turnout races where Sanders' supporters would be more numerous. However, Sanders' strategy was incomplete because caucuses tend to be conducted in rural areas, which in turn afforded him fewer delegates to the national convention to win. Sanders' caucus approach gained him significant amounts of media attention (from which Trump also benefited) but did not provide him enough momentum in non-caucus states to propel him to the Democratic nomination.

7.1   Primary Structure

Primary elections are a diverse collection of administrative methods. While the term primary election evokes a ballot process, the term subsumes a number of different processes. Nominating elections are not only conducted in traditional polling places with paper or electronic ballots. Political parties can conduct their primaries though caucuses as well, though they do appear to engender ideological and demographic biases that call the democratic contribution of the caucus into question (Fiorina et al. 2005; Marshall 1978; Norrander 1993; Panagopoulos 2010).

Even when restricted to ballot primaries, the rules by which voters are eligible to vote introduce significant biases. Closed primaries restrict voting in a party's primary exclusively to voters who have registered with that party prior to the election. In open primaries, voters do not identify their party preference (if any) at registration and can select the primary in which they want to participate when they arrive at the polling place. While the promise of open primaries is the expansion of representation among the electorate and an improvement in turnout, evidence suggests that open primaries do not significantly expand the primary electorate nor represent a more diverse population of voters (Schuman and Presser 1979; Kaufmann et al. 2003; Snyder and Ting 2011; McGhee et al. 2014). Closed primaries restrict the electorate, but from the perspective of parties, they are far superior. In a closed primary, existing party allegiance is necessary which reduces the opportunity for strategic voting, though evidence suggests that such "sabotage" voting is not widespread (Abramowitz et al. 1981). Noteworthy in the findings is that when strategic voting occurs it tends to favor candidates who have broader general election appeal. Thus, open primaries may encourage a crossover effect that would be particularly noticeable among independent voters.

Primary and caucus votes, regardless of rules, must translate into equivalent delegate support at the parties' national conventions. Since the McGovern–Fraser reforms incentivized proportional delegate allocations among Democrats beginning in 1972 (Hitlin and Jackson 1979), the two major parties have diverged greatly in their allocation rules. Republicans did not transition quickly to proportional allocation of delegates as Democrats did after McGovern–Fraser reforms (Meinke et al. 2006). Despite a stated desire to improve representativeness in the Democrats' delegate selection process, Ansolabehere and King (1990) found that nonproportional delegate allocation rules were more responsive to public vote shifts than proportional ones were.

The rules clearly matter in primary elections (Pomper 1979). Changes in rules can significantly influence the outcomes of those elections. As parties are private organizations and not legislative bodies, they are free to conduct their business with a wider scope of freedom than they would be if they were regulated similar to other entities of government. That freedom leads to a variety of different rules which range from byzantine to seemingly corrupt. The rules are rarely democratic, and in fact are often restrictive of voter choice. Closed primaries may be better for parties and democracies generally speaking, but they are more restrictive and to both academic and public critics they are antidemocratic.

Before the advent of primaries, when parties controlled their entire nomination process, there was no public scrutiny of candidate choice by parties. The parties would make their delegate allocation rules, delegates would show up to party conventions, and those delegates were free to make whatever decisions on candidates they desired. The voting public had little to no say in party nominations, which led to any number of concerns and contributed to the advancement of the Progressive Movement.

Since the 1968 Democratic convention, though, the public has strongly retrenched against the idea of parties having exclusive authority over nominations, especially for the presidency. The McGovern–Fraser Commission functionally forced the state parties to move toward direct primaries since the new demographic representation rules for delegates were so onerous as to be impossible with which to comply. As primaries have increased and become more prevalent the rules by which they operate have become more important as well.

Primary rules are set at two levels, complicating their behaviors. One determiner of primary rules is the state. Each of the states has the opportunity to control their own rules regarding the primary method and timing. The states set their own calendars for primaries, and can shift them from election to election. A state can also determine the method of election, usually by a ballot primary. Should the state choose to not hold a ballot primary, the other determiner of primary rules makes the decision: the party organization.

State parties conduct caucuses in conjunction with their state chief election officers, but their administration is wholly under the direction of the party organization. The party has even more control over the transformation of caucus and primary results into delegates to the national party conventions. Each party has its own rules and formulae to convert popular votes and participation into allocated delegates for their nominating conventions (Cook 2004).

For Democrats, the delegate allocation process is complicated by the addition of superdelegates (Southwell 1986, 2012; Mayer 2009). Unpledged delegates from the ranks of Democratic elected officials and party leaders have the effect of softening the impact of the popular will on nominations and provide the party with more leverage against outside candidates who may want to have access to the party's electoral support infrastructure but not pledge loyalty to the party's platform or agenda. Republicans have no such bulwark against a runaway primary, since most of their delegates are pledged through the primary process (Herrera 1994; Oliver 1996).

The march of frontloading creates a related problem for the parties (Mayer and Busch 2003; Cook 2004). In the post-McGovern–Fraser world of binding primaries and caucuses, the pivotal event in primary elections has become the opening caucuses held in Iowa. Momentum, media attention, and the ability to fundraise as a front-running candidate have created a circumstance where the Iowa primary sets the stage for the rest of the calendar. Without finishing in the top three in Iowa, candidates stand little to no chance at continuing to compete. So most candidates put all of their effort into Iowa in the hopes of making the next phase of the campaign (Redlawsk et al. 2011).

Other states saw the primacy of Iowa in the process, and began moving their primaries and caucuses ever-earlier in the calendar. During the 1960s, the primary calendar traditionally extended well into June. Indeed, John Kennedy did not enter the Democratic primaries for 1960 until March of that year. In the 2000s, nominees are usually determined by March. Frontloading has created problems for candidates, making campaigns much more expensive; and for the parties themselves, minimizing the role of the party apparatus in selecting a nominee. The Republican Party, facing an ever-shorter campaign calendar and a loss of influence over the process, decided to change its rules regarding the allocation of delegates in 2016 as a response.

For the 2016 presidential election, the Republican National Committee determined that any state which moved its primary or caucus to a date prior to March 1 where it had originally been later would have to allocate its national convention delegates on a proportional basis. For some time, most Republican primaries had been conducted as winner-take-all events. The idea was to lessen the influence of the early primary and thus remove the incentive to front-load the calendar (Putnam 2016a).

7.2   TRUMP STRATEGY

As rules have consequences, so did the change in Republican delegate allocation rules. Winner-take-all elections, especially early in the primary cycle, winnow large fields of candidates down quickly. A normal Republican field would number seven to nine candidates, with the pool quickly narrowed to three candidates after Iowa and its soon-to-follow counterpart in New Hampshire. Candidates without early success would drop out quickly, leaving a smaller collection of candidates to compete for the eventual nomination. Iowa represents a nearly all-or-nothing chance for the typical candidate. But the move to proportional primaries changed the strategy of the 2016 election.

The 2016 Republican primary was anomalous because of the large number of candidates who entered the field. The proportionality of early primary delegate distribution helped inspire the odd nature of the race. A total of 17 Republican candidates entered the race, 8 more than ran in the 2012 GOP nomination contest.

The 2016 candidates flooded into the field partially because there was no clear frontrunner entering and the proportional allocation rule meant that a clear frontrunner (or set of them) was not likely to emerge from the early primaries. Without that momentum-driven separation, it would be possible for lesser known candidates to cluster for a longer period and stay in the race longer.

By contrast, the 2012 Republican field looked remarkably different from the 2016 iteration. 2012's field looked much more similar to fields since 1976, with two or three eventual competitive candidates emerging quickly after Iowa and New Hampshire (Skelley 2016). No Republican primary from 1976 through 2012 featured more than nine candidates. The strategy was well established and stable through the 2012 primary, but the significant change in delegate allocation caused a significant shift in the strategic calculus of Republican campaigns for president. Thus, 2016 was more of a historical aberration in both number of candidates and strategy.

As Fig. 7.1 shows, a typical field of less than ten candidates with clear front-runners quickly evolves into three tiers of candidates. Some, as three did in 2012, will withdraw before ever contesting a primary. Front-runners emerge in Iowa and New Hampshire, and those three will contest the calendar longest. (Cohen et al. 2008; Aldrich 2009) Another group will contest the early primaries but by the third or fourth event in the calendar will withdraw.

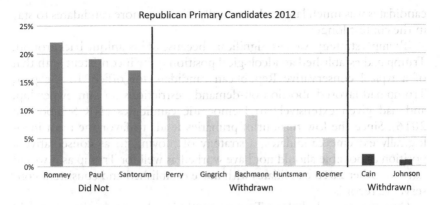

Fig. 7.1 Default Republican pre-2016 primary strategy

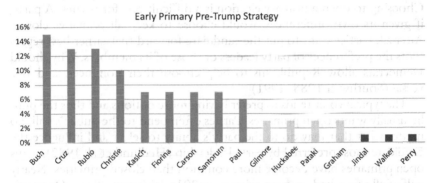

Fig. 7.2 Typical pre-Trump entry candidate strategy for 2016

The proportionality of 2016 encouraged a larger field that would sustain longer. As no early frontrunner emerged, the more likely it became that any given candidate could emerge. A field divided evenly among 16 candidates where the largest likely vote total was in the low 20 percent range opened an opportunity for a candidate with high name recognition to enter the field and counteract the effects of the new strategy. Donald Trump's entry into the Republican field may have been a result of the new rules presenting an opportunity for him to take advantage of the according vote dispersion (Krieg 2015). As Fig. 7.2 shows, based on pre-Trump entry polls, the clear delineation between a top tier of candidates that occurred in 2012 and below was not evident. The tier of competitive candidates was much larger, theoretically allowing more candidates to stay in the contest longer.

Trump's strategy was also significant because of his unique background. Trump had established an ideological position quite inconsistent with that of a typical conservative Republican candidate for office. In the past, Trump had favored abortion-on-demand, restrictions on gun ownership, and had given extensively to Democratic candidates (NR Symposium 2016). Since the low turnout of primaries tends to favor the most ideologically extreme candidates, a strategy of moving to as conservative a position as possible should not have worked as well for Trump as it would have for other 2016 candidates with more established and consistent conservative records.

One primary rule helped Trump greatly in addition to the large field stemming from the new proportionality structure: open primaries. Choosing to open a primary election is a difficult one for parties. A party, if given its own preferences, would choose to keep all primaries closed. After all, parties want to put the candidate forward that either best represents the preferences of party leaders or those of its members. Why should Democrats allow Republicans to help choose their nominees, and vice versa? (Southwell 1988, 1991)

The typical voter tends to prefer having more options and thus the public usually wants open primaries. Parties often bend to the public's will, no matter what that may do to the party's ability to select and influence the candidate most preferred by party leadership (Hedlund et al. 1982). Thus open primaries have become more common than closed primaries. Nearly half of all states had an open primary in 2016 (Fairvote 2016). Open primaries not only allow the other party's voters to enter in and sabotage, but they also enfranchise non-partisan disaffected voters into voting in primary elections. Closed primaries shut the unaffiliated voter out. With a significant portion of Trump's support coming from non-Republicans, we should expect to see Trump perform better in open primary states.

7.3   Sanders' Strategy

Sanders may not have been as successful as Trump, failing to secure a nomination, but it was equally important as it shows that Trump's hostile takeover was not unique to the Republican nomination process. The Democratic Party is just as susceptible to someone from outside the party mainstream entering the primary calendar and succeeding in moving the party's agenda to one ideological pole or another.

For Sanders, who was ideologically more extreme than the center-left campaign of Hillary Clinton, the key to success in the primary calendar would be to activate the more ideologically extreme liberal voters (Enten 2016). Caucuses, with their longer duration and requirements for speeches or other politicking, dissuade the only slightly interested and encourage those with the most commitment to engage. Caucuses traditionally have even lower turnout than typical primaries, themselves already known as low turnout affairs, and so Sanders' best opportunity was to focus on the elections where the lowest turnout battles could be fought.

As Trump rode a wave of expanding open primaries, Sanders' campaign was much more successful in a primary type that is shrinking. Democrats have been moving progressively away from caucuses and toward ballot primaries for the last 20 years (Putnam 2016b). In the 2016 primary season, only 12 states held Democratic caucuses. In 1976, the number of caucuses was nearly three times what it was in 2016. Sanders' caucus success was predicated on media attention that focused on the statewide wins, but not on his allocation of delegates to the Democratic National Convention. Caucus success, had it translated into mainstream approval and subsequent vote increases in ballot primaries, could have proven eventually successful for Sanders.

7.4   Hypotheses

Presidential nominating campaigns are highly strategic affairs, and every factor with the potential to influence that strategy must be accounted for. For Republicans, the strategic calculation involved a rules change altering pre-March 1 primaries to proportional delegate allocation. Theoretically, the larger field should have allowed more candidates a chance to stay later into the primary calendar. However, Donald Trump's entry into the race allowed him to leverage his name recognition especially in the later winner-take-all primaries. Thus, the first hypothesis to test is:

H1 The Donald Trump campaign performed better in later winner-take-all states than in early proportional primaries

Trump's broad name recognition and appeal, along with his lack of ideological consistency with other Republican candidates, should mean Trump's appeal should be stronger in states that allow non-Republicans to vote in their primaries. Thus Trump should out-perform other Republican candidates in open primary states leading to Hypothesis 2.

H2 The Donald Trump campaign performed better in open primary states than in closed primaries

Among Democrats, the strategic calculus is very different from what the Republicans experienced. Sanders' strategy was to focus on states where grassroots enthusiasm and mobilization would bring the most reward. Thus we should expect to see Sanders perform best in the type of primary that encourages mobilization, the caucus.

H3 The Bernard Sanders campaign performed better in caucus states than in ballot primary states

Caucus-first strategies are problematic in the current primary system, because most states are moving away from the caucus model and the caucuses that remain tend to be in smaller states. As a result, we should expect to see Sanders' success in caucus states to be limited in their overall impact on delegate allocation to the eventual nominating convention.

H4 The Bernard Sanders campaign would consistently underperform in delegate allocation compared with the Hillary Clinton campaign owing to his caucus-driven strategy

7.5   DATA AND METHODS

To empirically test the primary contest strategies of Trump and Sanders, the author collected data on all Republican and Democratic primaries conducted for the 2016 nomination cycle from the archives of the New York Times (Andrews et al. 2016). The site provided the vote totals and delegate allocations for all candidates who contested any Democratic or Republican primaries during the 2016 cycle.

For all territories, the vote totals for each of the 17 Republican candidates and 3 Democratic candidates in 2016 were collected. Delegate allocations for each candidate also were retrieved from the same site. For comparison with prior elections, the Times site was also used to collect vote and delegate data for the 2012 Republican and Democratic primaries.

Putnam's (2016a) Frontloading HQ website provided the delegate allocation protocol, calendar, and ballot type for each contest for each party in all 50 states as well as Washington, DC, and US territories. Dummy variables were produced to indicate whether a state conducted a ballot primary or caucus, whether the party registration for that primary was open or closed, and what delegate allocation model was used (winner-take-all or proportional).

7.6 RESULTS

Focusing first on the Republican field, correlations will prove instructive to determine relationships between data. Table 7.1 presents a series of correlations run against caucuses and open primaries for Republican candidates in 2016. The Trump campaign did not appear to focus on any one type of primary, and caucuses should favor more established and ideologically polarized candidates. Thus, Ted Cruz should have out-performed Trump in ballot primary states. We should expect to see Cruz's performance in caucuses as significantly superior to that of Trump's. In open primary states, we should see the most significant relationship between the primary administration type and Trump's overall vote. Trump's name recognition and crossover popularity among non-Republicans suggest that we should see much more success for him in open primary states.

Table 7.1 presents correlations of Trump's and Cruz's vote totals, percentage of the overall Republican primary vote, state victory, and in Trump's case his margin of victory in that state's total votes over the other GOP candidates. For Trump, the correlations between conducting a caucus and his vote totals, vote percentage, and victory likelihood are significantly and negatively correlated. Trump performed markedly worse in caucus states than did Ted Cruz, which is also reflected by the significant

Table 7.1 Republican primary correlations

	R caucus	Sig.	R open	Sig.
Trump's win	−0.506	0.003**	0.312	0.082
Trump's %	−0.521	0.002**	0.248	0.172
Cruz's %	0.391	0.031*	−0.254	0.161
Trump's vote	−0.522	0.001**	0.464	0.005**
Cruz's vote	−0.459	0.008**	0.413	0.019*
Trump's MOV	−0.271	0.116	0.108	0.539
Trump's share	−0.216	0.214	0.408	0.015*
Cruz's share	0.519	0.002**	−0.293	0.104

*Significant at 0.01

**Significant at 0.001

and positive relationship between Cruz's vote share of the GOP field and his percentage of the vote. Since caucuses tend to mobilize social conservatives among the GOP faithful, the result is not surprising.

Turning to open primaries, Trump's likelihood of victory is not significantly related to the primary type. Holding an open primary did not necessarily contribute to Trump's victory, but as Trump won most races the measure is an imperfect one. Instead, Trump's vote total and share of the Republican vote are very salient. Both variables emerged as positive and significantly correlated with open primaries. Cruz's data showed no significant relationships with open primaries, so we can see that there is a strong relationship between the manner of conducting a primary and the Republican voting tendencies from 2016. Cruz represented the GOP faithful, while Trump brought outsiders into the Republican camp.

Turning to the Democrats, we should expect to see Sanders outperforming Clinton in caucus states, while no necessary effect is expected among open primaries. As Table 7.2 shows, the hypothesized relationship is supported by the results. Sanders' win likelihood was correlated significantly and at an R value of 0.566. Sanders' percentage of the vote and vote share among Democrats were also highly and strongly correlated with the caucus method of administration. Sanders' campaign was thus stuck in a win-lose scenario. Caucuses were shrinking in frequency and influence, but the natural administration of caucuses worked strongly in his favor. In fact, with the tendency of caucuses to be held in rural Midwestern and Great Plains states, Sanders could have swept the caucuses and still not competed with Hillary Clinton's support even without

Table 7.2 Democratic primary correlations

	D caucus	Sig.	D open	Sig.
Sanders' win	0.566	0.000**	−0.125	0.473
Clinton's %	−0.31	0.07	0.333	0.051
Sanders' %	0.614	0.000**	0.077	0.66
Clinton's vote	−0.638	0.000**	0.322	0.072
Sanders' vote	−0.565	0.001**	0.382	0.031*
Clinton's MOV	−0.421	0.012*	0.131	0.452
Clinton's share	−0.604	0.000**	0.163	0.373
Sanders' share	0.604	0.000**	−0.163	0.373

*Significant at 0.01

**Significant at 0.001

her additional advantage in unpledged convention superdelegates. The smaller populations of caucus states also explain why Sanders' vote correlation was negative with caucuses, since the populations of the states were universally smaller than the ballot primary states.

The correlations suggest that the first three hypotheses find support with the data, but more evidence would be helpful. Therefore, a linear regression is a more appropriate measure of the relationship between the variables. With Trump and Sanders receiving the most attention among candidates in 2016, those two candidates will be the focus of the tests. For Trump and Sanders' vote total, delegates allocated, and margin of victory, I conducted a regression analysis against the presence or absence of a caucus and open primary, state population, total turnout of their party, and party turnout difference between 2012 and 2016. As Democrats allocate all delegates proportionately, I include a variable for the winner-take-all model of delegate distribution for Republicans only.

Table 7.3 reports the results from the three Trump regressions. As shown in the correlation data, the presence of a caucus was not a driver of Trump's success. Trump was a nontraditional candidate, so we should expect to see him do comparatively worse at caucuses. Across the board, in vote totals, delegates allocated, and margin over his closest competition, Trump showed no significant trends in 2016 among caucuses. While Trump did not see an increased likelihood of increased delegates, he did see a significant and positive relationship between margin of victory and open primary states. In other words, Trump did well across the board but truly dominated the field where non-Republicans were allowed to vote. Where Trump seemed to have the most success were in winner-take-all states. With non-Republican voters able to vote, we should expect turnout spikes in open primary states for Trump, and the results again support that assertion. While proportionality may have helped drive more candidates into the field, in vote totals, margin, and especially in delegates allocated Trump's results were significantly related to winner-take-all states. State population also was significantly related to Trump's votes, delegates, and margin of victory.

Turning to Sanders' results, the caucus-first strategy again shows to be significant. Sanders' vote and delegate totals both emerged as statistically significant and positively related to the state in question holding a caucus. Sanders' margin of victory did not emerge as significant, which suggests that not only did Sanders do well but that the Clinton campaign likely engaged in counter-mobilization. The fact that overall Democratic turnout was significantly related to all three measures of Sanders' success

Table 7.3 Donald Trump vote and delegate results regressed against primary type, delegate allocation rules, vote history, population and turnout

	Trump's vote	Sig.	Trump's delegates	Sig.	Trump's MOV	Sig.
Caucus	−21,161.605	0.566	−7.908	0.328	−7068.282	0.914
Open primary	−48,498.376	0.157	0.478	0.069	138,953.883	0.004**
Winner-take-all	64,280.106	0.006**	13.841	0.05*	−39,602.733	0.003**
Population	0.003	0.563	36,948,294.62	0.002**	0.004	0.611
2012–2016	282,813.974	0.147	−0.096	0.924	512,644.813	0.072
Total Republican turnout	0.341	0.000**	−13,555,369.21	0.196	0.235	0.001**
R^2	0.795		0.358		0.602	

*Significant at 0.01

**Significant at 0.001

Table 7.4 Bernard Sanders vote and delegate results regressed against primary type, delegate allocation rules, vote history, population and turnout

	Sanders' vote	Sig.	Sanders' delegates	Sig.	Sanders' MOV	Sig.
Caucus	45,968.19	0.029*	14.275	0.003*	83,534.69	0.04
Open primary	28,883.04	0.06	−1.433	0.646	56,868.77	0.056
Population	−0.013	0.000**	1.939	0.001**	−0.026	0.000**
2012–2016 turnout	85,767.99	0.49	35.698	0.189	106,827.5	0.656
Total Democratic turnout	0.541	0.000**	−2.4045	0.000**	0.094	0.087
R^2	0.971		0.857		0.659	

*Significant at 0.01

**Significant at 0.001

reinforces that likelihood. Open primaries and increased overall turnout were not significantly related to any of the measures of Sanders' success (Table 7.4).

7.7   Discussion

The rules matter, and they matter to a great effect in the administration of a party primary. As parties have become significantly weakened over the last decade while partisanship has been stronger, biases introduced by different primary administrative processes can have highly amplified effects. Candidates follow the primary calendar to develop their strategies, differences in the type of voter attracted matter more, and the variabilities between states can mean the difference between victory and defeat.

In the case of Bernard Sanders, the Vermont Senator had a narrow path to victory. Sanders' best opportunities for victory were in caucuses, but Democrats have been moving away from caucus primaries for some time and the remaining states are fairly small. The number of delegates available to Sanders through a caucus strategy was small, but the opportunity to win states and gain media attention through those wins represented his opportunity. Sanders would have needed to parlay the attention over to success in other states, which he could not do.

Regarding Trump, the results are only slightly less clear. The overall large field of candidates, which itself was driven by changes in delegate allocation rules by the Republican National Committee, helped Trump greatly. However, clearly Trump benefited especially from primaries where non-registered-Republicans could participate. In effect, Trump's victory could be compared to a hostile takeover in the business world. Trump could have run as a Democrat or Republican, but saw a strategic opportunity in the wide-open GOP field that he leveraged into the party's nomination and eventual general election victory.

Trump's victory, and Sanders' emergence, both reinforce the idea that the party organizations have been gutted of their power compared with even their state one decade ago. Supreme Court rules on outside electioneering such as the *Citizens United* and *SpeechNow* cases, a lack of coordination in the national party committees, and high turnover of executive leadership in the parties have contributed to a decay in party organizational direction that have allowed upstarts to threaten or completely take over the party apparatus.

For political parties, the next step is to reevaluate their primary election rules. The parties must make a case for why they should have more power in their own processes if the party as an information shortcut for voters will return to a place of value.

REFERENCES

Abramowitz, Alan, John McGlennon, and Ronald Rapoport. 1981. A Note on Strategic Voting in a Primary Election. *The Journal of Politics* 43 (3): 899–904.

Aldrich, John H. 2009. The Invisible Primary and Its Effects on Democratic Choice. *PS: Political Science & Politics* 42 (1): 33–38.

Andrews, Wilson, Kitty Bennett, and Alicia Parlapiano. 2016. 2016 Delegate Count and Primary Results. *The New York Times.* https://www.nytimes.com/interactive/2016/us/elections/primary-calendar-and-results.html?_r=0. Accessed October 10, 2016.

Ansolabehere, Stephen Daniel, and Gary King. 1990. Measuring the Consequences of Delegate Selection Rules in Presidential Nominations. *The Journal of Politics* 52 (2): 609–621.

Cohen, Marty, David Karol, Hans Noel, and John Zaller. 2008. The Invisible Primary in Presidential Nominations, 1980–2004. In *The Making of the Presidential Candidates*, ed. William G. Meyer, 1–38. Lanham, MD: Rowman & Littlefield.

Cook, Rhodes. 2004. *The Presidential Nominating Process: A Place for Us?* Lanham, MD: Rowman & Littlefield.

Enten, Harry. 2016. Bernie Sanders Continues to Dominate Caucuses, but He's About to Run Out of Them. *FiveThirtyEight.com.* https://fivethirtyeight.

com/features/bernie-sanders-continues-to-dominate-caucuses-but-hes-about-to-run-out-of-them/. Accessed March 20, 2017.

Fairvote.org. 2016. 2016 Primary Rules and Types. http://www.fairvote.org/primaries#presidential_primary_or_caucus_type_by_state. Accessed March 17, 2017.

Fiorina, Morris P. with Samuel J. Abrams, and Jeremy C. Pope. 2005. *Culture War? The Myth of a Polarized America*. Hoboken, NJ: Pearson Longman.

Hedlund, Ronald D., Meredith W. Watts, and David M. Hedge. 1982. Voting in an Open Primary. *American Politics Quarterly* 10 (2): 197–218.

Herrera, Richard. 1994. Are "Superdelegates" Super? *Political Behavior* 16 (1): 79–92.

Hitlin, Robert A., and John S. Jackson. 1979. Change & Reform in the Democratic Party. *Polity* 11 (4): 617–633. doi:10.2307/3234340.

Kaufmann, Karen M., James G. Gimpel, and Adam H. Hoffman. 2003. A Promise Fulfilled? Open Primaries and Representation. *The Journal of Politics* 65 (2): 457–476.

Krieg, Gregory. 2015. Why There Are So Many Republicans Running in 2016. *Mic.com*. https://mic.com/articles/119530/the-real-reason-so-manyrepublicans-are-running-for-president-nbsp#.jKHzLoen2. Accessed March 20, 2017.

Marshall, Thomas R. 1978. Turnout and Representation: Caucuses Versus Primaries. *American Journal of Political Science* 22 (1): 169–182. doi:10.2307/2110674.

Mayer, William G. 2009. Superdelegates: Reforming the Reforms Revisited. In *Reforming the Presidential Nomination Process*, ed. Steven S. Smith and Melanie J. Springer, 85–108. Washington, DC: Brookings Institution Press.

Mayer, William G., and Andrew E. Busch. 2003. *The Front-Loading Problem in Presidential Nominations*. Washington, DC: Brookings Institution Press.

McGhee, Eric, Seth Masket, Boris Shor, Steven Rogers, and Nolan McCarty. 2014. A Primary Cause of Partisanship? Nomination Systems and Legislator Ideology. *American Journal of Political Science* 58 (2): 337–351.

Meinke, Scott R., Jeffrey K. Staton, and Steven T. Wuhs. 2006. State Delegate Selection Rules for Presidential Nominations, 1972–2000. *The Journal of Politics* 68 (1): 180–193. doi:10.1111/j.1468-2508.2006.00379.x.

Norrander, Barbara. 1993. Nomination Choices: Caucus and Primary Outcomes, 1976–88. *American Journal of Political Science* 37 (2): 343–364. doi:10.2307/2111376.

NR Symposium. 2016. Conservatives Against Trump. *National Review*. January 21, 2016.

Oliver, J. Eric. 1996. The Effects of Eligibility Restrictions and Party Activity on Absentee Voting and Overall Turnout. *American Journal of Political Science* 40 (2): 498–513. doi:10.2307/2111634.

Panagopoulos, Costas. 2010. Are Caucuses Bad for Democracy? *Political Science Quarterly* 125 (3): 425–442.

Pomper, Gerald. 1979. New Rules and New Games in Presidential Nominations. *The Journal of Politics* 41 (3): 784–805.

Putnam, Josh. 2016a. 2016 Republican Delegate Allocation Rules by State. *Frontloading HQ.* http://frontloading.blogspot.com/p/2016-republican-delegate-allocation-by.html. Accessed March 10, 2017.

———. 2016b. 2016 Democratic Delegate Allocation Rules by State. *Frontloading HQ.* http://frontloading.blogspot.com/p/2016-democratic-delegate-allocation.html. Accessed March 10, 2017.

Redlawsk, David P., Caroline J. Tolbert, and Todd Donovan. 2011. *Why Iowa?: How Caucuses and Sequential Elections Improve the Presidential Nominating Process.* Chicago: University of Chicago Press.

Schuman, Howard, and Stanley Presser. 1979. The Open and Closed Question. *American Sociological Review* 44 (5): 692–712.

Skelley, Geoffrey. 2016. The Modern History of the Republican Presidential Primary, 1976–2012. *Sabato's Crystal Ball.* http://www.centerforpolitics.org/crystallball/articles/the-modern-history-of-the-republican-presidential-primary-1976-2012/. Accessed April 20, 2017.

Snyder, James, and Michael Ting. 2011. Electoral Selection with Parties and Primaries. *American Journal of Political Science* 55 (4): 782–796.

Southwell, Priscilla L. 1986. The 1984 Democratic Nomination Process: The Significance of Unpledged Superdelegates. *American Politics Quarterly* 14 (1–2): 75–88.

———. 1988. Open Versus Closed Primaries and Candidate Fortunes, 1972–1984. *American Politics Quarterly* 16 (3): 280–295.

———. 1991. Open Versus Closed Primaries: The Effect on Strategic Voting and Candidate Fortunes. *Social Science Quarterly* 72: 789–796.

———. 2012. A Backroom Without the Smoke? Superdelegates and the 2008 Democratic Nomination Process. *Party Politics* 18 (2): 267–283.

Chapman Rackaway serves the University of West Georgia as a professor and chair in the Department of Political Science. Previously, Rackaway was a faculty member, department chair, and dean at Fort Hays State University (FHSU). After serving as a political activist and consultant for ten years, Rackaway received his Ph.D. in political science from the University of Missouri in 2002. In 2007, 2010, and 2013, Rackaway was a nominee for the Pilot Award, FHSU's highest award for teaching faculty. In August 2015, Rackaway was named the FHSU President's Distinguished Scholar.

Chapman Rackaway is an avid believer in the role technology plays in both teaching and politics. Rackaway has published work on the use of technological and social media tools in state representative campaigns and multimedia supplements' effects on student learning outcomes in the American Government classroom. Rackaway uses instant polls, web video, lecture capture, social media, interactive graphics, and freeware tools to engage students in course materials.

A recognized expert in Kansas politics, Rackaway is regularly quoted in state, national, and international media. Rackaway's primary scholarly foci are on political parties as electioneering organizations and internal campaign strategy. Rackaway is the author of five books, including *Civic Failure and Its Threat to Democracy: Operator Error*. Interested parties can follow Chapman Rackaway on Twitter @DocPolitics or connect with him via Facebook or LinkedIn using the ID chapman.rackaway.

CHAPTER 8

Conclusion: The Paradox of Partisanship in 2016 and Beyond

Chapman Rackaway and Laurie L. Rice

Political parties are a paradox of human governance. Parties provide the laudable opportunity for individuals to organize and collectively act as republican democracy expects, but the public also reviles them for corruption of democratic intent and sometimes actual, corrupt acts. There is no more effective mobilization tool than the political party, and yet at least in the American context, they are terribly unpopular. No other representative democracy has the love-hate relationship with its parties that the United States does. This deep rooted ambivalence dates back to the Framers, who decried them as dangers for democracy and formed and joined them in nearly the same breath because of their usefulness. The relationship that developed over time, to take the analogy further, could be termed 'dysfunctional' or even 'codependent'. Parties and voters need

C. Rackaway (✉)
Department of Political Science, University of West Georgia,
Carrollton, GA, USA

L.L. Rice
Department of Political Science, Southern Illinois University Edwardsville,
Edwardsville, IL, USA

© The Author(s) 2018   189
C. Rackaway, L.L. Rice (eds.), *American Political Parties Under Pressure*, DOI 10.1007/978-3-319-60879-2_8

each other, and yet both try to control the other's behaviors in ways that are often destructive.

By the mid-2010s, parties and voters seemed to be diverging from each other in ways that brought newfound challenges. Parties were becoming weaker in the aftermath of decades of growth at the same time that partisanship was experiencing a limited revival after decades of decline. Entering the 2016 election cycle, the parties were trying to reassert themselves and harness the latent power within a more partisan electorate. Yet, once again, American political parties found themselves in a difficult position.

American political parties have to deal with problems and challenges that parties in other industrialized republics do not. Most notably, American parties have the scourge of primary elections that undermine their abilities to coordinate campaigns; select candidates who best represent the party's philosophy and strategic goals; and increase the costs of campaigns. American parties also have the larger electioneering environment including outside groups, restrictive campaign finance regimes, and an independent media that all serve to provide a hostile locus from which they operate.

Structurally, parties are weaker now than they have been at any time since the 1970s. Party rebuilding efforts of the 1980s and 1990s were undone by legislative and judicial intervention. The Bipartisan Campaign Reform Act 2002 and the twin *Citizens United* and *SpeechNOW* Supreme Court decisions served to remove the national parties and their electioneering subcommittees as the central coordinating hubs for political campaigns, the political 'nuclei' described by Schlesinger (1994). In this environment, political parties are just one of many potential sources of campaign funds. Meanwhile, wealthy donors, sometimes with distinctly different ideological agendas than the leaders of the party organization under whose name they field candidates, recruit and fund their own candidates, seeking to tip the outcome of primaries, and thus the party, in their favor.

Parties are so structurally weak in the United States that they are limited in their capacity to build the network of collective action necessary for governing (Aldrich 1995). The weak party structure has leeched into governance, with the parties in Congress becoming more polarized and deeply divided. The Tea Party on the right and the Occupy Wall Street movement on the left have fractured the Republican and Democratic parties in Congress, making compromise even within parties much more difficult.

While party organizations and the party in government find themselves in difficult circumstances, the party in the electorate is stronger than it has been in decades. American National Election Studies and private polls show a small resurgence in partisan identification since 2000, though a sizable proportion of the population still considers itself to be non-partisan. Despite a rise in self-proclaimed independents, the 2010s also saw strengthening partisan identification among those with a party (Twenge et al. 2016).

The partisans have become more polarized as well, leading to the phenomenon of 'negative partisanship'(Abramowitz and Webster 2015), where partisans are not necessarily as invested in their own party as they are convinced the other party is worse. Partisans tend to use negative adjectives to describe members of the opposite party and find political discussions with people they disagree with to be stressful and frustrating (Doherty et al. 2016). Meanwhile, the percentage of partisans with very unfavorable views of the opposite party has skyrocketed from around 20% in 1994 to over 50% in 2016 (Doherty et al. 2016).

Parties, who stand to benefit from a certain level of polarization at least, should see polarization as a sign that they are adequately differentiated from their opposing party and thus a distinct electoral choice. But parties also take risks when embracing polarization, because their adherents may gravitate toward political positions with which the party would have trouble integrating into an agenda. In this environment, the compromises often necessary to pass legislation become political liabilities.

Sociological changes, both in self-identification and migration patterns, significantly affect partisanship in the current day as well. As people relocate from place to place, they tend to cluster around like-minded individuals. Living patterns have created homogenous 'echo chambers' that encourage single-minded and polarized ideologies (Bishop 2009). Increasing diversity across the country has also led to a significant ideological division. Those who consider themselves Americans without modifiers are shrinking in population but becoming a more distinct portion of the voting public.

The ideological bases of parties are changing as well. Parties are not only rational electioneering bodies; they are collections of ideologically similar citizens. As polarization extended into both the electorate and government, so did the signs of ideological change begin to emerge. The very meaning of being a 'liberal' or a 'conservative' became fluid. Some issues, such as immigration, changed from being crosscutting to valence issues with well-defined partisan stances and little dissent within the parties on the issue. Others, such as same-sex marriage rights, began to moderate. Parties are their strongest when they can provide distinct differences between themselves and the 'other' party. The issues on which parties can campaign thus effectively change.

The state of the parties going into the 2016 elections was thus one of strong partisans and weak parties. The parties are in a particularly difficult position when one looks at them historically. Even though parties rebuilt themselves and returned to a position of strength in the 1980s and 1990s, they have been weak since the Progressive Era greatly diminished them in the early twentieth century. In addition, since that period of resurgence, parties have become weaker still over the last decade. Occasional attempts by the parties to reclaim some of their power, whether it be reforms like the Democrats' superdelegate system or strategic efforts like soft money state-level electioneering, have not been as successful in providing a stable return to prominence for the party organizations. The lack of success has not prevented the parties from trying to reassert themselves in the electoral milieu. Republican efforts to restrict the march of frontloading, for instance, emerged from the idea that the Grand Ole Party (GOP) must exert more subtle influence on the nomination process for its presidential candidates.

8.1   Parties Under Pressure

The 2016 election revealed parties under pressure from a variety of sources. Some of the pressure placed on parties comes from changes in the electorate. The number of unhyphenated Americans—white Americans who view their ethnic background solely as American—is growing as the nation becomes increasingly diverse. Arbour shows that Trump did quite well with this group. He provides evidence that this was not particular to Trump. Republicans have enjoyed a growing advantage in the regions where unhyphenated Americans are concentrated since 1992. While Trump's promises of bringing jobs back and making America great again resonate well with this group, past electoral results suggest that, as the Republican nominee, he would have done quite well with unhyphenated Americans regardless.

Other pressures come from the efforts of specific presidential candidates to build winning coalitions and the rhetoric they employed in doing so. Dulio and Klemanski examine the role of populism in propelling the campaigns of Bernie Sanders during the battle for the Democratic nomination and Trump's successful bid for the presidency. Their case study of Michigan, one of the 'blue wall' states that fell to Trump, reveals Trump's success in substantially increasing turnout in rural areas and areas with high concentrations of manufacturing or trade-related jobs.

The parties have faced increased pressure on the coalitions they have relied on in the past. Gooch's investigation of political polarization on the issue of gay rights reveals one of the issues that have placed strain on existing party coalitions. The polarization among the public may crosscut existing party coalitions. The parties have taken opposing stances on issues such as gay marriage but these stances are not shared by all of their regular members. Rural, conservative Democrats such as those in Michigan described by Dulio and Klemanski or the unhyphenated Americans written about by Arbour who have shifted their party allegiance over time may not have shared the liberalization of views on gay rights undertaken by the Democratic Party.

The 2016 election also revealed substantial debates within each party about ideology. Romance's examination of the state of ideology in the Republican and Democratic Parties helps reveal another source of pressure within the parties. As Romance reveals, conservatism within the Republican Party contains several distinct strains including social conservatism, libertarian conservatism, and Burkean conservatism. These offer distinctly different worldviews and lead to different issue positions. The candidates for the 2016 Republican nomination were positioned across these and united or divided these distinct ideological camps in various ways and in a crowded field of candidates, Donald Trump won with a brand of conservatism that does not fit neatly into any of these camps. Meanwhile, the battle for the Democratic nomination revealed clear divides in what it means to be liberal. Sanders drew some aspects of socialism into the mainstream while Clinton focused on a broader view of human empowerment and what it means to be a member of society.

Romance concludes that Clinton, Sanders, and Trump all spoke to different elements of disempowerment. For Sanders and Trump, this involved blaming the establishment. This, too, put added pressure on the parties as part of the establishment. The weakness of party organizations was put on full display in 2016 and as Rackaway shows, some of this was made possible by rules enacted by the party establishments. Rackaway reveals a key rules change that inadvertently helped Trump—requiring states that moved their primaries up before March 1 to allocate their delegates proportionally. This meant the unusually large field of candidates would not be winnowed as quickly. Meanwhile, the small number of states using caucuses on the Democratic side undercut Bernie Sanders' ability to ride a wave of strong caucus support to secure the nomination.

As Gooch shows, the underlying issues that compose ideologies and campaign rhetoric shifts constantly, and as they morph so do the component strategies of the parties seeking to capitalize upon them. Polarization is seen as a given, especially among the market press, but understanding why the electorate appears more polarized remains an elusive element. Gooch shows that polarization is partly determined by the shifts among and between those issues. As issue stances moderate among voters, as in the case of support for same-sex rights, electioneers have a greater incentive to delineate their differences. Where conflict appears on its face to be softening, partisan stances around the issue in question may polarize, creating the appearance of greater dissonance on the topic than exists among the voters. Furthermore, Gooch's work suggests that parties have a strong incentive in their rhetoric and electioneering efforts to push issues out to the edges of the ideological spectrum. Put directly, when everyone agrees, there is nothing to campaign around, no reason to raise money, and no reason to mobilize people for a fight.

The business world is accustomed to the concept of hostile takeovers and as Rackaway points out, Trump's victory could be interpreted as a hostile takeover of the Republican Party. Trump's focus on the economically disempowered, written about by Dulio and Klemanski and Romance, worked. Rice's analysis shows that Trump did better in areas with higher unemployment. Yet, Rice reveals another important factor that left the party vulnerable—lack of attention from the party's presidential candidates in previous election cycles. Rice argues that campaign visits by presidential primary candidates strengthen voters' ties to their party and help expose them to the variety of views within it. She finds that Trump did significantly better in those areas that had been ignored by Republican candidates in previous election cycles. And, to the extent contest rules set by the party organization shape where candidates visit, that, too, helped leave the door open for Trump.

8.2   PARTIES MOVING BEYOND 2016

Throughout the 2016 campaign, pundits focused on the strain Donald Trump was placing on the Republican Party—they presented it as a party about to break apart. However, the result of the 2016 election changes the narrative about parties under pressure. As the results of the November 2016 election rolled in, pundits began to proclaim that it was the Democratic Party in trouble and that the Republican Party was strong and unified. Rackaway points out that Bernie Sanders' campaign exemplified the split among Democrats between the 'mainstream' wing of Hillary Clinton and the more progressive strain led by Sanders. Sanders' vote shares and delegate wins were strongly disproportionate to the media attention he gained for state-level victories in strategic locations. Using the press' interest in state-level victories, Sanders was able to project a following far beyond that of his actual vote results, and built a cadre of passionate supporters that continued to support him at the Democratic National Convention.

Trump's eventual victory had pundits questioning the future of the Democratic Party and its leadership, noting it was a deeply divided party, with no clear leader left at its helm. Meanwhile, they portrayed the Republican Party as unified around common goals. However, the Republican Party's electoral success belied deep divisions that became clearly apparent in the efforts to repeal and replace the Affordable Care Act (ACA). Republican members of Congress, many wary of their prospects for re-election in 2018, were less unified over the vote to repeal and replace the ACA once on the legislative floor than they were on the campaign trail in support of Trump's presidential bid. Democrats, finding a unified voice in support of the former President's legacy program, quickly emerged in media reports as a resurgent force preparing for a competitive 2018. Over the course of two months, the national narrative shifted from a fractured Republican Party against a dominant Democratic Party, to Democratic collapse under shocking Republican victories, and back to a deeply divided GOP with a strong and vocal Democratic Party. Which is to say, that public perceptions may change quickly, but those perceptions are of a moment and analogous to Plato's cave. The cave wall shadows we see are imperfect and often distorted representations of reality.

Pundits are prone to speak in bold, sweeping statements that make for good television. Their pronouncements about both party's demise were deeply exaggerated. Still, the fact remains that both the Democratic and Republican parties are under pressure. As the electorate changes, party elites struggle to hold their traditional coalitions together and face challenges from various wings within the party for control. The tripod on which the party rests is no longer steady and party elites must strategically adapt. The nuclear party model that emerged in the 1980s has also been rendered archaic by legislative, electioneering, and finance changes. What the party looks like today is as much a mystery as it has even been. If the tripod does still exist, the legs are drastically different, with only one leg supporting most of the three-legged stool. For the network model of parties, the central server is down. Coordination is banned (though some extra-legal means of coordination are still done) and so the central routing point of money, expertise, and personnel is missing.

The party organizations have thus become rather passive organizations. The parties have little control over their nomination processes and whichever candidate (no matter how appealing or unappealing to the party organization) wins the nomination gets control over the party's still-strong electioneering apparatus. Party leaders may have preferences for which candidate they would like to see at the top of their Presidential ticket, but even if their choice does not win the party is bound to support its nominee. For voters, the fact that a party can be taken over by a hostile force means that the label, or 'brand identity' of the party can be drastically undermined by its candidates. Donald Trump is a prime example of a candidate who does not fit the mold of a 'preferred' party candidate and yet still was able to use the Republican National Committee and its affiliated entities for his general election purposes. For traditional mainline Republicans, though, a candidate like Trump who obviously deviates from the party's traditional stances means either they will have to shift their ideological preferences toward those of Trump, deal with the cognitive dissonance of being in schism with their party, or find another political party home. With only one other electorally viable option, the Democrats, we might expect to see those disgruntled anti-Trump Republicans shifting to the other party. But negative partisanship suggests that instead, the disgruntled Republicans will become non-partisan. We can then expect the resurgence in partisan identification to be brief.

The future of American political parties at the federal level looks quite bleak, then. Losing the capacity to coordinate campaigns and be the central throughput for electoral money has made the parties much weaker, and the primary system makes them susceptible to capture from either outside groups or non-aligned candidates. Ideological shifts mean that the parties will have a progressively more difficult time connecting to voters on a stable basis, suggesting a higher volatility of partisan identification. If the party organization and the party within the electorate weaken, we can expect to see a similar shift among those elected.

An opportunity exists for more research into the internal operations of the party organizations. Do party organizations have a reduced role in campaigns, or have they simply been co-opted? How will parties cope in the future? Would other structural reforms to nomination and electioneering practices provide a stronger system into which parties could rebound?

What value does a political party have to the voter? In a day where the largest portion of the electorate often self-identifies as non-partisan, is the label that comes with being Republican or Democrat worth the challenges and negatives that accompany it? With more externally imposed reforms such as top-two primaries and public campaign funding challenging parties further, is the American public considering a wider-scale rejection of parties?

Finally, a comparative opportunity for study exists at the state level. While the national parties appear to be struggling, there are examples across the country of resurgent state party organizations such as in Kansas. State parties, which were moribund until the soft money area allowed the cash-rich national committees to subsidize and rebuild them, are stronger in any number of areas. Why, if national parties are weaker, should state parties appear to be getting stronger?

While parties face more challenges than they have in decades, history also reveals American parties possess a remarkable amount of adaptability to circumstances. They have survived both internal and external challenges from popular (and fleeting) movements in the past. They persisted through declines and resurgences in partisanship. They found ways to claw back from Progressive era reforms aimed at gutting their power. They created new tools for influence when they lost most of their power to pick their party's nominees in the late 1960s. While the specific challenges facing the parties has changed substantially, parties under pressure is nothing new. To survive, they must do what they have always done—adapt to a changing electorate.

References

Abramowitz, Alan, and Steven Webster. 2015. All Politics Is National: The Rise of Negative Partisanship and the Nationalization of US House and Senate Elections in the 21st Century. Paper Presented at the Annual Meeting of the Midwest Political Science Association, April 16–19.

Aldrich, John H. 1995. *Why Parties?: The Origin and Transformation of Political Parties in America*. Chicago: University of Chicago Press.

Bishop, Bill. 2009. *The Big Sort: Why the Clustering of Like-Minded America Is Tearing Us Apart.* Boston: Houghton Mifflin Harcourt.

Doherty, Carroll, Jocelyn Kiley, and Bridget Jameson. 2016. Partisanship and Political Animosity in 2016: Highly Negative Views of the Opposing Party and Its Members. Pew Research Center. June 22. http://www.people-press. org/2016/06/22/partisanship-and-political-animosity-in-2016/. Accessed April 29, 2017.

Schlesinger, Joseph A. 1994. *Political Parties and the Winning of Office.* Ann Arbor, MI: University of Michigan Press.

Twenge, Jean M., Nathan Honeycutt, Radmila Prislin, and Ryne A. Sherman. 2016. More Polarized but More Independent: Political Party Identification and Ideological Self-Categorization Among U.S. Adults, College Students, and Late Adolescents, 1970–2015. *Personality and Social Psychology Bulletin* 42 (10): 1364–1383.

Chapman Rackaway serves the University of West Georgia as a professor and chair in the Department of Political Science. Previously, Rackaway was a faculty member, department chair, and dean at Fort Hays State University (FHSU). After serving as a political activist and consultant for ten years, Rackaway received his Ph.D. in political science from the University of Missouri in 2002. In 2007, 2010, and 2013, Rackaway was a nominee for the Pilot Award, FHSU's highest award for teaching faculty. In August 2015, Rackaway was named the FHSU President's Distinguished Scholar.

Chapman Rackaway is an avid believer in the role technology plays in both teaching and politics. Rackaway has published work on the use of technological and social media tools in state representative campaigns and multimedia supplements' effects on student learning outcomes in the American Government classroom. Rackaway uses instant polls, web video, lecture capture, social media, interactive graphics, and freeware tools to engage students in course materials.

A recognized expert in Kansas politics, Rackaway is regularly quoted in state, national, and international media. Rackaway's primary scholarly foci are on political parties as electioneering organizations and internal campaign strategy. Rackaway is the author of five books, including *Civic Failure and Its Threat to Democracy: Operator Error.* Interested parties can follow Chapman Rackaway on Twitter @ DocPolitics or connect with him via Facebook or LinkedIn using the ID chapman. rackaway.

Laurie L. Rice is an associate professor of political science at Southern Illinois University Edwardsville, where she teaches classes in American politics, including the presidency, presidential campaigns, and political parties and interest groups.

She received her Ph.D. in political science from the University of California, San Diego. Her research appears in journals such as *Congress & the Presidency*, *Presidential Studies Quarterly*, *Social Science Computer Review*, and *Social Science Quarterly*. Rice is a co-author of the book *Web 2.0 and the Political Mobilization of College Students* and a contributor to *Technology and Civic Engagement in the College Classroom*. Rice has also written pieces for *The Hill* and *The Huffington Post* and provides expertise on elections, social media, and the presidency to regional, national, and international media.

INDEX[1]

[1] Note: Page number followed by 'n' refers to notes